Texas Shrimpers

TEXAS SHRIMPERS

Community, Capitalism, and the Sea

by Robert Lee Maril

TEXAS A&M UNIVERSITY PRESS
College Station

Library of Congress Cataloging in Publication Data

Maril, Robert Lee.
    Texas shrimpers.

    Bibliography: p.
    Includes index.
    1. Shrimp industry—Texas. 2. Shrimpers (Persons)—
Texas. I. Title.
HD9472.S63U545   1983   338.3′7253843′09764   82-45897
ISBN 0-89096-147-6

Manufactured in the United States of America
FIRST EDITION

For Andrea Fisher Maril

Contents

TABLES

Preface

This book is about Texas shrimpers. It is about their work, their families, their dreams, and their frustrations. It is also about their place in their communities and about how their communities respond to them. Finally, it is about shrimping as an industry and about how shrimpers are affected by big business, big government, and the larger economic forces, such as inflation, that affect us all.

This book was written for everyone who, like me, has watched from a pier, a passing car, or a cozy dockside restaurant as shrimpers and their boats head for the Gulf sea, rigging framed against the sunset—and has wanted to go with them. It is written for those who wish they could see what shrimpers see, when far from sight of land, or work as they must work, if only for one day. It is directed, too, to anyone who has ever yearned to go on board a shrimp boat, sit and talk for a while about the weather or the fishing, and try to learn a little about these men who fish for a living. It is for those who wonder, too, what shrimpers do when they return with their catch—whether they lead their lives as other men do or whether the work at sea makes them somehow different from the rest of us.

The shrimp industry is the most important fishing industry in the United States.[1] Landings were valued in 1976 at $331.4 million, with production at 403.6 million pounds. While Texas was third in volume of landings among all states, it ranked first in value of shrimp landings, with $119.9 million. Texas is also a major importer of foreign shrimp.

Yet it was not the money or the importance of the industry that first drew my attention. The boats, the shrimp trawlers, were what caught my fancy. I was a sophomore in college in Iowa. It was 1967. The winter had been very hard, as Iowa winters usually are, and some friends and I planned a trip during spring vacation to the sunny

[1] See U.S. Department of Commerce, Data Management and Statistics Division, *Fisheries of the United States, 1980.*

beaches of Texas. The plan was to forget term papers and exams for a week and to get as sunburned as possible.

We took a train from Des Moines to Oklahoma City, where I was born and raised. I remember staying up most of the night, then watching the sun come up over the spring stubble of the Kansas cornfields. We rented a car in Oklahoma City and drove the rest of the way to Galveston. When we got there, tired, pleasantly hot, a little dazed from the long trip, we all took a long walk along the beachfront, staring at the seafood restaurants, the gift and tourist shops, the cruising college student traffic, and the shrimp boats proudly docked in the harbor.

The boats affected me as only images of life at sea could attract a landlubber locked into academic life among Iowa winters. They were at once foreign and majestic, their riggings forming an intriguing asymmetry, while at the same time mundane, putrid in their smells of diesel fumes and dead fish. I took photograph after photograph, later developing pictures filled with ropes, anchor chains, steel outriggers, winches, and bows with names like *Conchita*, *Cajun Lady*, and *Sea Witch*, all facing the foggy Galveston mornings.

Some years later I pulled the photographs out of their envelope, again staring in fascination at their proud images. But if the boats were still haughty in their seedy dignity, they now appeared to me also entirely lifeless. I still had never met or even seen a shrimper.

In 1975, when my wife and I moved to South Texas, I found myself drawn time and again to the jetties at South Padre Island. Using the subterfuge of fishing for trout and flounder, I would sit for hours watching the shrimp boats head down the ship channel and out the Brazos-Santiago Cut to the Gulf of Mexico beyond. Perched on a piling no more than one hundred yards from the boats as they chugged slowly by, I would bait my hook with frozen shrimp, toss the line with heavy sinker over the jetty rocks, and hope that, for a while at least, no crabs or fish would disturb me. More often than not the whole fishing apparatus of hook, line, sinker, and shrimp would catch itself in a bottom crevice; then I would do some ritual pulling to appease my fellow fishermen and happily cut the whole lump free from my rod.

But if it was the boats that had originally kindled my imagination, it was increasingly the shrimpers themselves to whom I was drawn. In part this was because, whenever I mentioned the word *shrimper* to friends or acquaintances, I received amazingly negative reactions. I could not believe that any group of people could be as bad, as irresponsible, and as wild as everyone said shrimpers were. And if the fishermen were really like that, then I wanted to meet them all the more.

As I began to study Texas shrimpers formally and to talk, to interview, and to work with them, I began to understand in part the contradictions in their public image. On the one hand, there is a certain romanticism associated with men who earn their living from the sea. It was this romantic notion that had first attracted me, as no doubt it has many others, many years earlier: those of us who spend the majority of our time on land assign a special significance, known only to ourselves, to those who leave the relative safety of the land for the vagaries of the sea. On the other hand, this romanticism seems to be mixed with an equal measure of disdain for men who work with their hands, smell like dead fish, and return to port eager to raise a little hell after two weeks of hard labor on a cramped boat. In the landlubber's eyes, shrimpers do not seem to obey the rules by which most of us have tacitly agreed to live.

Just exactly who are Texas shrimpers, what is their work at sea, what do they do when they are on land, and, more important, what are they like and why? These are the central questions that this study seeks to answer. But larger than these concerns are other issues, which emerged as my involvement with shrimpers increased. In studying shrimpers, I began, after a certain point, to realize that I was studying less a certain identifiable occupational group and more the economic structure, the communities, and the general society out of which these fishermen come. By studying men who work at sea, I began to have new insights into those who work on land. To some degree, then, this book focuses not just on a specific group of skilled and semiskilled workers, regardless of their intrinsic interest and importance, but also on the social, political, and economic systems of which they are a small part. Thus, to study Texas shrimpers is both to consider the social dynamics of the Texas coastal towns in which they live and to scrutinize their entire industry.

In order to accomplish these objectives, the book is divided into three parts. The first, "At Sea: Big Men in Little Boats," takes as its central task the description of the shrimpers' daily work and their attitudes toward it, emphasizing what those of us who spend most of our lives on land find difficult to understand: the sea is a totally different living and working environment that demands of the shrimper a unique set of responses and a unique pattern of behavior. The sea dominates life on board a shrimp boat, not only because it is constantly life-threatening, as indeed it is on all workboats, but also because it hides the shrimp that the fishermen seek. The work and the social structure of the crew are adaptations to the ocean's demands, whether the wind blows gently or with hurricane force.

Part Two, "Landfall: When Shrimpers Come Home," describes the social history of shrimpers and the coastal communities in which they reside, because the demands of their work directly affect these men's families, friends, and neighbors; in fact, anxieties among some shrimpers are greatest when they return to the dock after several weeks of fishing. In addition, the impact of the stereotype of shrimpers as hell-raisers and alcohol abusers on the fishermen themselves, those close to them, and their communities is analyzed.

Major economic forces that influence the shrimping industry and directly affect the individual shrimper are studied in Part Three, "In the Marketplace: Shrimpers, Big Business, Big Government, and Unions." Shrimpers are, in an economic sense, slaves to the price they receive for their catch. Who determines that price and who profits most by it are considered in this section, and the federal government's successes and failures in its attempts to help the shrimping industry are assessed. Also considered is the problem of labor-management relations: other fishermen on the East Coast and West Coast are unionized, but Texas shrimpers are not. The reason why they have not been successful in their attempts to unionize is examined through an analysis of one shrimpers' strike in a Texas port.

I am a sociologist by training; thus, the themes and concerns of this volume are ones of sociology and anthropology. I have borrowed three approaches from these disciplines. First, I have tried to look at shrimping through the eyes of the men who do the job. In that respect, this book contrasts sharply with most previous studies, which focus on specific aspects of these men's lives, most commonly their annual production or the technology of their fishing equipment. As a result of studies like these, we know more about the shrimp, their diseases, their migration patterns, and their life cycles and about the boats, their hull lengths, their tonnage, and their latest gadgets than we do about the shrimpers.[2] One major exception to this observation is the excellent work by David White.[3] Like White, I have attempted to study and write about shrimpers with the implicit acceptance of their own perceptions of their daily lives, their personal realities. Michael Orbach's fine work on the tuna fishermen of San Diego has also served as a model for this project.[4]

Second, I have tried to study these fishermen and their families in ways that generate analyses that make sense both to shrimpers and to me. I have tried to ask these men what they think is most important to them and to their lives; then I have measured their answers against what I have learned from participant observation, general interviews, and a survey. When something has not made sense to me, I have gone back to particular shrimpers, owners, and industry experts and have asked them to explain it to me again.

Third, I have tried to write this essay in understandable English by avoiding as much academic terminology as possible. Unfortunately, this plan has not always been feasible, as, for example, in the chapter on pricing and price fluctuations. I hope that, as a result of this attempt, the general reader may find this book more accessible than most. I hope, too, that the serious student of the social and behavioral sciences will not think this book less informative because of the absence of academic jargon.

Open-ended interviews, participant observation, and a random sample were employed to study Texas shrimpers and the shrimping industry. The combination of these three approaches was particularly well suited to the methodological problems that arose during the course of the project.

I began this work in the spring and summer of 1977 by interviewing fleet owners, brokers, marine agents, fishhouse operators, working shrimpers, retired shrimpers, and others associated with the industry in two Texas ports. In addition, educators, social workers, police, and

[2] See M. Estellie Smith, ed., *Those Who Live from the Sea*, for a critique of the focus of studies on fishing communities, as well as James M. Acheson, "Anthropology of Fishing," *Annual Review of Anthropology* 10 (1981): 275–316.

[3] David R. M. White, "Environment, Technology, and Time-Use Patterns in the Gulf Coast Shrimp Fishery," in Smith, *Those Who Live from the Sea*, pp. 195–214.

[4] Michael K. Orbach, *Hunters, Seamen, and Entrepreneurs: The Tuna Seinermen of San Diego*.

others who daily come into contact with these commercial fishermen were contacted. The open-ended interviews centered on issues of concern to the shrimping industry, including fuel prices, the ban on fishing in Mexican waters, the future of the industry, and the role of shrimpers in their respective communities. These questions often served as a springboard to related issues of concern to the respondents. The interviews lasted from ten minutes to two hours: the average was about forty-five minutes long. Approximately fifty interviews were conducted in this manner.

These first interviews served as a preliminary data base. Since I lacked sufficient data and information, they helped bring into focus the concerns of those in the industry and acquainted me with the work that shrimpers do at sea. They also allowed me to become familiar with the terminology that shrimpers and those in the industry use daily.

Crucial differences in perspectives on work and other important issues between shrimpers and other community members were immediately evident. From the first, shrimpers I interviewed emphasized certain aspects of their work at sea that they said could be fully understood only if one worked as a shrimper. On the other hand, members of their communities, with a few exceptions, showed little knowledge of the day-to-day work that shrimpers do. To some degree I felt, at times, as if I were talking about two completely different kinds of work, one described by the fishermen and the other by those who had never left the dock.

In order to comprehend fishing from the viewpoint of the shrimpers themselves, I spent three weeks working as a shrimp header during the summer of 1977. My stint in the Gulf provided invaluable insights into the nature of shrimping as routine work. During this period of participant observation I kept a twenty-four-hour-a-day log of all activities on board the trawler. In this way over the three-week period a work routine emerged, including various contingencies depending on the demands of the fishing, the sea, and the men.[5]

At first I found the work almost impossible to perform, but within a week I had recovered sufficiently from my seasickness to be able to head shrimp at a reasonable rate. In addition I cooked meals, cleaned

[5] Robert Lee Maril, "Shrimping in South Texas: Social and Economic Marginality Fishing for a Luxury Commodity."

the boat, and occasionally stood watch at the wheel when other crew members were busy with their jobs.

Although the crew realized I was not just another shrimper, the work and the sea made all four of us friends from the first day out. I learned firsthand from the crew their anxieties about the changing wage shares, the effects of rising fuel prices on their earnings, and the low price for shrimp they often received at the dock and their thoughts about being away so long from home and family. The three-week trip into the Gulf was an intense experience that provided perspectives on the men, the work, and the industry that would have been impossible to acquire simply by interviewing those on land or with a land-bound point of view.

The in-depth interviews were continued in the summers of 1978, 1979, and 1980. A total of approximately 150 interviews from eight different ports was eventually collected.

Finally, with the aid of funds from the Sea Grant Program at Texas A&M University, a random sample of Texas shrimpers was conducted during the summer and fall of 1980. This survey consisted of 143 interviews with captain-owners, captains, riggers, and headers from four major shrimp ports in Texas. The questions were aimed at gathering basic demographic data and attitudes toward shrimping as an occupation. Demographic data collected included job status, age, education, religious preference, marital status, health status, race, annual income from shrimping, secondary indicators of economic status, family size, place of birth, and work status of the shrimper's wife. Additional sets of questions explored the fisherman's attitudes toward his work, his industry, and his community and sought to determine patterns of alcohol use and consumption. Finally, several open-ended questions probed other areas of concern to these men. The questionnaire was translated into colloquial Spanish, and approximately 30 percent of the interviews were administered entirely in that language. Several more began in English but switched to Spanish when it became apparent that the respondent was more comfortable with the latter.

Only shrimpers who regularly fish in the Gulf of Mexico were interviewed. Those fishermen who net shrimp in the Texas bays and channels were excluded from the sample. These bay shrimpers fish on a daily basis, returning to shore when the sun sets; their work on the water and their lives on land are very different from those of the men who fish for shrimp in the open Gulf.

Fifty-eight captains and captain-owners were interviewed, along with forty-eight riggers and thirty-seven headers. From previous experience I knew that riggers and headers would be the most difficult to interview because they were the hardest to find; headers, in particular, are a marginal work force, often with limited social ties. Of equal importance, I recognized that riggers and headers, a significant number of whom were undocumented workers, were less likely to respond to an unknown interviewer.

Several methodological problems developed during the pretest of the interview. The most important concern was maintaining randomness in the selection of shrimpers on the trawlers. A variety of methods for selecting vessels was considered, and several methods were discarded because they were impractical: for example, because shrimpers and their boats are highly mobile and do not stay in one place very long, problems occurred in tracking down the trawlers once they had been selected and in finding the shrimpers once they had hit the docks after a trip. In the end, after several weeks of experimenting with various methods of selection (some of which sounded superior on paper but were unworkable at the dock), I decided upon random selection of trawlers at particular fishhouses. These fishhouses, themselves randomly selected, were visited every day of the week but Sunday, when they were usually closed. The random selection of different crews unloading shrimp at the dock thus was biased only in that it excluded one major category of shrimpers—namely, those who were not working, most commonly because their boats were being repaired.

Permission to interview crewmen on a boat was requested first from the boat owner or manager, if possible, and again from the captain on board. Unless he was too busy, the captain was always interviewed first, which both demonstrated to the rest of the crew the importance of the interview and provided them with a sample of the process, since many of the fishermen stood around listening and discussing the questions while the interview with the captain was being conducted.

When possible, the entire crew of captain, rigger, and one or two headers was interviewed. Frequently, however, at least one crew member, most often the header, would disappear almost as soon as the boat had landed at the fishhouse. Reasonable attempts were made to locate all the crew members, but this was not always possible. As a result, the number of captains, riggers, and headers who were interviewed are unequal, with sixty-six different trawlers represented in all.

Another problem grew out of the fact that many shrimpers were undocumented workers from Mexico and Central America. When asked directly about their legal status in this country, these men either would lie or would not answer and would refuse to respond to other questions for fear of losing their jobs. In order to avoid confronting these men with their illegal work status, I asked a series of questions designed to determine their status as workers and their place of birth. The sum of these questions, which included' length of work as a shrimper, how the respondent began working as a shrimper, number of other family members who fished for a living, and language of choice, made determination of these men's country of origin possible: once I had gained their confidence, I would ask them, toward the end of the interview, whether they looked forward to returning home; the majority answered yes, and almost always they also named their own country.

My experience working as a shrimper and my fluency in colloquial Spanish facilitated interviews with these undocumented workers, who in other circumstances would have been far more hesitant to answer questions from someone they did not know. As my skill in interviewing them increased, however, a different problem emerged: having never had anyone solicit their opinion on any issue, or ask such questions before, many were confused and puzzled by the purpose of the interviews. As a result, there is a good deal of data missing for this group. In some cases an interview-naive respondent had a friend who would explain the importance of a question and why the respondent's answer was being elicited, but this help was not always available.

The insights from the participant observation were particularly helpful in getting interviews from shrimpers on their boats. I used a variety of approaches if a particular fisherman did not at first seem to want to be interviewed. (For example, shrimpers sometimes said they did not have time to be questioned; I responded, depending on the circumstances, either that I would be glad to wait until they had finished what they were doing or that I would come back the next day.) Most of the time, however, the fishermen were openly friendly and curious about the questionnaire and, once the first questions had been asked, were quite vocal in their opinions and free with information about themselves. Again, my experience as a shrimper in the Gulf helped me enormously in asking the questions and interpreting the replies, particularly in a few cases in which the fishermen tested my knowledge of shrimping by responding with unlikely answers. In all, only four fishermen on the selected boats refused to be interviewed: one shrimper said he was sick and did not want to talk, another said he never answered questions people asked him, and two others were undocumented workers who were afraid to respond.

Every attempt was made to select Texas shrimping ports that were representative of all Texas Gulf Coast ports from Louisiana to Mexico. The four major ports along the northern, central, and southern coast that were selected for the sample contain the largest fleets in Texas: about eight hundred Gulf trawlers, out of a total of approximately three thousand trawlers in all of Texas, fish from these four ports.

One port selected was some distance from any town or city; another was an integral part of the town. One was adjacent to a highly industrialized coastal area, while another was situated in one of the poorest areas in Texas. Two ports contained trawlers that were owned by very large companies; the other two provided services for smaller fleets and independent boat owners. One showed signs of inept management by the port authority, while the others did not. In all, the four ports surveyed represent a wide range of ethnic, economic, and geographic characteristics.

In order to protect the privacy of the respondents, any characteristics that may identify them have been changed. All unreferenced quotations in the text are taken directly from the interviews.

I myself am not a shrimper, nor do I pretend to be. When a shrimper chooses to tell his own story, it will undoubtedly be far different from the one set forth in these pages. My goal is to explain the relationships that exist between shrimpers, their work, the sea, and men who, like me, seldom venture far from the sight of land.

Fishing on a pier, walking along the beach, or standing at the bar, we watch the trawlers slowly disappear from sight. Regardless of how much we love our families, how hard we work at our jobs, or how much we fear the sea, there is a part of each of us that at times yearns to go with that trawler and those men, that wants to throw away the commonplace for that which is different and exciting. Shrimpers have done just that: they have exchanged the demands of land jobs, family, and community for fishing at sea. But they have not escaped the expectations, the limitations, of working and living on land; they have only temporarily postponed them. Each day and night of fishing at sea is juxtaposed against their realization that eventually they must return to port and, once again, rejoin society.

Acknowledgments

I would like to express my thanks to the people who made this book possible. William Kuvlesky, M. Estellie Smith, Dorothy Mariner, Michael V. Miller, and Lauriston R. King all contributed critiques to drafts of this project; I am grateful for their help. I would like to acknowledge the support of Albert Besteiro, Julie Garcia, and Robert Shaw, all at Texas Southmost College. I thank Mary Chipley for her work as computer assistant. Jo Ann Tomlin, typist, did an excellent job on the drafts of this manuscript. Cypriano Cardenas translated the questionnaire from English into colloquial Spanish. Charles Fincher and Daniel Bourbonnais of Island Studios contributed the illustrations. Andrea Fisher Maril contributed significantly in her role as editor and proofreader; this book would have been much less than it is but for her. Finally, I must acknowledge a special debt of gratitude to Michael V. Miller for his intellectual integrity and collegiality throughout this project.

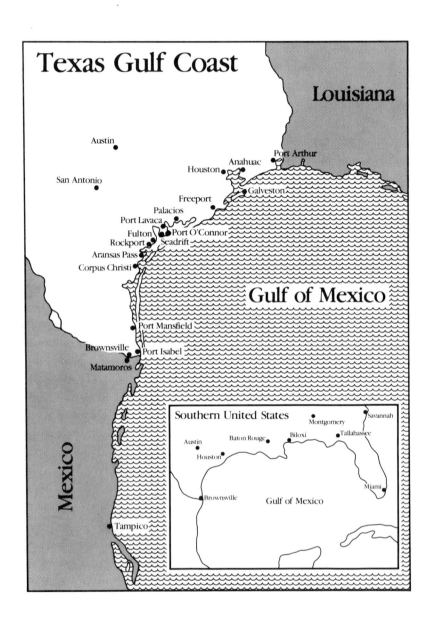

Texas Gulf Coast

Louisiana

Austin

Port Arthur
Anahuac
Houston
San Antonio
Galveston
Freeport
Palacios
Port Lavaca
Fulton Port O'Connor
Rockport Seadrift
Aransas Pass
Corpus Christi

Gulf of Mexico

Port Mansfield

Brownsville Port Isabel
Matamoros

Mexico

Tampico

Southern United States
Montgomery Savannah
Baton Rouge Biloxi Tallahassee
Austin
Houston
Miami
Brownsville Gulf of Mexico

PART ONE

At Sea: Big Men in Little Boats

1. The Sea

"My father was a captain. Now he's retired. When he stands in the living room he moves back and forth like he was on the boat. He can't stop."

"I get cold and wet. I can't get warm in the winter. It gets bad out there."

"One of these days a hurricane is going to come along and wipe out the whole fleet."

The sea is an alien environment that not only hides the shrimp from the shrimper but also constantly gets in his way and makes his work harder. Even in good weather it complicates his job tremendously: it tears up his equipment, confuses his senses, and, worse, physically isolates him from the rest of humanity.

The life cycle and migration patterns of brown shrimp (*Penaeus aztecus*) and white shrimp (*Penaeus setiferus*), the two most common species fished in Gulf waters, are hidden by the ocean depths. Far from the sight of man, the shrimp spawn, develop through five larval stages, and migrate into the estuaries, bays, and marshes of Texas, Louisiana, Mississippi, Alabama, and Florida.[1] From there, having grown to a juvenile stage, they migrate back out through coastal passes and cuts in the barrier islands to the Gulf beyond. It remains unclear just exactly where the mature shrimp then go, although there is an extensive literature on the life cycle of shrimp and a copious, sometimes contradictory one on their migration patterns.[2] General patterns of seasonal move-

[1] See Eugene A. Laurent, "Description of Industry: Economics," in *The Shrimp Fishery of the Southeastern United States: A Management Planning Profile*, Technical Report No. 5, ed. D. R. Calder; and Gulf of Mexico Fishery Management Council, *Draft Environmental Impact Statement and Fishery Management Plan for the Shrimp Fishery of the Gulf of Mexico, United States Waters*.

[2] See, for example, Wade L. Griffin, Melvin L. Cross, and George W. Ryan, *Seasonal Movement Patterns in the Gulf of Mexico Shrimp Fishery*, Department Technical Report No. 74-4. Migration patterns appear to fluctuate because of a variety of variables, so exact predictions are impossible.

ment have been noted, however, and shrimpers have their own ideas on patterns of migration.

Both juvenile and adult shrimp are omnivorous bottom feeders. They eat any and possibly almost all organic material found on the ocean floor, including "fragments of higher plants, foraminiferans, hydroids, nematodes, mollusks, polychaetes, crustaceans, tunicates, and fish larvae, as well as sand, mud, and organic debris."[3] Active at night, they are primarily nocturnal feeders, although both brown and white shrimp sometimes feed during the day.

These important behavioral characteristics determine to a great degree how shrimp must be caught. Dragging his nets all night along the bottom of the Gulf in searching for and harvesting his elusive prey, the shrimper is put in the position of a blind man in a storm trying to find his lost umbrella with his cane: if only he can find his umbrella (the shrimp), he can protect himself from the storm (the sea) and go home. Each time the shrimper thinks he has found shrimp, however, they may mysteriously move on; or, worse, the sun rises and they disappear.[4]

The sea constantly tears up the shrimper's equipment, rusts his metal winches, sucks his nets and doors into its mud and unseen obstructions, and tumbles his cable, nets, and chains into huge balls that must be painstakingly unraveled. In summer he hides from the tropical heat during the day in makeshift tents tied to the rigging. In the fall and winter even the warmest clothes cannot keep the wind and spray from chilling him to the bone; he stays wet and he stays cold.

Besides water and weather, shrimpers have to contend with constant, grinding sensory deprivation. There are no trees, no houses, no sidewalks, no familiar shapes and colors. In vain the eye searches for some comforting reinforcement from the environment, but all one sees, out of sight of land, is waves reaching toward the horizon.

One of the first things I was told was not to look at the individual

[3] Laurent, "Description of Industry: Economics," p. 76.

[4] See David R. M. White, "Environment, Technology, and Time-Use Patterns in the Gulf Coast Shrimp Fishery," in *Those Who Live from the Sea*, ed. M. Estellie Smith, pp. 195–214, in which the author emphasizes in some detail the interaction between shrimp and shrimp fishermen by stressing the need for shrimpers to adapt their techniques as well as their life-style to the feeding habits of their prey.

waves, waves that have no texture or uniform shape and reflect a monotonous color spectrum. I was told, "Look at the horizon; it looks more like land." It does. The distance smoothes out the chop, gives a uniform, solid line to the fluid. Still, there is nothing to look at except the occasional immense tanker, offshore oil rig, or other shrimp boat.

But the sensory deprivation, a minor result of which is being seasick, goes beyond the visual. The smells, the sounds, the tastes were incredibly uniform. The wind blew constantly and the diesel groaned on and on, emitting its smells of Mexican bus stations. Instinctively I moved closer to the crew, and they to me, as the Gulf closed in around us. Their faces took on lines of character, reflecting my growing knowledge of them. The captain changed most of all. A friendly, quiet, but compassionate man, his sea skills gave me confidence in my own ability to learn to adapt to the sea changes around me. The rigger, who works the nets, was an articulate man who had traveled widely and had a story for every country; he was, in fact, one of the best storytellers I have ever heard. The header, who snaps the heads off the thousands of shrimp, was less interesting, but a talkative and open person.

The sea and the work brought us together. The galley table was a renewable resource of land senses, of the smells of food cooking on the stove, of jokes repeated for the fifth, sixth, and seventh time, of shared experiences from the past.[5] I looked forward to the evening meal, the only regular one, as much for the food as for the reaffirmation that we were all men, of the same species, working, if temporarily, in an alien environment.

I cannot, of course, talk about the sea without talking about its quiet times, its intense beauty, its ability not only to deprive the senses but to overwhelm them. One hot afternoon I awoke to the squawking of the sea gulls on the rear work deck. They would regularly roost on the rigging or rails until we had all fallen asleep inside the cabin. Then the bravest among them would hop around the deck foraging for food. On this particular afternoon one gull, the one that had waked me from the heat-dulling afternoon sleep, stuck his head in the cabin door to see what was going on.

I staggered out of the doorway, heavy with sleep, chasing the gull

[5] Joseba Zulaika, in *Terranova*, focuses on the importance of the galley as a locus for sharing thoughts of home, social ties, and sea stories.

away. The boat creaked on its anchor line. Then a loud splash drew my attention to the port side. Not twenty feet away three porpoises were gracefully jumping completely out of the water, turning, and falling headfirst back into the Gulf. I watched intently. Four more porpoises showed up, then another group of three, and another, and another, all playing the same games. I counted fifty of the grey-backed shapes before losing track of their movements. Then, just as suddenly as they had appeared, they were gone.

There were the sunsets, the phases of the moon, the black skies with stars the brightness of mountaintop stars. There was the incredible cleanness of it all, a space so untouched, so immense, that it defied words created to describe places inhabited by humans.

Did these shrimpers see this incomparable liquid beauty that is the Gulf of Mexico? Some did and some did not. Many ignored it, regularly dumping garbage into the water, or belittled it in our constant conversations. Sitting at the table each night, the rigger would finish his Coke and, stopping to make a particular point in his story, unconsciously toss the can over his shoulder, out the port window, to the sea below. It was not an act of a litterer; it was the act of someone who simply was not aware that it was possible to litter the ocean. It was indeed possible, I soon came to realize, as later in the voyage I watched patches of oil, clumps of bilge, and other garbage float by. I was shocked when we hauled up, in thirty fathoms, more than twenty beer bottles from the muck below, each with two or three baby octopuses lodged within.

Yet, because the sea is the shrimper's workplace, he must be aware more of how it can hurt him than of whether it possesses any aesthetic values that please him. It can and does kill him. It can and does permanently injure him, cut off a finger or a hand, crush or infect a leg, or slice an arm. It drowns him. Its sixty-mile-an-hour "northers" scare him, and its seasonal hurricanes drive him to port, where he still cannot be sure of protection. Texas shrimpers will never forget Hurricanes Beulah and Allen and all those storms that preceded them.

The sea tires a man. It etches lines of fatigue and stress permanently into his skin, from his cheekbones to the corners of his mouth. It crinkles the back of his neck, and it turns his hands into thick, scarred members. Most of all, though, it threatens his life, and thus it directly threatens his family.

For all these reasons the sea can and must be learned by the crew. But I think the sea is rarely ever loved, its beauty appreciated for its own sake, because it does what no shrimpers, or other commercial fishermen, or merchant mariners, or sailors can ever forgive it for—it totally isolates them from those they love and from the society to which they belong.

The crew can give some shelter from the pressure of the sea, especially if crew members include family. Yet friendship and support from a shrimper's coworkers can never replace family and land friends. Moreover, the shrimper must contend with special problems brought on by the sea. When he leaves the shore, he totes along with him his store of unresolved family problems and troubled relationships and the myriad anxieties we all share; yet he is frequently isolated to the point that he knows that even if an emergency occurs, he can do nothing to help. Unlike the rest of us, the most he can do is wait and worry. He must and does, then, learn to accommodate to these anxieties and to set them aside if he can.

Marine radio phone calls are possible and are at least better than nothing. Important messages are sometimes relayed to waiting family, and family and friends are called if the boat must go into a port for repairs. Still, it is the sea that isolates work from home and community. Almost all the shrimpers I talked with mentioned distance and isolation from family, friends, and community as one of their most serious problems.

As the trip wore on, my appreciation for my surroundings lessened considerably. I began to share the attitude and feelings of the crew toward them. My frustrations with being physically isolated grew and my anxieties and worries about my family doubled. My sensitivity to the beauty of the Gulf correspondingly decreased: almost unconsciously I began to throw my own garbage into it. (Other shrimpers I later interviewed had experienced similar feelings.)

A few shrimpers (less than 5 percent of those interviewed) said that they preferred being out at sea to staying on shore. I believe them. I think that for one reason or another these men have grown to appreciate the distancing from their families and other land problems that the Gulf affords them. But I think their preference is less a comment on their ability to adapt to an alien environment than it is a reflection of their devaluation of their personal relationships on land.

In other words, for those few their land problems are so great that they would rather not go back to them. These men may regard fishing far from home as a blessing. If they had to stay at home more, they would be forced, one way or the other, to improve, change, or live with whatever their problems might be. The sea gives them a way not to have to make decisions.

Despite the tremendous isolation, regardless of the physical pressures, and even in the face of danger, many of the fishermen I talked with suggested that they were not wholly unaware of the beauty of the sea. They spoke of the tranquility they at times felt at sea, of the freedom, of the time to think about their lives on land. There is a beauty in the immensity of the sea, a beauty in its alienness, a beauty to the challenge it offers. Some shrimpers thrive on the sea. They respect it, and they feel a sense of loss as the environment they live and work in is destroyed by the carelessness or neglect of others.

For all that it takes from these men, in return the sea gives shrimp—tons of the tiny crustaceans they seek. Many of the men, when asked what they liked best about shrimping, said simply that they liked catching the shrimp. When probed further, they said they liked the feeling, the sensation, the emotion in their gut when the nets were hauled in and hundreds of pounds of shrimp dumped on the rear deck. The shrimp are money, anything from two to five dollars or more a pound depending on size. But, more than that, the shrimp are proof that the shrimper has not wasted his time, that he knows his job, that he is a good fisherman.

2. The Work: Header and Rigger

"Work is work. Shrimping is no different than any other job, say construction."

"Es muy peligroso." (It's very dangerous.)

"I like being out there. As long as you do your job, no one bothers you."

The work of a shrimper is determined by the sea and by the particular habits of the shrimp themselves. A shrimper works all night because that is when shrimp are most active. He fishes by dragging huge nets along the ocean floor because that is where the bottom-feeding shrimp are found. He is constantly searching for them because they move from one area of the bottom to another without apparent cause. Sometimes they simply disappear.

The social structure on board the boats for captain, rigger, and header, the specific set of relationships and expectations, emphasizes the need for cooperation, flexibility, and interdependence in all the work that is done. While the shrimper's major motivation is to catch as many shrimp as possible, to earn as much money as he can in one trip to feed himself and his family, he does not want to take too many unnecessary risks. He wants to live to fish another day using his same expensive equipment. His daily work is a delicate balance between the need to take risks (some but not all of which exist because he is at sea in a boat) to earn a living, his fatigue, his experience, and his luck.

The Boats

The boats themselves are designed and built to facilitate the harvesting of shrimp. Crew comfort comes a distant second, safety third. The majority of the vessels are between forty-five and eighty-five feet long. The largest on which I interviewed was eighty-three feet and constructed of steel, as are most of the newer boats. The smallest was

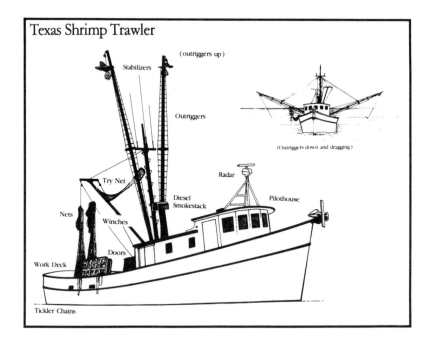

Texas Shrimp Trawler

forty-two feet and made, like all the older boats, of wood. The wheelhouse sits forward, along with accommodations for the crew. The engine room, most often containing a 300- to 350-horsepower Cummings, General Motors, or Caterpillar diesel engine, is directly under the wheelhouse. The rest of the hull is for shrimp storage. In this area the shrimp are packed in ice, which is brought aboard by conveyor belt in large blocks and is later chopped up into smaller pieces by the rigger and spread in layers over the shrimp.

On the rear deck, directly behind the pilothouse, sit the hydraulic winches used to work the nets. The outriggers, which in port are raised and folded together, are lowered at sea and support the two or four nets, the latter now the most common, that are towed along the Gulf's bottom. The nets are usually either thirty-six or forty-five feet in length. In the twin-trawl rig, most common among Texas shrimpers, the boat pulls sleds, or "dummy doors." These large wooden doors keep the mouths of the four nets open to catch the shrimp. Tickler chains at the nets' bottoms stir up the shrimp and, at least theoretically, drive them into the nets.

The bags of the nets are attached with a rope, or "lazy line," that allows the nets to be swung on board more easily when they are hauled out of the sea. In addition, a try net, a much smaller net used to search for and sample the abundance of the shrimp below the surface, is fixed to one outrigger. It is checked periodically to see if the amount of shrimp it reveals is worth the time and effort to lower the larger nets. When the nets are being dragged, the try net is also used to estimate the amount and kind of shrimp being netted.

The shrimp, along with everything else that is caught from the bottom, are winched up out of the sea, swung over the rails, and dumped on the rear deck. Then they are sorted out and deheaded, thrown in laundry baskets, washed in a preservative that controls decay, and stored and frozen below in ice. On the few freezer boats, those with refrigerated holds, the shrimp are washed in saltwater, put into thirty-five-pound net bags, and stacked.

Most but not all boats had Loran-A at the time or have since converted (as of January 1, 1980) to Loran-C, both of which are electronic locating systems that allow the shrimper to pinpoint within several hundred yards his location or the location of a good place to fish.[1] Before Loran, captains depended entirely on their compass readings and their experience. For example, one captain who had fished off Louisiana before coming to Texas in the 1950s said simply that when he left port headed southeast he knew that in order to return he had to set a northwest course until he saw land.

The wheelhouse also contains marine CB, marine radio, at least one depth finder and sometimes up to three, and other nautical aids. All boats have regular AM-FM radios; a few even have stereo and television. In general the boats provide the minimum necessities for living, although this has not always been the case. Several of the longtime shrimpers mentioned that when they started fishing in the 1940s, most boats lacked toilets, showers, beds, and adequate heating. (One shrimper told me that he used to sleep in the engine room during the winter; he said the noise was deafening but it was the warmest place on the boat.) Since the early 1960s crew accommodations have gradually improved, and almost all boats I saw appeared to provide the basic necessities. But they still were a far cry from the passenger liners,

[1] See "Loran-C Completes Transition January 1," *Texas Trawler* 7 (1980): 1.

sport fishermen's boats, or commercial fishing vessels that many of us think of when we envision ships at sea.

Header

The primary task of the header, or *descabezador*, is to remove the heads of the shrimp as soon as possible after they are netted. He also performs a wide range of tasks that are necessary to the running, maintenance, and fishing of the boat. In contrast to the rigger and the captain, who earn a share of the boat's profits after the shrimp are sold, the header is most commonly paid in direct proportion to the number of shrimp he heads, with his rate per box determined by his skill and experience. Thus, his major economic motivation is to work as fast and as efficiently as possible to increase his payoffs at the dock; the faster he heads the shrimp, the sooner they will be iced and the higher the price they will bring.

After the rigger has dropped the catch into large piles on the work deck—piles that may contain hundreds of pounds of shrimp, as well as fish, crabs, squids, octopuses, mud, and man-made objects such as tin cans—the header must sort through the "trash" and head the good shrimp. Sitting next to the large pile of dead and dying organisms, he sorts out the desirable shrimp—those that are not too small and those that have not been damaged in the nets or torn apart in the pile.

The first time I was faced with this huge pile of dead fish and other junk, among which I could see thousands of squirming shrimp, I was overcome by it all. If you have ever been to a slaughterhouse you will know the effect. There is so much of the sea matter, all dead and dying, that it is at first overwhelming. When the pile first hits the deck (and remember it is usually in the dead of night, the first drag usually being hauled up about midnight or later), the crabs scramble like crazy for their freedom. The spider crabs, some of which grow to a large size, are perhaps the most ominous: they look like great ugly spiders. Inevitably several wind up on your blind side, near your feet. The rigger first told me, when I commented on the incredible number of crabs that were all walking as straight at me as they could, "All they want to do is shake hands with you." I ignored their friendship.

As the header sorts through the shrimp, he deheads them. Grabbing several of them at a time in either hand, if he heads "two-handed," he pinches their heads off between thumb and forefinger. In the "one-handed" style he grabs the shrimp with one hand and pinches their heads off with the other. (The two-handed style is faster but harder to learn.) Headers often argue over subtleties in style, each claiming his own particular variation of these two methods to be superior.

After deheading the shrimp, the header tosses the tails into plastic laundry baskets at his side. The shrimp are now said to have their hats (that is, their heads) off. Each basket can hold from sixty to seventy pounds of shrimp tails; one hundred pounds of tails equals a box. The header is paid a given rate for each box of shrimp he heads—typically, in 1980, from ten to twenty-four dollars—depending on what the captain decides the particular header is worth to him.

The header sits on a small wooden stool with three- to five-inch legs, spreading his own legs out in front of him for balance and comfort, and stoops over the pile to rake the fish toward him in smaller amounts. For this purpose he uses a rake with a wooden or metal handle from six to ten inches long, which is attached to a dull blade five to eight inches long and three to five inches wide. The rake allows him to reach into the pile and not get surprised by a friendly crab or stuck by a fish fin or other sharp object. He can also keep the crabs away from his feet, toward which they continue to gravitate until they are swept over the side.

To protect his hands, the header wears thin rubber gloves, thicker than surgical gloves but much lighter than most gloves worn to wash dishes. Some headers use baby or talcum powder in the gloves or homemade solutions designed to protect the hands from being pricked by the shrimp. Extending up to an inch or more over the shrimp's head is a lancelike projection with tiny spaced barbs. If the header grabs the shrimp the wrong way, he gets stuck: the barbs can easily pierce the rubber gloves. I felt a slight pinprick at first. Then, as I continued to work, the acidic fluids produced by the shrimp and the other dead organic matter began to seep into my gloves through the small holes and, eventually, into my fingers; several of my fingers swelled. (Sometimes headers' hands turn yellow and the top layer of skin peels off.) With attention and care these shrimp prickings can be minimized, but every header I talked with had had similar experiences. The shrimpers call the whole process shrimp poisoning, and it is one of the reasons there were few headers who said they really liked the job.

The inexperienced header soon develops large protective calluses on his hands. The hands of the experienced header usually show a number of minor scars and scar tissue from handling the shrimp and the other dead fish and refuse. Some headers appeared to have hands that had turned a muted but permanent yellow.

Headers, along with other crew members, usually wear distinctive white boots. The boots are calf high, with thick rubber soles and heels that protect their feet from the pile, especially from the crabs. To some extent these boots have become a symbol that readily identifies shrimpers. In fact, some people refer to them simply as shrimper boots, although they are commonly worn also by the men who unload the boats and by those who work in the freezer warehouses.

The header's work requires coordination, dexterity, and at least minimal concentration. He must balance himself against the seas at the same time he heads the shrimp. I found that when I lost my concentration I got stuck more by the shrimp or grabbed onto something I should have left alone. The jellyfish must be avoided, as well as a tiny fish, called squirrel fish by other shrimpers, that was said to have a harmful poison in its fins.

Heading shrimp is similar to agricultural stoop labor in that it puts a tremendous strain on the worker's back. While the header sits on his short stool, he must bend his back in order to keep his balance on the stool and reach for shrimp from the catch. It is a very awkward position in which to work. Raking part of the catch toward him, he can raise his back only slightly. Except for infrequent breaks for coffee and perhaps a smoke, he sits in this position all night and into the next morning. Headers in fishhouses stand at long tables to do their work; this puts much less strain on their backs. On a workboat, however, it would be impossible to stand because of the pitch of the seas.

My back never did stop aching the entire trip. My hands grew hard calluses, but I could head shrimp only thirty minutes or so before I would have to stop, hobble over to the rails, stretch out my back, and then return to the stool. I'm not soft. It was not because I was in poor health, or even because I was new at the job, that my back ached: it was and is simply because the job is very hard on everyone's back. All the headers I talked with said the same thing. While to some extent a person can get used to the requirements of the job, it is simply an unnatural position in which to work. Many headers either quit or become riggers as quickly as they can.

The men head shrimp regardless of weather. Thus, those who head shrimp, and all the crew takes a turn at it, are exposed to a variety of weather conditions, ranging from extreme heat, exacerbated by diesel fumes, in the summer months to freezing temperatures and rains in the winter months. Temporary canvas tents are often strung up to protect headers from the sun and the heat.

It is very easy to fall on the work deck. A fall on the steel decks, or even on slippery wooden decks, hurts. If a shrimper falls on the pile, it can be very painful, because he is exposed to the glass, tin cans, fish fins, and other sharp objects that are dredged up from the bottom. And while the short rails on the sides of the vessel make it easier to swing the shrimp on board, they reach only knee high on the average person, making it easy to roll against the sides in a rough sea and go sailing overboard into the water below.

Once I saw that almost happen. The other header was helping me sweep the trash fish over the side. We were using long push brooms. The trash fish often compose 95 percent or more of the hundreds of pounds that are captured in each net, and in order to get the pile moving, to get some momentum, the header shoved as hard as he could. The trash moved, the boat happened to lurch, and the header barely caught himself as his knees hit the rails.

One rigger whom I interviewed told me about an incident that occurred when he was working as a header and was intent on his work. A bigger than usual swell came along, the boat happened to turn at the same time, and he slid on his stool to the starboard side. He hit the rail hard and broke three ribs.

Although a header spends the majority of his time sitting on his stool, back bent, heading shrimp, he also does his share of the maintenance and running of the boat. He is the rigger's right-hand man. He constantly cleans the rear work deck after each pile is worked through for the shrimp. He sweeps the trash over the side, helps wash the shrimp in the preservative, and helps pack it in ice in the hold. Keeping the boat clean is no easy task. The decks must be as clean as possible both for health reasons and for safety's sake. He hoses and mops the deck five times or more in a twenty-four-hour period.

Depending on his individual skills, the header aids the rigger to some extent in setting the nets and picking them up, and when it takes two people to do a job, like weighing anchor, he does his share. Dishwasher, "gofer," and general handyman, the header sometimes will even take his stand at the wheel, especially if the captain and rigger both need a break. He is called upon to do anything and everything he can to keep the boat fishing.

Headers, as mentioned above, are usually paid a piece rate, unlike captains and riggers. Green headers may be paid as little as three to five dollars a box the first few trips they make. This is because inexperienced headers really are not worth the groceries they consume: they head shrimp slowly and get in everyone's way. But they have to learn somehow, and so they are tolerated. Captains prefer headers who are experienced, but they have to take what they can get or find, and sometimes headers are in short supply.

Income of Headers

Of the thirty-seven headers I interviewed, those with some experience and expertise received in 1979 between fifteen and nineteen dollars per box, while the best paid earned between twenty and thirty dollars (see Table 2-1). Inexperienced men and other headers who received lower wages earned between ten and fourteen dollars. Three headers interviewed earned seven dollars or less per hundredweight of shrimp tails. The most common wage that headers reported was fifteen dollars per box.

Undocumented workers, most often from Mexico, were commonly paid less than those with American citizenship, regardless of experience. In fact, undocumented workers employed as headers were the only headers who had more than three years of work experience; the majority of the other headers, after at most two years of experience, would commonly move up to a position as rigger. I encountered one other exception to this general trend: several Anglo men in their fifties and sixties who were working as headers. These men were former riggers but were no longer employable in that position.

TABLE 2-1. Wages per Box Received by Headers, 1979

Dollars	Frequency*	
10	8%	(3)
10–14	27%	(10)
15–19	40%	(15)
20–24	19%	(7)
25–29	3%	(1)
30	3%	(1)

*N = 37.

The median annual income in 1979 for headers who responded in the survey was $6,400. Riggers' median annual income was more than twice as much, $13,200, and the median for captains was $22,400. One reason for headers' low annual income is that the shrimping season is best for only a few months out of the year. While theoretically shrimpers can go out all year round, in practice the months of December, January, and February are the dog days, when it does not pay to go out or the weather is so bad only a few boats will fish. Shrimpers make the majority of their incomes from mid-July up to Christmas.

The header may do just as well as the captain and the rigger, who work for a percentage of the total profit, when there are few boxes of shrimp netted, but he does not fare nearly as well when shrimp are abundant. Thus, in order to supplement their income from shrimping, some headers I talked with worked at other odd jobs, such as electrician's helper, mechanic, welder, and migrant farm worker. In almost all cases, however, this supplementary income was less than two thousand dollars.

While headers do in effect get room and board on the boat, their wages still do not amount to a minimum wage ($3.10 an hour, at the time of the survey) if all their time at sea is counted. They are expected to work around the clock, if necessary, for two to three weeks or more; then, after three to four days of rest, they are expected to go out again. If they go out for fourteen days during the late summer and the catch is reasonably good, they may earn in the neighborhood of $700 before taxes and Social Security deductions are taken out. This paycheck, when divided by the number of hours they are at sea, 336, equals $2.09 an hour before taxes and Social Security.

Of course one could argue, as do some trawler owners, that it is fair to count only the actual number of hours that are worked. This point of view discounts the fact that the crew does, in fact, sometimes work twenty-four hours a day and that being in a boat at sea—running it, fishing it, maintaining it—is all work in and of itself, whether or not any shrimp are caught at all. The point remains that the header is paid relatively little, in comparison both to the other crew members and to the rest of society, for the hard work that he puts in.

Because these wages are substandard, most novice headers go out for one or two trips, then call it quits and seek other work. I have talked with many people in the communities that were surveyed who had given heading a try. Some hated the sea, some hated the work, and almost all hated the wages. The smart headers, or the dedicated ones, or the young ones, or the ones who cannot or will not do anything else, or the ones who like shrimping and take to it naturally, stick with it and in six months to two years have their first job as riggers. As mentioned, I have talked to very few shrimpers who said that they liked working as a header.

The men who advance watch and learn from the rigger or the captain. Gradually they pick up the skills, gaining valuable experience each trip. Usually a captain or rigger will decide at some point that a certain header is worth the time and trouble to train. He then will actively and patiently teach the header the trade.

Heading is dangerous work, as are rigging and being a captain. But the safety factor is compounded by the fact that inexperienced headers constantly are in the wrong place at the wrong time. They do not know the right place to stand when the nets are boarded, and they grab a line that should be left alone or take an unnecessary risk because they do not know any better. One rigger summed it up this way: "Usually I'm pretty cool out on a trip. The only time I ever yell is at a green header."

Heading shrimp is repetitive and boring work that requires some dexterity but pays a substandard wage, and the header is the low man on the boat, regardless of his position or status on land. Unlike most other jobs in which the man at the bottom is treated badly, however, headers usually are treated well by the captain and rigger because the header is indispensable: the crew must all work together if any money is to be made. The demands of the work on board bring about a cooperation and equality among the crew that do not reflect the great disparity in their skills, experience, and incomes.

Rigger

The rigger, rigman, or *huinchero* operates and maintains the nets that catch the shrimp and is an experienced and skilled fisherman. He is usually paid 40 to 50 percent of the boat's share of profits, with the remainder going to the captain. The greater the number and size of the shrimp, the more the rigger will earn. The rigger tries to increase the number of shrimp and the condition in which they arrive at the dock by working efficiently and safely. The better the rigger, the more he will earn in the long run.

The rigger's major responsibilities can be divided into five categories: preparation of the nets; dragging; picking up; freeing the boat from bottom obstructions; and general chores, like those of the header, that involve running and maintaining the boat. By tradition, for instance, the rigger is usually the cook.

The rigger spends a great deal of his time preparing the nets and the other gear for fishing. Because nets and other gear must be properly maintained in order to avoid returning to port for repairs or making repairs at sea, since these decrease the amount of time for fishing, he is constantly repairing the nets and maintaining the equipment. In fact, one rigger, when asked what he liked least about shrimping, quickly responded, "Cleaning the fucking eels from the nets."

The rigger, with the header's help, lowers the outriggers by winch as soon as the boat is clear of the dock and other boat traffic. Then, while the vessel chugs to the fishing grounds, the stabilizers—large triangular pieces of metal that minimize the rocking of the boat as it plows through the waves—are lowered in place from the outriggers. When the captain is ready to fish, the rigger hauls in the stabilizers and detaches the doors on either side of the boat from their fastenings so that they swing freely at each outrigger's tip. Assuming no problems develop, the outriggers and doors are left in this position until the end of the trip.

Particular care is taken when the doors are lifted from their resting place by winch and pushed over the boat's sides. Each set of doors weighs several hundred pounds; the arc in which they swing is determined by the rocking of the boat against the seas, and the rigger must avoid a blow from the doors as well as keep them from hitting the side of the boat. Wooden-hulled boats are especially susceptible to serious damage by swinging doors, which, in a rough sea, can hit the sides with considerable force.

Once the doors are in place, the rigger lays out his nets on the work deck, closely inspecting all four nets to be used. Broken or damaged nets have been painstakingly repaired by the net shops at the home port; riggers can do temporary minor net repair themselves, but there are enough problems without having to repair torn nets. As a result, the rigger takes his time in straightening them out, for the thirty-six- to forty-five-foot nets can become easily entangled. To the observer the whole contraption looks like an unwieldy and cantankerous glob of ropes, lines, and floats, and during fishing it flops around, gets sticky with jellyfish and trash fish, and clings to other gear or bottom of the Gulf. It is a mess.

The rigger ties the bags of a net and checks and tests the knot several times. The knot must be secure enough to withstand the weight of the catch but must release the catch with a hard tug; if the bag of the net is not properly tied, the catch may be lost. This rarely happens, however. What is more important is that the rigger is able to place the catch wherever he wants it on the work deck. This is possible only if the knotted rope quickly and consistently releases the hundreds of pounds of catch. In turn the rigger checks each of his nets and ties their bags.

Most riggers have a system that they faithfully follow as they work at their nets. They keep to the same routine so consistently that their work eventually becomes more or less automatic. Thus, when fatigue begins to wear riggers down, they can function without having to think about each little, but possibly critical, detail.

Signaling the captain to reduce engine speed, the rigger places the nets, one by one, on the rail of the boat and plays them over the side, bag first. He must play the nets so that they fall out and away from the boat to avoid the vessel's propeller. If done properly, the weight of the doors in combination with the boat's speed will draw the nets out. As each bag is pushed over the side, it drags the rest of the net with it with increasing speed. At this point the nets circumscribe an arc from the doors to the boat while being dragged along in the water.

When the nets have been pushed over the side, the rigger signals the captain to increase the vessel's speed. Simultaneously, the doors on either side of the boat are lowered by winch. Swinging back and forth until they hit the water, the doors slowly submerge as the cables are played out, and they open the mouths of the nets as the whole apparatus of nets, doors, chains, and cables sinks to the bottom. The lazy line, the rope attached from the stern of the boat directly to the nets, is tied off.

More and more cable is played out, depending on the depth in which the boat is fishing. Shrimpers most often fish in the thirty- to fifty-fathom waters. The cable is sometimes marked along its length in fathoms; the rigger always checks with the captain to ascertain the approximate desired fishing depth, and when enough cable has been played out he shuts off the winch. The captain then assumes a dragging speed of three to five knots, depending on weather conditions.

If the try net is not already in the water, it is lowered over the side and fished at this time. The same procedure is used for the try net as for the other nets, although it is more easily raised and lowered.

Once the nets are being fished—that is, the boat is in the process of dragging them—the rigger usually takes a well-deserved break from his work, generally at the galley table drinking coffee or on the rear deck smoking a cigarette. He will remain constantly alert, however, to any change in engine speed, sudden turning of the boat, or other indication that the nets have become fouled on bottom obstructions or stuck in the mud.

The rigger and sometimes the captain will check the try net periodically, depending on their estimates of how large the catch in the try net may be. This estimate is based on the previous fishing, the try net's most recent catch, and hunches. Usually the try net will be fished from thirty minutes to an hour before it is brought up from the bottom. Only if a very large catch is expected will it be fished for a shorter time.

The rigger will extend his break until he decides it is time to take a look at the first catch in the try net. Using the winch, he signals the captain to reduce engine speed, then slowly hauls up the cable attached to the net. As the try net reaches the surface of the water, he gathers it in by means of a rope with a blunt hook at its end by tossing in the hooked rope on the far side of the net and dragging it through the water until it engages the net's webbing (this is sometimes done by the header). He then pulls in the net as quickly as he can: if the catch is left bouncing at the water's surface for more than a few minutes, it can be damaged.

The try net is pulled over the side of the boat, bag first, and falls heavily onto the deck. Then the knot in the bag is jerked, releasing the catch inside. Hundreds of half-dollar-sized crabs scatter in all directions; fish flip and jump; rock shrimp go through a series of dying gyrations. Shrimp that will "make count," that are of legal size, are quickly sorted out, counted, and thrown into a plastic laundry basket, to be headed with the larger catch from the regular nets. The trash fish are swept over the side.

Riggers and captains have their own opinions on how to estimate the eventual catch from the try net, which is used to tell them whether it is worth their time and effort to fish their larger nets, and they realize that the try net can be a misleading indicator of what they may eventually catch. But if in forty-five minutes' time they net one hundred or more good-sized brown shrimp with little trash, they can with confidence look for a good catch when they haul in their nets.

If the try net looks good, the crew will become excited in anticipation of the catch. If not, someone may comment that the try net sample does not always coincide with the catch in the nets or, if the crew has lost confidence in the captain's ability to find shrimp, that they should move to better fishing on up the line. The captain makes a decision, based on the try net, on how much longer to continue dragging the nets. The try net is immediately tossed over the side and lowered by winch into place. Dragging speed is resumed. Not more than five minutes have passed since the try net was boarded.

If the rigger has no other immediate tasks, he will, after lowering the try net, catch a few hours' sleep. There is always other work to be done, however, such as relieving the captain at the wheel or repairing or checking equipment. The rigger has up to three hours until the nets will be hauled in; after the first catch of the night, he knows that he may not get another break until midmorning. If he does find some time to catch a little sleep, the header or the captain will check the try net periodically.

When the boat is dragging its nets, the rigger's primary concern, although it is the captain's responsibility, is that nothing go wrong with the nets, that no hang-ups occur. He knows that if there is a hang-up it will happen instantaneously and that time lost in correcting the problem inevitably leads to further complications, which can involve damage to the boat and the equipment and possible risk to the crew. As a result, dragging time is, for the rigger, paradoxical: he is constantly waiting, regardless of what other work he may be doing, for hang-ups, yet hoping they will not occur.

Assuming there are no problems, the nets are picked up when the captain, often after discussion with the rigger, estimates that they are as full as possible. Unless the catch is extraordinary, the boat usually makes two to three drags and pickups each night. The boats begin dragging shortly after sunset, so their first pickup is usually around 1:00 A.M. The second pickup, assuming the fishing is good, may occur between three and four in the morning and the third, if there is one, at sunrise. If the catch is fair to poor, the second pickup will be skipped and at sunrise the nets will be winched in. If the shrimping is very good, more frequent pickups will be made.

Should there be too many jellyfish that foul the nets, no shrimp, shrimp not worth the harvesting effort, or other difficulties, the captain may decide to fish somewhere else. In that case, he will run until he finds a place to his liking, then start dragging again. If possible, running at night is avoided, since it means the loss of valuable fishing time.

The schedule for pickups during the daylight hours depends entirely on what the shrimp seem to be doing. For instance, the nocturnal brown shrimp can sometimes be netted close to shore during daylight hours. White shrimp, which are often more active during the day than at night, can also be netted close to shore, often during the morning hours but sometimes into the afternoon as well. Shrimpers play it by ear during the day, using the try net frequently to test the waters. Most captains and riggers agree that daytime fishing can be more profitable, because they can net white shrimp, which bring higher prices at the dock; but it is also more uncertain and, after a full night of working, hard on the crew.

White shrimp off the Texas coast are more desirable than browns. Not only do they bring a higher price per pound at the dock, but they are often larger than browns, which means fewer have to be netted; and their large size—the largest can go five to seven tails per pound— makes them easier to head than the smaller brown shrimp, for they can be more easily sorted from the pile and handled by the header.

Less work is required although a better price is earned. Box after box of white shrimp is a shrimper's dream.

The main drawback is that whites are harder to find and more easily fished out; many tries usually have to be made before they are located. Many captains and riggers have related how they will hit a large cache of whites, only to have it play out after the first pickup. When they return to the place where only minutes earlier they netted a box or more of whites, their nets come up empty.

When whites are being harvested, fishing may continue around the clock, for browns at night and whites during the mornings and early afternoons. But, although the crew may be glad to be hauling in so many boxes, the strain of this schedule can be debilitating. When the crew can no longer do the work that is required of a twenty-four-hour schedule, the captain will take a break, anchor up, and let everyone get a well-deserved sleep. One captain, an exception, said he would fish only for whites, during the day; he did not fish at all for browns at night.

At the captain's signal, the rigger, with the header's help, begins hauling in his nets, or picking up. The captain reduces his dragging speed and, depending on his own preference, may put the wheel on automatic pilot and join his crew on the work deck; picking up requires either two very skilled men who work well together or, more commonly, three or more crew with an acknowledged leader, most often the rigger but sometimes the captain. Slowly, the winch begins hauling in the steel cables with the attached nets; it may take twenty minutes or longer for the nets to be retrieved, depending on the depth of the water and the weather. Meanwhile, the rigger and the captain both watch and listen for any hang-ups or other problems, which could damage or destroy the catch and ruin a half a night's fishing.

The outriggers strain against their cables as the doors emerge from the depths and are jerked up against the blocks at each outrigger's tip. At this point the nets are slowly being dragged along the surface of the water. Their bags must be retrieved immediately or, as with the try net, the catch will be damaged by the action of the water. To do this, the lazy line is tossed around each of the nets in turn—first one side, then the other—in order to reach them; then a rope is thrown around the nets as soon as they can be grasped by hand. First one net is hauled by winch toward the boat and over the side. Then a line is secured farther down the first net, and the winch hauls the remaining net and bag with catch over the low sides of the boat.

At this point, both bags from the two or four nets are suspended several feet over the afterdeck. The rigger, with help from the header, tries to place the catch where it can be conveniently headed. This is at best difficult to accomplish, since each bag, with five hundred pounds or more of catch, swings slowly from one side of the work deck to the other. Skilled riggers, however, can place the catch exactly where they want it by timing the swing and yanking on the knot at the end of the bag.

The bags release their catch, and the rigger quickly shakes the nets to free any debris stuck in the upper webbing, being careful to avoid jellyfish or falling fish that may have been trapped in the webbing. The nets then are swung into a new position and dropped on deck where they are out of the way. The rigger goes to the other side of the boat, where in a similar fashion the other net is boarded, dropped, and placed on deck.

Assuming there is going to be another drag, little attention is given to the catch until the rigger quickly checks his nets, reties the bags, and goes through the same procedures he carried out previously. If no problems occur, within ten to fifteen minutes of the catch's being boarded the nets have again been pushed over the side and the cables have lowered the doors beneath the waters. Fishing once again resumes.

Hang-ups are the dread of all shrimpers; it is the rigger's responsibility to help untangle the mess. Hang-ups result when the nets during dragging become entangled with a bottom obstruction, with each other, with the boat itself, with some other boat, or with some combination of boat and sea bottom.

Hang-ups are inevitable, in part because bottom obstructions, upon which the doors, nets, cables, or chains may become entangled and damaged, have only recently been charted.[2] Obstructions are difficult to locate and are constantly changing; although a captain may avoid

---

[2] See Gary Graham and Jim Buckner, *Hangs and Bottom Obstructions of the Texas/Louisiana Gulf: Loran-C.*

all documented ones, as well as those known by him alone from his fishing experiences, an unlucky skipper may drag his boat over a large rock, an old wreck, or mud and, as a result, lose a night or more of fishing.

Technological innovations have meant larger nets, which make possible larger catches and greater profits. As the nets have increased in size, however, the possibility of hang-ups has similarly increased. This requires greater expertise and more work from all the crew, including the rigger.

Human error also makes hang-ups inevitable. Mistakes in judgment on the part of the crew can occur, particularly as work exhaustion gradually impairs the crew's perceptions and decision-making abilities. Human error in reacting to a hang-up can further complicate a particular situation and decrease fishing time. An experienced and cooperative crew will, all things being equal, encounter fewer hang-ups than one less skilled, but they will still make mistakes.

The inevitability of hang-ups is affected by weather conditions. The small problem, quickly attended to in a light sea, grows geometrically into a major difficulty in a heavy one, and even the smallest task can become the most difficult in bad weather, when mistakes are compounded.

Some causes for hang-ups while dragging remain undetermined. After the captain and the rigger have first rectified the problem, which may take many hours, they will later analyze what happened—over a cup of coffee, if they are still speaking to each other. Usually they will have a few clues and, based on their experience, can piece together a likely chain of events; but this is not always possible, and there is little else they can do to ascertain the cause, short of going back to the exact spot and dragging it again. This is not to mystify what causes hang-ups, only to emphasize that often the exact cause is unknowable.

The maxim that trouble comes in threes holds true on board ships. One net, for example, will become entangled just as the rigger is reaching for a rail that is inexplicably covered with grease. Then, as the boat jerks in its course from the tension of the net, the rigger stumbles and falls on the work deck. At this point, either the men and events straighten themselves out as before, or the situation gets worse.

The boat, when hung, will make a sharp turn, possibly a dip to one side, and the steel cables attached from the outriggers to the nets

below will groan mightily. The captain then will slack off speed immediately and run back to the work deck to check for possible damage.
The captain and the rigger must yell over the engine noise and seas to
be heard, and in the excitement the yelling can turn to abuse and
blame for what has happened. At best, however, each will give his
opinion of what happened and what is to be done. Then the captain
will take charge, yelling orders, making decisions, and working toward
a solution.

Regardless of the cause of the hang-up, there are four things that
usually result: some part of the nets or other gear gets stuck to something on the bottom; some part of the nets or other gear becomes
entangled with some other part of the nets or gear; the nets wrap
around some part of the boat; or some combination of all three circumstances occurs. There are a limited number of options that the captain
has to choose from. If, for example, the nets and doors are caught on
the bottom, the boat must be maneuvered so that the nets are freed
with minimum of damage. All other nets, including the try net, are
quickly winched in to avoid any further entanglements; then either the
boat is turned by the captain to maneuver free of the obstruction or the
engine is revved to pull against it. In either case, something, usually
the weakest part of the netting gear, has to give. As soon as the net is
pulled free, the cable is winched up to assess the damage.

If the nets become entangled one with another, they are quickly
brought to the surface. A medium or heavy sea can further complicate
this situation, because the nets, doors, chains, and ropes can become
uselessly wrapped in a thousand-pound ball of webbing, iron, and
wood, which somehow must be untangled if fishing is to continue. If
the damage is slight, however, it is just a matter of straightening out
the mess at the tip of the outrigger. This requires that someone, usually the rigger, climb out on the outrigger and work free whatever is
encumbered. In a smooth sea this is not a big problem, but when the
seas get over seven feet, the wind is gusting to thirty-five or forty
knots, and the cold has seeped into a man's bones, it can be quite a
chore.

If the mess cannot be straightened out, it is brought over the side
and dropped on deck. This is a time-consuming, risky task, for the
tangled nets may sway erratically as they are brought over the side,
especially in a high sea. Once the nets are boarded, which may take up

to an hour, the task begins of sorting out the nets; repairing or replacing the doors and nets with extras, if necessary; and returning the nets and doors to their outriggers. Additional equipment is kept on board for just such problems. This operation may take from four to eight hours or longer and in rough seas up to twenty-four hours or more, depending on the skills of the crew. Sometimes the boat is forced to seek the nearest port for repairs.

More rarely, the nets can become enmeshed with the boat's propeller or rudder, or—and this is a rigger's nightmare—the fishing gear can become entangled with that of another shrimp boat. These problems are avoided at all costs by captains and riggers with years of experience as shrimp fishermen.

The rigger, in addition to his main job of preparing, fishing, picking up, and helping the captain with hang-ups, also does his share of the heading. His other major tasks take priority, but he may spend a great deal of his time, along with the header, bent over on his stool, raking the catch toward him, deheading the shrimp, and throwing their tails into his basket. If the catch can be handled adequately by the header or headers, then the rigger will head only if he is needed—when the catch is large, for example, or the header is not very good. The rigger is always a former header, however, and often can head as well as or better than the header.

The rigger is normally responsible for the more demanding daily chores on the boat for which the header lacks the skills. These might include changing the oil filters and lubricating the engine, servicing the electronic devices in the wheelhouse, and periodically troubleshooting the boat for possible problems. The extent of the rigger's responsibility for these chores depends on his individual skills and the degree to which the captain sees the chores as part of his own or the rigger's domain.

Two other specific tasks complete the rigger's work responsibilities. Except on freezer boats, where this is not necessary, the rigger ices the shrimp. After the shrimp have been headed, thrown into plastic baskets, rinsed by hose in seawater, and dipped into the preservative, the rigger climbs down into the hold to prepare a bed of ice for them. First he chops up three hundred-pound blocks of ice and shovels the fragments into a chosen bin. Then the baskets are handed down from the work deck by the header, and the rigger meticulously spreads a layer of shrimp over ice, adds ice to cover them, and puts down another layer of shrimp. This ice-and-shrimp layer cake is finally topped off by a foot of ice. The shrimp, thus frozen, remain untouched for the remainder of the trip.

Icing the shrimp is complicated by the extreme difference in temperature between the work deck (in summer 90° to 100° or more) and the ice-filled hold, where the cold fogs glasses, cracks foul-weather gear, and numbs the bones. Crushing the ice, shoveling it, and lifting and pushing seventy-pound baskets of shrimp are all hard work in any situation. At sea the temperature differential and the rocking of the boat make them especially demanding. To make matters worse, after working in the hold, the rigger may return to three or more hours of deck work in the hot summer sun or the freezing rains of winter, compounding his discomfort.

Finally, the rigger is the cook. Mealtimes are determined entirely by the work load, but the big meal is usually eaten about an hour before sundown. The crew commonly eats two meals and occasional snacks in a twenty-four-hour period. Although a few captains are known for providing little money for food, or for having peculiar tastes in food, while at sea the crew usually eats quite well. The rigger does his best with what he has, and there is rarely a shortage of food. While crew members, like the rest of the population, have limited nutritional knowledge, they eat as much as they want in order, they say, to have the energy to work the boat.

If the rigger is a good cook, then the crew is riding high. The rigger on my boat was from Florida and liked to smother everything in thick southern gravies; he was good at spicing up bland foods and serving balanced meals. Unfortunately, the few fresh vegetables lasted only through the first week at sea, and toward the end of the trip we began eating some of the canned goods. I was working so hard that I would have eaten horsemeat without complaining; the rigger commented one morning that I was eating so much I was eating up their profits.

A shrimper's diet is determined by ethnicity, but it is always high in proteins and carbohydrates, with eggs, meats, breads, and canned and processed foods preferred. It is low, as suggested, in fresh vegetables and fruits. Shrimpers seem to eat at sea what they would, if they had the money and the opportunity, eat on land, except more of it because of the demands of the work. Refrigeration and cooking facilities on boats do not greatly limit the preservation or preparation of food, although this was, according to old-timers, not the case until recent years.

Income of Riggers

Riggers earn considerably higher incomes than do headers—in 1979, a median of $13,200, compared to $6,400 for a header—because their earnings are based on a percentage of the crew share, commonly referred to as the boat's share, as opposed to the header's piece-rate wages.

The boat's share is a fixed percentage of the boat's profit after the shrimp have been sold and the owner has taken his cut. Typically, the owner of the boat keeps 65 percent of the total profit from the sale of the shrimp at the dock and pays the rest to the captain to divide as he sees fit. The remaining 35 percent of the profit, less certain fixed expenses, is the boat's share.

A majority of riggers earned 40 to 50 percent of the boat's share (see Table 2-2), although a greater range of percentage cuts was reflected in those who earned 35 percent or less. Three riggers interviewed earned 19 percent or less. The percentage cut a rigger earns depends on his experience and the particular arrangements he can make with the captain, who decides how the boat's share is divided. Riggers who received the higher cuts often were men who had been captains themselves. Those receiving the highest cuts often were riggers who worked without the benefit of headers and split the tasks on board fifty-fifty with the captain, thus justifying an equal split in pay as well.

On all five of the boats in the sample that were captained by black shrimpers, the boat's share of the catch was divided fifty-fifty between captain and rigger. In all these cases, the captain, when asked, said they split their money equally because that was the way it was done in Georgia, their original home.[3] They went on to say that they had never heard of any other way to split the boat's share until they first came to Texas.

[3] For a complete discussion of shrimpers in Georgia, see Harold L. Nix and Muncho Kim, *A Sociological Analysis of Georgia Commercial Shrimp Fishermen, 1976–77.*

TABLE 2-2. Riggers' Percentage of Boat's Share, 1979

Percentage	Frequency*	
15–19	7%	(3)
20	7%	(3)
25	4%	(2)
30	11%	(5)
35	4%	(2)
40	11%	(5)
45	41%	(19)
50	15%	(7)

*N = 46.

Those who earned considerably less than the 40 to 50 percent share fell into two categories. In the first category were novice riggers —men with limited experience as riggers, usually less than six months, who were learning the skills of the netman from the captain. In the second were undocumented workers. Like those undocumented workers who were employed as headers, these men, though few in number, received less, on the average, than did those who were doing the same work with identical experience but who were American citizens. On one boat I found two undocumented workers, employed as riggers, who were splitting their share of 40 percent equally, each earning 20 percent. When I asked these men whether they had been working very long as riggers, expecting the pay arrangement to reflect their inexperience, I was surprised to find that each had more than two years' experience as a rigger.

3. The Work: Captain and Captain-Owner

"It's all up to the captain. If I have a good captain, I don't worry."

Captains are the backbone of the shrimp industry, for on their shoulders rest the responsibility for fishing the boats and the pressure to harvest the shrimp. Captains pit their skills and experience against the demands of the sea, the work, the crew, and the owners. In general, a shrimp captain has four major responsibilities: he runs the boat and is responsible for the crew at sea, he finds the shrimp, he oversees the harvesting of the shrimp, and he returns the shrimp safely to the dock and the fishhouse. Just exactly how each of these responsibilities is met is up to the individual captain.

Captains and captain-owners (captains who are part or full owners of the boat) vary somewhat in their economic motivations and, thus, in the decisions they make in shrimping. These distinctions will be discussed as they arise; normally, however, the observations made regarding captains apply equally to captain-owners.

Running the Trawler

The captain runs the boat at sea: he must pilot, navigate, and maintain it. If he is a captain-owner, he must also see that it is kept shipshape at the dock. Piloting the boat appears deceptively easy. The captain stands at the wheel or, more often than not, sits in a comfortable chair while the automatic pilot holds the boat to a course. A few times while I was out fishing it was necessary for me to watch the wheel because the captain, rigger, and other header were busy trying to unhang the boat. Steering the boat on a straight course is relatively easy in a calm sea; it gave me a tremendous sense of power, the power felt when driving a tractor-trailer or, closer still, an amphibious tank. I kept looking behind me, realizing that I was controlling the bulk weight of tons of steel that were being hauled awkwardly through the waves.

This experience made me appreciate the expertise required to maneuver and handle the vessels in close quarters and in rough seas. While the Gulf is largely clear of other vessels, it takes only one unseen obstruction, such as a pipeline from an oil rig, or one mistake in judgment in port for the vessel to do serious damage.

As the number of shrimp boats has steadily increased in recent years, piloting has become even more demanding. Sometimes dragging at night resembles nothing so much as a two-lane interstate overpopulated by eighteen-wheelers: the boats often come very close to each other, and, inevitably, one boat on a dragging line does not want to give way to another. Horns are tooted; captains and crews may shine their spotlights on each other in hopes of intimidation or take to shouting obscenities. One captain told me that he had been harassed several times in Louisiana waters by Louisiana shrimpers who knew he had a Texas boat. In any case, as the number of shrimp boats continues to increase, dragging requires more and more of the captain's skills just to stay out of the way of the other boats.

The captain is aided in piloting his vessel by his automatic pilot, which is, in a word, indispensable. It relieves him of the monotony of constantly correcting a course and gives him the freedom to leave the wheelhouse completely. Some captains routinely will work at a variety of tasks on all parts of the boat—helping the rigger on the work deck, for example—while the automatic pilot holds a course; they will, however, keep one eye out for approaching boats. On the other hand, some captains never leave the wheelhouse. For them the device is less useful but necessary all the same: with their hands freed, they can eat a meal, smoke a cigarette, tinker with a piece of equipment, or simply move around the small wheelhouse to stretch their legs and add some variety to the often monotonous task of piloting.

Almost all boats now have radar. Radar allows the captain to avoid unseen obstructions, especially while dragging, when the boat is going at a very slow speed. In addition, because captains steer wide courses around freighters and tankers (which do not stop for other, smaller boats, regardless of who has the right of way), radar gives the captain the time to change course to clear the major ship channels. Finally, it is very useful in bad weather when leaving or returning to port.

The usefulness of Loran-A and, more recently, Loran-C has already been discussed. Loran is easily the captain's most valuable piece of electronic gear. Not only can he plot his position or set a course, but he also can chart where he last caught eight boxes of shrimp or meet a friendly captain at a certain reading where the shrimping is supposed to be good.

Captains use depth finders with varying success. Some use them sparingly; others, with regularity, in order to avoid bottom obstructions marked in their "hang book." If a captain does hit an uncharted obstruction, he will usually mark it down and often will tell his friends about it so they can steer clear of it in the future.

While these and other technological aids provide invaluable navigational information to the captain, it is ultimately the captain's expertise that determines whether or not the obstructions are avoided, a course is properly set, and a destination reached. Even the most expensive and accurate of navigational devices are of little use in the wrong hands, and in addition this sophisticated machinery has been known to malfunction, often at critical times: the radar can vary decisively depending on its most recent tuning; depth finders can go on the blink; the Loran equipment can be misleading if the captain, under pressure and fatigue from the trip, misuses it; and automatic pilots, even in the newest boats, can fail to function, inevitably when they are needed the most.

A very few of the older captains know enough celestial navigation so that in a pinch they can avoid disaster. Most captains, however, rely on their many years of experience, with support from their navigational aids. Technological sophistication in navigational devices has undoubtedly decreased costly errors at sea and maximized fishing time, all things being equal, but it remains no substitute for experience. If the captain is a poor navigator, and there are some, he not only wastes valuable fishing time but endangers the safety of crew and boat as well. If he hears from a friend of good fishing at a certain Loran reading but then cannot get his boat to that exact spot, he is not going to catch as many shrimp as the next man. Finally, if he relies on line-of-sight navigation for docking and visibility becomes poor, then, like

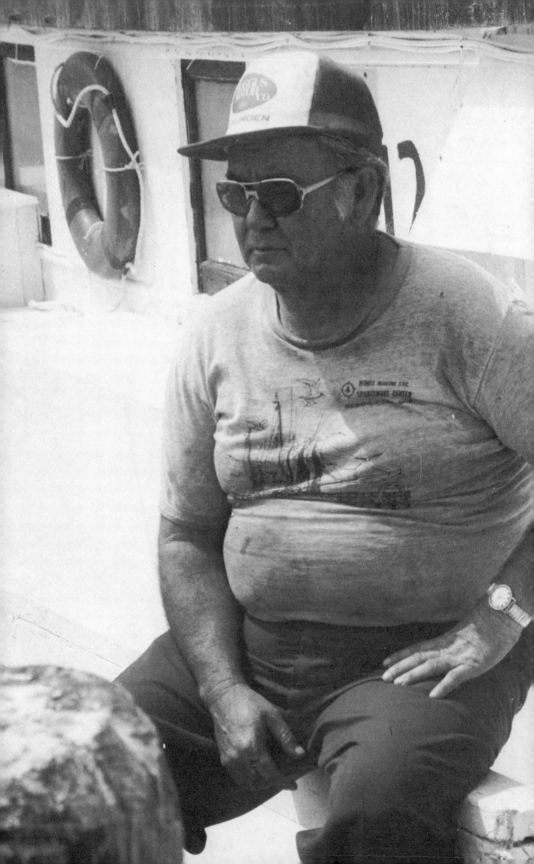

others before him, he may ground his boat on the beach or run into a jetty.

Captains realize that their decisions are affected by exhaustion and lack of sleep. Consequently, they regularly switch wheel watches with the rigger while they try to get a few hours' sleep or rest. Usually the captain takes the first wheel watch, the rigger the second.

Most captains, like the rest of the crew, drink monumental amounts of coffee in order to stay awake during the long night hours, although a few, like some riggers and headers, use over-the-counter or prescription drugs. In addition, most have various methods and routines for staying awake. Many captains pace the wheelhouse, take a walk around the boat, splash water on their faces, eat something for energy, or have a long talk with another crew member. One captain told me of his foolproof method for staying awake: if he thought he might fall asleep, he stood at the wheel, avoiding the comfortable captain's chair; then, if he did go to sleep, he would fall down, waking himself up in time to maintain control of the boat. Several captains said that they had dozed off at the wheel and awakened to find that several hours had passed by; for this reason, captains are always on the lookout for other shrimp boats that might be piloted by a sleeping crew member.

Piloting is the most hazardous when returning to the dock after a long trip, when dragging, and in northers and hurricanes. Returning to port is a particularly hazardous situation, because everyone, including the captain, is worn down by the exhaustion of the trip and more likely to make mistakes in judgment. More than a few boats have grounded in sandbars or jetties when coming in. For this reason, after a long trip most captains prefer to enter port during the daylight hours, realizing that darkness brings with it an even greater chance of getting into trouble.

Shrimpers are more adversely affected on a day-to-day basis by northers than by hurricanes. Although the danger of hurricanes cannot be overstated—the effects of Hurricane Beulah in 1967, for instance, were devastating to the shrimp fleets in South Texas—northers with winds gusting up to forty knots or better can cause permanent damage to the boats and put the safety of the crew in jeopardy. The northers often seem to come from nowhere, and, frequently, the captains say, the weather service cannot or does not accurately forecast them. Captains anchor up to ride out the blow if they cannot reach port before the storm. More than one captain told me of the times he had stood at the wheel, anchor in place, riding out a storm whose waves crashed down on the pilothouse as if to tear it to pieces.

Dragging, as suggested earlier, also requires the best of the captain's piloting skills, not just for the safety of the boat and crew but also to increase fishing time by minimizing hang-ups. Should a hang-up occur, the captain must attempt a series of maneuvers that will free the gear with a minimum of damage. The captain has a limited number of things he can do, and his alternatives may be further limited by weather conditions, including wind, current, and wave action; but it is his responsibility nevertheless to get the boat unhung, even if the other crew may in some way have fouled things up originally. As one captain succinctly put it, "Even if the crew screws up, it's my ass that gets chewed out by the owner."

The captain is in charge of not only piloting and navigating the boat but also maintaining it at sea and at the dock, especially if he is a captain-owner. The boat represents a large capital investment (in 1980 a new boat could cost $300,000 or more); the investment must be protected. Proper maintenance is mandatory if as many shrimp as possible are to be harvested; if the boat has engine trouble on a trip, or the equipment is not in top shape, a captain or captain-owner can lose thousands of dollars. For this reason, captains gravitate toward owners with the best-maintained boats.

Actual mechanical ability of shrimp captains varies. A few captains and captain-owners, especially the ones who started off as diesel mechanics, possess the knowledge to overhaul any piece of equipment on their boats. Most, however, know enough to maintain their equipment in good working condition and, at best, to prevent some of the more common problems: although diesel engines must be carefully checked for any changes in oil pressure or other indications of a malfunction, they require only regular oil filter changes and little else that cannot be done between trips.

Since electrical systems on most boats cause many problems at sea, an experienced captain will know his boat's electrical system backwards and forwards. In addition, all the machinery on the rear deck must be regularly lubricated and cleaned, and cables and ropes, as well as the other fishing gear, must be periodically checked for signs of wear. The list goes on and on: there is always something on a shrimp boat that requires fixing or cleaning, and the captain must either do it himself or see that it gets done by the crew. One captain-owner put it this way: "Even if I worked twenty-four hours a day on this boat, I'd still not get it all right."

Many captains are adept at "jerry-rigging," or temporarily replacing a broken part with a substitute that will last until a permanent onshore repair can be made. Since almost all captains worked their way up through the ranks from header to rigger, their capabilities are limited only by their individual talents. There are a few captains who will depend entirely on their rigger to provide needed repairs or, when they have mechanical problems with their engine, get on the CB and yell for a tow back into port. In general, however, the demands of shrimping many miles offshore and away from home port in all kinds of weather have created captains who know their boats' strengths and weaknesses and do their best to keep them in good shape. From getting good ice in the hold to making certain that the nets are properly repaired, captains seek to minimize the effects of equipment breakdown or damage.

At sea, captains often help each other out. They will provide cigarettes to a boat whose crew has smoked up their supply; they offer mechanical advice; they warn each other of bottom obstructions and weather conditions; and they will lend each other a door or other needed piece of equipment. In particular, if the captains in a given area hear that a crew member has been lost overboard, they all stop their fishing to begin their search; though they are in direct competition with each other for shrimp, that competition is founded on the mutual understanding that shrimpers at sea must stick together.

The captain often oversees minor in-port boat maintenance, unless he is a captain-owner. Normally, he will ask his crew to meet him at the dock a day or two after they have returned to do minor repairs and attend to any cleanup that was missed when the boat unloaded its catch. If the captain owns the boat, he will see that any welding, mechanical work, or replacement of gear is done properly and with the best service available.

A captain-owner who has three or more boats most often has his own welders, mechanics, and general repairmen or has made some kind of permanent arrangement with another captain-owner to use his men. This both saves the former money on the constant upkeep of the boats and guarantees him that he will get good service since the work is done by his own men. A few of the captain-owners interviewed had built their own boats; these men had special knowledge of their vessels and, in general, had fewer maintenance problems.

A captain is always in the position of having to explain to an owner in what way or under what circumstances a piece of equipment was damaged. Sometimes the cost of the gear, if the owner believes it was damaged through negligence, will come out of the captain's paycheck; this is just one more incentive to the captain to know his own equipment well and to maintain it properly.

One retired captain told me about an owner who, while interested in how many boxes the captain had caught, was always interested more in how his boat had fared on a trip. He would make a close inspection of the boat after each trip. When the boat was eventually sold, the captain said, the owner loved the boat so much, and had taken such good care of it, that he had tears in his eyes.

Other owners appear to take minimal care of their boats. One small fleet I inspected showed years of neglect; the owner apparently did not want to spend the necessary money to keep the boats in good shape. The captains who worked the boats were frustrated with their condition, and one complained that he was not making the kind of income he usually did and was therefore looking for another boat to captain.

While a captain's responsibilities for his docked vessel may vary, depending on the agreement he has with the boat owner, hiring crew is always left to the captain himself. Riggers are almost always selected on their reputation: sometimes the captain will call another captain whom the rigger worked for to check him out, or he may ask around town about the man, talking to his friends in bars or cantinas.

Experienced headers, as suggested, come and go. While some headers who were interviewed had worked for up to a year for the same captain, most switched captains and boats regularly. A majority of headers seemed to switch because a personality problem developed between them and the other crew or because they just got tired of working on the same boat. One header was representative of a common situation. He related that he had just been fired from a boat he had worked on for six months. When I asked him why he was fired, he said it was because the captain told him that he was always trying to tell the rigger what to do and that his job was to head shrimp, not work the nets. This header did not seem at all worried; he said he had a good reputation and would easily find work on another boat. He also figured that after the captain had gone out with his replacement, who was sure to be a poor worker, the captain would rehire him at a higher rate per box.

Hiring a header is sometimes harder than taking on a rigger because captains often do not know the kind of man they are getting. Headers are, as one captain put it, "come-and-go people." Captains would like to hire experienced headers, but often that is impossible, so they try to make character judgments based on their first impression of the man. Sometimes this works and sometimes it does not. As a result, some captains find themselves taking on men who do not work out, who have no experience and no desire or aptitude for heading shrimp, while others will hire two headers, one they have some faith in and one who might never have been out before. Sometimes the header is so worthless, or hates the work so much, that it is easier to drop him off at the nearest port than to put up with him for the rest of the trip. During a year when shrimp are abundant, riggers and headers may both be in short supply.

Availability of good crew is a primary reason many owners in Port Brownsville and Port Isabel gave for coming to, and staying in, South Texas. Many owners felt that without the presence of the Mexican, Central American, and Mexican-American crews they could not stay in business. The owners said that these men were more willing to do the hard work required and were more accepting of the long hours and isolation from family because of the relatively high salaries they earned. Several said that it was unfortunate that citizenship was required for captain's papers because they had Mexican-born riggers who would make good captains.

There is no written work agreement between captain and crew. The agreement is only as dependable as the captain's word. The vast majority of times there is no problem with the lack of a written contract, but occasionally a header will complain to local legal-aid services that he was not paid what he was promised (this is more likely to happen if the header is an undocumented worker). In general, however, a captain will go out of his way to pay a header what he promised, even if the header was not worth the money.

Maritime law differs substantially from the civil and criminal codes. The captain and captain-owner have a legal responsibility for the crew that borders on paternalism. This responsibility developed, sensibly enough, from the dependent relationship of crew to captain during the frigate-and-schooner days of the eighteenth century. As a result, captains do not want to hire crew who look like trouble; trouble-makers can mean lawsuits and safety risks at sea. They look for hard workers with experience and an acceptable personality: crew compatibility is important on a trip.

Interestingly, only a few of the crews interviewed were composed entirely of family members.[1] Most often the captain had hired his sons, his first cousins, or close relatives of a well-known family friend; particularly during the summer months, many captains take on their sons or cousins as headers so that the younger men can earn some vacation money and also get firsthand experience on a boat. More rarely, a cousin, uncle, or in-law is hired on as rigger or header. Yet, while there were many shrimpers interviewed who came from fishing families and had gotten their first jobs as headers from their fathers or uncles, there were relatively few boats that were run exclusively by family members.

On one such boat the father was the captain of the boat and his oldest son, about twenty-one and engaged to be married, was the rig-man. The rigger said that he hoped someday to be a captain and own his own boat; he was saving regularly to achieve that goal. On the other hand, the header, another son in his junior year in high school, wanted to be an architect or to do some other kind of work that required a college education. He did not mind shrimping, he said, but it was strictly a summer job to make money to buy clothes and entertainment when school started in the fall.

Captains would ideally like to maintain year-round crews. At first glance it would seem that hiring family members would be the ideal solution. The captain could be assured of the character and personality

[1] Kinship is not a major concern of this study. For a more complete discussion of the importance of kinship among commercial fishermen, see J. Anthony Paredes, James C. Sabella, and Marcus J. Hepburn, "Human Factors in the Economic Development of a Northwestern Florida Gulf Coast Fishing Community."

of his crew, and the household would benefit from the extra incomes. That there are so few family-crewed boats is, again, a comment on the demanding nature of the work. To expect a father and sons, or other close family members, to work together for months at sea and then endure family relationships at home is to expect what appears to be beyond the capability of most shrimpers.

Several crew members who got their start on their fathers' boats expressed surprise at the personality changes their fathers went through at sea. They spoke of their fathers' authoritarianism at sea, the fact that they rarely yelled at home but rarely stopped yelling on the boat. Those few family who crewed boats that did seem to work usually were run by a captain father and a rigger son who lived either by himself or with his own wife and family.

It is easy to understand, therefore, why the sons of shrimpers would eventually want to be their own bosses and captain their own boats. Kinship plays an important part in the training and development of the crew, and the sons get their first jobs as headers and advance quickly because they are often given more time and notice than someone else. Then, having gained valuable work experience from their fathers, they naturally would desire to graduate to running their own boats or at least to strike out on their own as riggers. From the captain father's perspective, one shrimper put it very simply when he said, "I have enough to worry about at home without taking my own family out and worrying about them on the boat."

Despite the problem of working with family members, fishing does seem to run in families. Kinship ties among Texas shrimpers and other fishermen are quite strong (see Table 3-1): of the shrimpers responding, for example, 27 percent had fathers who either were or had been commercial fishermen, while 30 percent had brothers in the industry.

A majority of undocumented workers from the cities of Matamoros, Tampico, and Veracruz reported that they came from fishing families. Those in Matamoros had family members or close relatives who fished in the large bay systems near that city for trout, redfish, flounder, and shrimp. Those from Tampico and Veracruz had family who worked as part of the extensive Mexican shrimp industry.

Captains establish more or less permanent working relationships with riggers. A majority of the riggers interviewed had worked for the

TABLE 3-1. Kinship Ties of Texas Shrimpers to Other Commercial Fishermen

Relationship of Commercial Fisherman to Shrimper	Frequency*
Father	27% (39)
Brother	30% (43)
Uncle	23% (33)
Cousin	15% (22)
In-law	9% (13)
Son	8% (11)

*N = 142.

captain for six months or more, many for a year or more, and a few men had worked off and on for the same captain for five years or more. Most captains try to hire riggers who are likely to stay with them for at least the season. At the same time, however, they may have one or two backup riggers they have worked with before and will call in a pinch.

Fishing Strategies

A captain who regularly docks a lot of shrimp is considered successful, regardless of his abilities as pilot, navigator, mechanic, or foreman. Usually, of course, it all goes together: the best captains harvest more shrimp because they know how to handle their boats, their crews, their shrimp, and their owner. What counts most, though, is production, including the amount, size, and condition of the shrimp. It is shrimp production that makes or breaks a captain.

Each captain tries, of course, to catch as many shrimp as he can. If he is to keep his job, he must catch no less than the average number of boxes netted by other captains in port or in a particular fleet of boats under one owner. Luck is believed to be a temporary phenomenon that may bless one captain on a single trip or even over an entire season, but over the years a man's luck will ebb and flow. Owners know who the best captains are; they keep lists of the production from each boat and they rank the captains accordingly. Captains who do not net enough shrimp, as determined by the owner, lose their boats and go back to rigging, if they can find a job.

The key to being a good captain, one who consistently harvests more shrimp than the next man, is to find the shrimp in the first place.

While dragging and picking up are no picnic, the hunt for shrimp is complicated further by the pressure to use as little fuel as possible. As fuel prices have skyrocketed, costs have dug into the owners', and now the captains', pockets. As a result, captains have developed three basic strategies for minimizing searching, or running, time: depending on the circumstances, they go where all the other captains go, trawl off by themselves, or employ some combination of the two.

Migration patterns of shrimp, as mentioned earlier, for the most part remain a mystery. After two or three nights of good fishing, sometimes fewer, the shrimp can disappear. Thus, in port captains listen for all kinds of information on where the shrimp are being netted; they may buy their friends a few beers, for example, in order to hear the latest news on the best fishing. Often the owners give them advice, although unless the owner has been a captain himself, his information is usually ignored.

Once at sea, a captain will monitor his marine CB for additional information. If he has friends who are out fishing in a nearby area, he will in addition contact them to check out their luck, although he will often ignore information passed from one shrimper to another if he does not know them because there is a lot of misleading information purposely broadcast over the CB.[2] He also will scan his radar unit to determine where a large number of boats are anchored to fish for the night and will put out feelers to other captains he knows in order to receive accurate information about the previous night's fishing.

Many captains fish only when and where everyone else is fishing. There is some variation in the amount of shrimp netted by different shrimpers in a given area, but if, for example, several boats are netting three to five boxes a night, it is generally rare that another shrimper will catch fewer than two or more than six boxes in the same area on the same nights. Conversely, if a few shrimp are being netted by all the boats, then the captain will do no worse than any other captain. This is particularly important if the captain is directly accountable to a boat owner. He can justify his small catch by pointing out that no one else caught much either. Fishing where others fish entails less overall risk to the captain and makes finding the shrimp an easy task. All the captain has to do is find the other shrimp boats.

[2]See, for example, J. Stuster, "Where 'Mabel' May Mean 'Sea Bass,'" *Natural History* 87 (November, 1979): 76–81.

Shrimping off by himself is, from the captain's viewpoint, a much riskier strategy. In the optimum scenario, he may run into large numbers of desirable shrimp; if no other or few other boats hear of his good luck, then he may be able to net many boxes before the shrimp eventually play out. In this way a captain who finds his own shrimp may return to port with a catch superior to that of other boats in his fleet, and his profit may be increased still further if he has spent less travel time and fuel than have the rest of the shrimpers.

On the other hand, a captain who fishes by himself or with one or two other boats may come up empty-handed or with fewer shrimp than the others. If he has adopted this strategy over a period of months, he may have a lot of explaining to do to the boat owner, who is less interested in explanations than he is in the size of the catch. If the captain himself owns the boat, then he risks a direct, substantial loss.

If he decides on the third fishing strategy, a captain will fish where everyone else is fishing but will leave and run all day, if necessary, to find a better spot should he judge the catch meanwhile to be better elsewhere. In effect, he will simply have switched fishing groups. More rarely, a captain will leave a group of boats to fish in a particular location that has been productive in the past.

Strategies for finding shrimp are reasonable attempts to minimize financial risk, but it is also possible, when all costs are totaled, for a trip not to have been worth their time for the captain and the rigger or, more rarely, for the owner actually to lose money. Factors beyond the captain's control, including bad weather, fluctuations in shrimp population, low dock prices, inflation, and skyrocketing fuel prices, all augment this risk. In order to increase their chances for financial success, therefore, some captains have developed "protective fishing strategies," which are intended to reduce risk and increase income.

There are three popular protective strategies and one less common approach. The first method is sometimes referred to by shrimpers as mixing shrimp and involves netting and keeping undersized shrimp that by law should, when caught, be shoveled overboard along with the trash. Usually, when the catch is composed largely of undersized shrimp, the captain will haul in his nets and fish elsewhere. If he is found at the dock by the game warden with shrimp that don't "make count," meaning shrimp that take more than sixty-five tails to make a pound, he is fined two hundred dollars, has his catch confiscated, and, most important, loses valuable time from an unproductive trip.

In mixing shrimp, the captain keeps the undersized shrimp in the hope that later on in his trip he will net larger shrimp. He then will mix the smaller shrimp with the larger so that the overall count per pound will not exceed the limit. Or, failing to catch the larger shrimp, he will simply take his chances with the game warden at the dock. Maybe he will get caught, but most probably he will not; although his catch will bring far less than if he had caught larger shrimp, he will at least have something to show for all his effort, time, and expense.

The captain and crew justify this vaguely illegal sleight of hand by pointing out that since the shrimp are dead when boarded anyway, it makes little sense to throw them away, the law and game warden notwithstanding. Shrimpers would genuinely prefer to net larger shrimp, the larger the better, but undersized shrimp to some shrimpers are better than nothing. Ironically, the intent of the law is to protect juvenile shrimp so that they may grow into adulthood and then be harvested for a higher price.

In addition to mixing shrimp, some captains poach. This means they fish illegally for shrimp in areas closed to fishing during certain times of the year. Although many gaps remain in the knowledge of shrimp maturation and migration, it is known that shrimp in the juvenile stage remain inshore to feed and grow in size before moving offshore to deeper waters. As a result, it is illegal to fish within a ten-mile limit of Texas shores from June 1 to July 15 in order to protect the juvenile shrimp; more rarely, when there are two separate populations of juveniles in one year, there is an additional closed season, although shrimpers can still fish outside the ten-mile limit during these periods. In June, 1981, a new law became effective that makes poaching much more difficult.

Not all shrimpers poach. Many are outraged by the poachers, realizing that they cut into everyone's profits. Several shrimpers even suggested stiffer fines; they felt that a few thousand dollars' fine after a third conviction of poaching did nothing to stop the crime. Fines and increased surveillance were seen as the only solutions to a serious industry problem.

All shrimpers who were interviewed showed disgust over the recent Mexican ban on shrimping inside a 200-mile limit. Up until 1977, American shrimpers fished extensively off Mexican shores. At that time the Mexican government, under President Echeverría, imposed regulations banning foreign shrimpers from Mexican coastal waters unless they purchased expensive licenses. Captain-owners and owners who could afford the licenses found the fishing as good as always; those who did not have the money at the beginning of the season had to fish elsewhere. But the licenses were phased out, and by 1979 no U.S. boats were legally allowed to shrimp within the 200-mile limit. In general, shrimpers remain bitter over this fishing policy and feel that the U.S. government did nothing to help them.

Some few captains still fish in Mexican waters, or "south of the river," the Rio Grande. They risk losing their gear, their shrimp, their boats, and the cost of expensive bribes to Mexican officials if they are caught by the Mexican patrol boats. But they do it anyway, which is a comment both on how good the fishing can be in Mexico and also on the chances that captains, with the owners' encouragement, will take. The dockside price is likely to be high for a captain who will, in effect, bet his boat and crew against the probability of netting and docking Mexican shrimp. One rigger justified the risk when he said, "Shrimp is shrimp. It's the same whether it's on this side of the river or the other."

The third way in whch some captains reduce their own economic risk in shrimping and increasing their profits is to steal shrimp from the boat owners or from themselves, if they are a captain-owner. At sea, the captain and crew are the only ones who have a good idea of how many shrimp have been harvested; there are a variety of innovative ways in which shrimp may be stolen, but each method essentially relies on the ignorance of the boat owner about the real amount of shrimp netted on a particular trip. Shrimp can be off-loaded before a boat returns to its home port, for example, or removed from the boat while it is docked, although this is much more difficult. They are then sold outright to a buyer for cash and the transaction is not recorded.

A captain-owner may also steal from himself—that is, sell shrimp to a buyer who will not record the transaction. Since the exchange is made in cash, both buyer and seller avoid tax. No one is seen as getting cheated but the government, which, it is reasoned, wastes taxpayers' money anyway.

It is impossible accurately to assess in dollar figures the amount of shrimp that is stolen by crews each year. Based on interviews with shrimpers and others in the industry, however, a conservative estimate is that 5 percent of the actual catch is never recorded.

The last, and by far least common, protective strategy is smuggling. This area of illegal activity is beyond the interest or scope of the present study but is mentioned here because occasionally the Coast Guard does catch a shrimp trawler filled with marijuana from Mexico. Smuggling in South Texas dates back to the early 1800s, when American entrepreneurs smuggled wood, furniture, and bulk goods into Mexico. A few shrimpers have, in the twentieth century, found it to be a very lucrative sidelight to their fishing efforts.[3]

The captains' protective fishing strategies, while more often than not illegal, must be analyzed within the context of the economic forces at work in the shrimp industry as a whole. In the first place, captains and crews believe that price-fixing and payoffs among the owners are rampant. (There is some evidence to support this assertion.) In addition, the captains know that any extra money they earn will even out the fluctuations in their seasonal income. Consequently, in light of the interplay of economic forces beyond their control, the captains' attempts to even the odds are at least understandable and their behavior certainly little different from that of those in similar positions in other industries such as the automotive or liquor industries.[4]

Harvesting and Docking the Shrimp

After having determined a good place to fish, based on his fishing strategy, the captain oversees the netting of the catch. Usually he will remain in the wheelhouse to pilot the boat as the nets are prepared and lowered over the side for the first drag of the night. As soon as the catch from the first try net is boarded, the captain's choice of fishing spots is either confirmed, as mentioned earlier, or called into question. A few captains will haul in the nets immediately if the try net is disappointing; they are betting that to continue dragging in the chosen area is more of a waste of resources than the effort already spent. The majority, once having made the commitment to drag, will fish regardless of the sample catch in the try net.

The captain decides when the nets are picked up. He bases his decision on the catch in the try net and on his future plans for dragging

[3] See, for example, "Local Investigators Say Mafia Has Hands in Gulf Drug Trade," *The Facts* (Freeport, Texas), October 7, 1980, p. 1.
[4] See Norman K. Denzin, "Notes on the Criminogenic Hypothesis: A Case Study of the American Liquor Industry," *American Sociological Review* 42 (1977): 905–920.

that night. If the shrimping looks good, he will make three, four, or more pickups. If it looks bad, he may make as few as two.

During pickups, as in dragging the nets, the captain is ready for any problems that may occur. If he has a good rigger, then the chances of something's going wrong are reduced. Some captains will join the rigger on the afterdeck to help pick up the nets; others will never leave the wheelhouse.

The captain watches the condition of his ice carefully. After fourteen days of summer heat, most ice boats must soon consider returning to the dock or the shrimp will begin to spoil, developing black spot, a discoloration on the outer shell that considerably lowers the dockside price. The captain must gauge the last few days of his fishing so that he does not find himself so far from port that his shrimp will spoil by the time he has made the trip back. While he makes his final run to port, he will, particularly if the fishing has been poor, periodically stop along the way and lower his try net, hoping he can add an extra box or two to his catch below.

On reaching port, the captain docks briefly at the owner's pier to check in with the owner and have the secretary arrange for the pay advances for himself and his crew. He then motors the boat over to the fishhouse and watches while the shrimp are unloaded.

The fishhouses hire men at the minimum wage to unload the shrimp. Often they are older shrimpers who either no longer want or cannot find work at sea, or younger men looking for a job on the boats. Large vacuum hoses suck the shrimp out of the trawler's hold and onto the conveyor belts that carry them from the dock into the fishhouse. Inside, the shrimp are automatically sorted, graded, and boxed in five-pound quantities. If the shrimp are brought in with the "hats on," then other workers, primarily women and older men, dehead them. The shrimp are then frozen a second time in the large freezers of the fishhouses, where they await distribution to wholesale and retail markets.

The rigger and header finish cleaning the boat while the captain waits for a final count from the fishhouse. He then returns to the owner's office, gets the pay advances for himself and the crew, locks the boat, and heads for his family or the local bar. The captain and crew usually return the next day for their checks, minus their advances; at that time they may do a final cleaning or minor repair of the boat.

Depending on the season and how good the fishing has been, the crew may take two or three more days off before the next trip. The day before the next trip out, the rigger, and sometimes the header, return to the boat to help the captain with any work that must be done. (They are not paid for this time; it is considered a part of their job.) The captain, almost always accompanied by his wife or girlfriend, buys the groceries and their supplies for the trip. An experienced captain's wife knows exactly what to buy and in what quantities. Other supplies, such as gloves, are also purchased at this time.

On the day of the trip the crew appears at the boat around 10:00 A.M. Now final preparations are made: the captain fuels the boat (this takes several hours), the rigger checks his nets, and the header helps with whatever he can. Many captains make themselves lists so that they will not forget any last-minute details.

Income of Captains and Captain-Owners

Annual incomes vary dramatically among captains, depending on their percentage cut with the owner, their cut with the crew, their expenses incurred while fishing, and their expertise in netting shrimp. The median income for captains surveyed in the sample was $22,400; some captains, however, earned less than $15,000 and others more than $30,000 (see chapter 4).

Almost all captains interviewed received a 30 or 35 percent boat's share from the owner (see Table 3-2). Those earning higher boat's shares tended to be from the two southern ports or to work for smaller fleet owners. In general, the larger the employing company, the lower the captain's percentage of the boat's share is likely to be.

As evidenced in examining the rigger's share of the boat's share, there is a considerable range of percentage cuts between captain and rigger (see Table 3-3). The captain decides what his split with the rigger will be, depending on his assessment of the rigger's worth to him. Captains reported that they most commonly split the boat's share 55-45 with the rigger or retained more than 60 percent of the boat's share for themselves.

In 1980, many captains paid a percentage of the fuel costs for the first time. In the fall and winter months of that year, fuel cost approximately ninety cents a gallon; since it is not unusual to burn several thousand gallons of fuel in one trip, a total fuel bill of from $3,000 to

TABLE 3-2. Captains' Boat's-Share Agreements with Owners

Boat's Share (%)	Frequency*	
30	37%	(18)
35	53%	(26)
40	4%	(2)
50	6%	(3)

*N = 49.

TABLE 3-3. Captains' Cuts with Riggers

Captain's Cut (%)	Frequency*	
50	14%	(7)
55	41%	(20)
60	12%	(6)
65	39%	(19)

*N = 49.

more than $5,000, depending on the size of the trawler, was common. The percentage varied from 10 to 20 percent of the total fuel consumption during the trip. Thus, captains and crews could pay $400 or more per trip, assuming an arrangement in which they paid 20 percent of the fuel bill.

Captains and crews normally pay a percentage of the costs for the ice stored aboard to preserve the shrimp. In 1980 this cost ranged from $50 to $100 per trip. In addition, they always pay for their own groceries while fishing; though costs again vary, depending on the individual preferences of crew members, in 1980 it was not unusual to spend $300 for three men on a fifteen-day trip. Finally, captains and crews always pay for their own personal equipment, including gloves, boots, foul-weather gear, and other incidentals.

There were a variety of arrangements between captains and owners to pay for minor repairs. Sometimes the owners required the captain to pay a percentage of the costs in order, they said, to discourage carelessness with equipment. Many captains were expected to pay 50 percent of the cost to repair the nets.

Based upon data collected in the survey sample, we can calculate the results of a typical trip in the summer of 1980. The trip lasted seventeen days; thirty-seven boxes of shrimp, 3,700 pounds of shrimp tails, were sold at a price averaging $3.50 per pound, for total revenues of approximately $13,000. The owner received $8,450 and the boat $4,550, assuming a typical 65-35 owner's share–boat's share split. Expenses deducted from the boat's share included wages for the header, $555 (37 boxes at $15 a box); ice, $75; fuel, at a rate of 20 percent of the total cost, $300; groceries, $300; repairs, $50; and gloves and other incidentals, $50. The captain earned a 55 percent cut of the boat's share, less expenses, while the rigger received 45 percent. Thus the captain received $1,771 and the rigger, $1,449.

The wages for the captain and rigger may seem excessive, except when one remembers that they are receiving a salary for seventeen work days, that the fishing season is limited, and that the captain and crew have avoided serious repair bills or downtime for their equipment. It is interesting to note that the captain in fact received 13.6 percent in wages of the total profit from the sale of the shrimp, the rigger 11.1 percent.

The owners do not, of course, earn as clear profit their 65 percent share from the sale of the shrimp. Various expenses, to be discussed in later chapters, must be deducted before they see a real profit. Those men who are sound money managers, however, have fared well over the years.

These figures for a typical trip emphasize that the captain's actual income is based not just on how many shrimp he nets but on other costs as well, some of which can considerably affect his wages. For this reason, captains have a wide range of incomes.

Luck in harvesting shrimp was not seen by most captains and owners as a reason why one captain might consistently do better than another and, theoretically, earn a higher annual wage. Owners believed it was question of which captains were willing to work the hardest. Many owners reported that income for a captain and crew depended solely on how hungry they were and how hard they worked for the shrimp. Captains, on the other hand, saw their income as closely related to factors increasingly outside of their control, including fuel prices, inflation, and the abundance of the fishery. Most captains said shrimp production depended on a good crew, especially a competent rigger. These men felt that if they had a good rigger, then even if the header was inexperienced they still would net their share of the shrimp.

Captain-owners earned substantially more than captains (see Table 4-5). Based on the incomes of the five captain-owners for which data are available, it can be observed that most captain-owners earned between $40,000 and $100,000 or more in 1979. The differences in the extent to which these men are not only successful captains but also good managers of their boats explain the wide range of incomes.

4. Demographic Characteristics and Attitudes toward Work

"Shrimpers are like men who work out of civilization."

Attitudes of Texas shrimpers toward their own work as fishermen reflect an ambivalence grounded in the nature of their work at sea, its long-term effects on their families, and their place in their own communities. When certain demographic characteristics of Texas shrimpers are considered, their complex feelings about working as fishermen become clearer. The economic benefits of shrimping and, by some, the enjoyment of the work militate against what are perceived as two major drawbacks, the time one must spend away from family and friends and the relatively low status accorded many shrimpers in their communities.

Ethnicity

Texas shrimpers sampled were composed of six major ethnic groups: Mexican-born, Anglos, Mexican-Americans, blacks, Cajuns, and Central Americans.

The largest group of respondents interviewed was composed of undocumented Mexican workers, who represented 30 percent of the sample (see Table 4-1). The majority of the Mexican workers (65 percent) lived in Matamoros, Tamaulipas, directly across the river from Brownsville. Other cities of origin were Tampico (9 percent) and Veracruz (5 percent). The remainder (21 percent) were from small towns and villages in northern Mexico.

The second-largest group interviewed was composed of Anglos. Anglos who worked as shrimpers were predominantly Texas-born, although a number of other states, including Florida, Louisiana, California, Oklahoma, and New York, were represented in the sample, albeit by no more than one shrimper apiece. Texas Anglo shrimpers tended

TABLE 4-1. Ethnicity of Texas Shrimpers

Ethnic Affiliation	Sample Frequency*		Corrected Estimate
Mexican	30%	(43)	20%
Anglo	27%	(39)	27%
Mexican-American	21%	(29)	20%
Black	9%	(13)	20%
Cajun	7%	(10)	7%
Central American	6%	(9)	6%

*N = 143.

to be from small rural towns from all parts of the state and from small towns in the other states mentioned (the Louisiana and Florida shrimpers were from fishing communities in these states). Large metropolitan areas were underrepresented.

Mexican-Americans comprised the third-largest group of Texas shrimpers interviewed, 20 percent. Almost all were born and raised in Texas, in contrast with Anglo and black shrimpers. They were most often from small fishing communities and nearby cities.

Blacks made up 9 percent of the sample. These fishermen were born and raised in small towns in Georgia, North Carolina, and Florida. None were born in Texas.

Cajuns represented 7 percent of all shrimpers interviewed. These fishermen came predominantly from East Texas and Louisiana; they are culturally distinct from any of the other groups. Their historical influence on the Texas shrimping industry has been impressive and is described in detail later.

Central Americans made up the smallest group of shrimpers sampled, some 6 percent. Those interviewed came from Guatemala, Belize, and Nicaragua. Like the Mexican shrimpers, these men were undocumented workers.

Based on my observations and knowledge of Texas shrimpers, Mexican shrimpers were somewhat overrepresented in this survey sample, and blacks were underrepresented. This occurred for two reasons. First, undocumented Mexicans are much more likely to work as shrimpers along the border than they are in more northern ports. Since approximately one-half of the shrimpers interviewed were at Port Brownsville and Port Isabel, the sample reflects this bias. This is not to suggest that there are few undocumented workers in the central and northern ports of Texas, but rather that the selection of the two border ports led to an overrepresentation of this group in the sampling frame. Taking this bias into consideration, it is reasonable to estimate that approximately 20 percent of all Texas shrimpers are Mexicans, rather than 30 percent represented in the sample.

Second, the reason blacks are most probably underrepresented in the present survey is that in Freeport I missed by only a few days interviewing a large number of black shrimpers from Florida who fish in Texas six months out of the year. A corrected estimate, based on data collected from interviews with black Florida shrimpers plus information from others in the industry, is that black shrimpers comprise approximately 20 percent of all Texas shrimpers, rather than the 9 percent reflected in the sample.

Each of the six major ethic groups has its own more or less distinct values, customs, and traditions. Even this observation, however, masks a greater ethnic diversity among Texas shrimpers. For instance, Mexican-Americans from South Texas certainly differ from nonborder Mexican-Americans. Florida blacks interviewed were more likely to reflect an urbanized life-style than those from other southern states. Central Americans were clearly representative of distinct cultures. These observations underscore the cultural diversity among these Texas fishermen, a richness of customs and traditions that cannot be overlooked.

Income

Texas shrimpers in 1979 earned a wide range of incomes from their fishing (see Table 4-2). Of the 133 fishermen for whom gross-income data are available, one shrimper earned $1,800, while another earned $85,000. With a median of $15,000, annual incomes can be placed into four major groupings: the first consists of those who earned less than $8,000, 24 percent of those sampled; the second, those earning between $8,000 and $14,999 (26 percent); the third, fishermen whose annual wages fell between $15,000 and $23,999 (28 percent); and the fourth, those earning more than $24,000 (22 percent).

The annual earnings of shrimpers can be viewed in another way that reflects what a wide range of incomes these fishermen earned.

TABLE 4-2. Gross Annual Fishing Income of Texas Shrimpers

Income	Frequency	
$ 1,800–$ 1,999	1%	(1)
$ 2,000–$ 7,999	23%	(31)
$ 8,000–$14,999	26%	(34)
$15,000–$23,999	28%	(37)
$24,000–$30,999	14%	(19)
$31,000–$37,999	5%	(7)
$38,000–$85,000	3%	(4)

*N = 133.

Seven shrimpers reported gross annual earnings of $4,000, eight made $5,000, eight made $6,000, and three made $7,000. At the same time, at the other end of the income scale, one shrimper earned $37,000, three earned $50,000, one earned $80,000, and one earned $85,000.

Those men earning in the lowest quarter of all Texas shrimpers were also those most likely to report that they supplemented their shrimping income with odd jobs during the off-season. This additional income rarely amounted to more than $2,000, however, and these men rarely reported any additional family income from other wage earners. Therefore, the data suggest that this group of shrimpers is at, or slightly below, the federal poverty guideline.

This considerable disparity in incomes among shrimpers is also reflected in other economic indicators, including quality of life, dependence on federal subsidies, and other related data that were collected. Questions used to determine quality of life, for example, at first glance appear to undermine the annual-income data for shrimpers, the QOL data (see Table 4-3) apparently reflecting fishermen who, on the whole, earn substantially less than the findings have shown.[1] For instance, 32 percent of those sampled responded that they frequently had problems with having enough food to eat.

These economic data must be interpreted in light of the fluctuating wages of shrimpers, which depend on a variety of factors, some of which have been suggested and others of which are detailed in later

[1] For a discussion of the relevance and limits of quality-of-life indicators, see, for example, Angus Campbell, Philip E. Converse, and Willard L. Rodgers, *The Quality of American Life: Perceptions, Evaluations, and Satisfactions.*

TABLE 4-3. Quality-of-Life Indicators for Shrimpers

	Frequency					
	Frequently		Seldom		Never	
Do you get behind in your rent?*	46%	(56)	7%	(8)	47%	(58)
Do you have enough food?†	31%	(39)	11%	(13)	58%	(72)
Are your utilities cut off?‡	25%	(31)	9%	(11)	66%	(81)
Are you late paying big bills?†	32%	(40)	15%	(18)	53%	(66)
Can you afford medical bills for family members?†	32%	(40)	15%	(18)	53%	(66)

*N = 122.
†N = 124.
‡N = 123.

chapters. The important point here is that even shrimpers in the second and third income groups are sometimes unable to pay their rent on time or afford their family medical bills. Furthermore, there is a core of shrimpers—the first group, with incomes of less than $7,000—who frequently face economic hardships.

Dependence on government subsidies is another indicator of economic status. One-quarter of the shrimpers interviewed said they received food stamps in 1980, while almost that many received unemployment compensation (see Table 4-4). Only one shrimper out of 141 reported that he or his family received AFDC, SSI, or a rent subsidy. These figures, again, point out the importance of the fluctuating and inconsistent incomes that shrimpers earn from fishing, which during one month may be more than enough money to get by, but the next month, too little.

The figures regarding unemployment compensation and food-stamps are particularly telling, for two reasons. First, the majority of shrimpers expressed the view that they would not accept food stamps unless there was absolutely no other option; many were too proud to accept government subsidies even if they were in genuine need. These figures, then, actually understate those who are in real need of assistance. Second, undocumented Mexican and Central American workers cannot qualify for food stamps and unemployment, and this group of shrimpers tends to be the most poorly paid. Therefore, shrimpers who do apply for food stamps and unemployment benefits are not solely

TABLE 4-4. Texas Shrimpers' Use of Government Subsidies

Subsidy	Frequency			
	Yes		No	
Food stamps*	25%	(35)	75%	(107)
Unemployment*	22%	(31)	78%	(111)
AFDC*	1%	(1)	99%	(141)
SSI†	0%	(0)	100%	(141)
Rent subsidy†	1%	(1)	99%	(140)

*N = 142.
†N = 141.

TABLE 4-5. Shrimpers' Income by Job, 1979

Income	Header		Rigger		Captain		Captain-Owner	
$ 1,800–$ 1,999	1	(3%)	0		0		0	
$ 2,000–$ 7,999	25	(67%)	6	(14%)	0		0	
$ 8,000–$14,999	7	(19%)	19	(45%)	8	(16%)	0	
$15,000–$23,999	3	(8%)	13	(31%)	20	(41%)	1	(20%)
$24,000–$30,999	1	(3%)	4	(10%)	14	(29%)	0	
$31,000–$37,999	0		0		7	(14%)	0	
$38,000–$85,000	0		0		0		4	(80%)

representative of the poorest group but also include those earning substantial annual wages.

Fully 27 percent of all shrimpers interviewed said they had to borrow money in 1979 from banks, finance companies, or employers. Again, some of these shrimpers were undoubtedly from the poorest group, but others with whom I talked represented the other three income groups, even those making the highest annual salaries.

The disparity in annual incomes and the other economic indicators clearly reflect the differential job status of headers, riggers, captains, and captain-owners (see Table 4-5). Fully two-thirds of all headers interviewed earned less than $8,000 in 1979, while almost one-third of the captains received at least three times that amount. Captain-owners topped the income scale, although information is available for only five men. Incomes of riggers, while substantially better than those of most headers, fell far short of the incomes of most captains: almost half of the riggers interviewed earned between $8,000 and $14,999. The respective median-income figures demonstrate the significant differences in earnings: the 1979 median income for headers interviewed was $6,400, while for riggers it was $13,200 and for captains $22,700.

Age

Shrimpers interviewed represented a wide range of ages, the youngest sixteen years old and the oldest sixty-nine (see Table 4-6). In general, however, the sample suggests that shrimping is a young man's work. Seventy percent of those interviewed were thirty-nine years old or less, with 39 percent between the ages of twenty and twenty-nine. Only twelve percent were fifty or older.

When the age of shrimpers is broken down by crew position, it becomes evident that headers on the average are much younger than captains and captain-owners, with riggers falling somewhere in between the two groups. Eighty-nine percent of all headers were less than thirty-five years old, compared to 34 percent of all captains and captain-owners. There was no significant difference in the ages of shrimpers on the basis of their respective counties.[2]

Education

Shrimpers' educational attainment does not differ significantly from that of others in the labor force in their respective counties.[3] The mean number of school years completed for the sample of shrimpers interviewed was 9.6 (see Table 4-7). Thirty percent of those sampled had a sixth-grade education or less, while 27 percent were high-school graduates. Eleven percent had gone to college; 2 percent were graduates of a four-year college program. The most common number of years of schooling completed was six, attained by 20 percent of all shrimpers interviewed.

Others in the fishing communities and the surrounding counties had approximately the same level of educational attainment. Adults twenty-five and over in Cameron, Brazoria, and San Patricio counties,

[2] U.S. Bureau of the Census, *County and City Data Book, 1977*, section 45, pp. 761–894.
[3] Ibid.

TABLE 4-6. Age by Crew Position

Age	Header		Rigger		Captain/ Captain-Owner	
16–19	5	(14%)	3	(6%)	1	(2%)
20–24	17	(47%)	11	(23%)	6	(10%)
25–29	6	(17%)	10	(21%)	6	(10%)
30–34	4	(11%)	6	(13%)	7	(12%)
35–39	0		8	(17%)	10	(17%)
40–44	0		4	(8%)	10	(17%)
45–49	0		2	(4%)	9	(16%)
50–54	1	(3%)	3	(6%)	4	(7%)
55–59	0		0		5	(9%)
60–70	3	(8%)	1	(2%)	0	

TABLE 4-7. Education of Texas Shrimpers

Years of Education	Frequency*
0– 6	30% (42)
7– 9	21% (30)
10–12	38% (53)
13–16	11% (16)

*N = 141.

for example, averaged 8.5, 12.0, and 9.5 years of education, respectively, as compared to the average for surveyed shrimpers of 9.6.[4] It should be noted, however, that shrimpers' educational attainment is significantly lower than that of the work force in nearby Texas metropolitan areas such as Houston, Galveston, and Corpus Christi and much lower than the national average.

Marital Status and Children

The majority of Texas shrimpers were married (see Table 4-8). Single shrimpers, including divorced fishermen, represented over one-third of the sample, with those widowed and "other" accounting for 3 percent.

[4]Stanley A. Arbingast, ed., *Atlas of Texas*, pp. 50–72.

TABLE 4-8. Marital Status by Crew Position

Marital Status	Header		Rigger		Captain/ Captain-Owner	
Single	24	(73%)	18	(39%)	6	(11%)
Married	9	(27%)	25	(55%)	48	(87%)
Widowed	0		1	(2%)	1	(2%)
Other	0		2	(4%)	0	

Marital status is strongly related to crew position, which in turn is related to age. While almost three-quarters of all headers, who comprise the youngest segment of the age spectrum, were single, 87 percent of all captains interviewed were married. The high percentage of headers, particularly undocumented headers, who were single thus can be accounted for by age. The marital status of riggers falls approximately between that of headers and captains.

As with the comparisons to county data for education, the sample of shrimpers interviewed did not differ significantly with regard to marital status. There are a greater number of Texas shrimpers who are single (36 percent, compared to a national average of 23.3 percent), but, again, the younger ages of headers must be considered.[5]

Data were also collected from 109 shrimpers on the number of children residing with them. The most common responses were no children, 20 percent; two and four children, both 17 percent; one child, 12 percent; and five children, 10 percent. The mean number of children who lived with the shrimpers sampled was 3.82.

Attitudes toward Work at Sea

The ambivalent attitudes of shrimpers toward their work at sea are reflected in their responses to the survey questions. On the one hand, when asked whether in general they liked their work, an overwhelming majority of men (78 percent) said they did, while only 22 percent responded that they did not (see Table 4-9), and, when questioned further, 80 percent of those responding said they were proud to be known as shrimpers. On the other hand, shrimpers' generally positive attitudes toward their work took another turn when they were asked

[5] U.S. Bureau of the Census, *Statistical Abstracts of the United States: 1980*, p. 5.

whether, given the option, they would again choose shrimping as an occupation; although two-thirds said they were more or less satisfied with shrimping as their chosen line of work, fully 29 percent said they would rather choose another career. Moreover, a marked dissatisfaction with shrimping as work is apparent in the responses to the question of whether fishermen would like their sons to follow in their footsteps, with only 54 percent of those surveyed responding that they would and 37 percent replying that they would not. Finally, there is an even stronger disagreement among shrimpers as to the dangers and risks of working at sea as fishermen.

To some degree, income, ethnicity, and education of Texas shrimpers explain their attitudes toward work at sea. Fishermen are attracted to the work because of what they perceive as the potential for earning high wages. While most headers interviewed agreed that they did not want to continue working as headers because of the repetitiveness and boredom of heading shrimp, combined with the low wages, the majority looked to better times, when they would advance to the job of rigger and, eventually, to captain.

TABLE 4-9. Shrimpers' Attitudes toward Work

	Strongly Agree	Agree	Not Sure	Disagree	Strongly Disagree
In general I like being a shrimper.	5%	73%	0%	20%	2%
I'm proud to be a shrimper.	5%	75%	0%	20%	0%
If I had to do it all over again, I'd be a shrimper.	1%	66%	4%	29%	0%
I'd like my son to be a shrimper.	2%	52%	9%	35%	2%
Shrimping is dangerous work.	0%	57%	2%	41%	0%

NOTE: N = 100.

Headers in particular repeatedly suggested that they did the dirty work in order to learn the ropes so that they could advance to a rigger's pay and, in some distant future, a captain's fortune. Riggers seemed of two persuasions: one group definitely saw themselves as soon advancing to the status of captain; the other seemed quite satisfied to remain in their present position. The latter group expressed the opinion that being a captain was not worth the extra responsibility and worry; the former were outwardly more ambitious, expressing a confidence that soon they would be given their own boats. Again, increased wages were the major motivation, although many suggested they wanted to be captain also so that they would not have someone always looking over their shoulder.

Undocumented Mexicans and Central Americans found working as headers or, more rarely, riggers to be suited to their skills. An important part of the work force, they were very positive about their jobs as fishermen. Shrimping offered easy access to a wage that, though minimal by American standards, was superior to any they might have expected south of the Rio Grande. Undocumented workers were able to save most of their wages because they were at sea, with room and board provided; when the boats docked, they most often continued to live on board until the next trip.

While the potential for earning a captain's salary remains a lure for many shrimpers, the absence of any real job alternatives certainly is one explanation of why men turn to fishing for a living and remain shrimpers over the years. The average shrimper has a very limited education by contemporary standards. He realizes that, regardless of his skills, lack of formal education precludes many job opportunities. Even other jobs on commercial boats, which would seem to be one possible alternative for shrimpers, often require formal licensing of skills and, for some, entrance into a union. Shrimping requires minimal licensing and no formal testing of basic skills, although recently there has been a move in that direction.

Shrimpers, then, have become and remained shrimpers because of the promise of high wages and because of limited job options. When they responded overwhelmingly in the interview that they liked their work, they did so because they realized that the possibilities of other kinds of work were severely limited. They were proud to be shrimpers because shrimpers can earn good incomes, incomes beyond the reach of most men with ninth-grade educations. Thus, many, when asked whether they were proud to be shrimpers, responded, "Damn right I'm proud."

Since 1979, however, shrimpers have felt that their wages have not kept pace with inflation. Many shrimpers talked about the good and bad years before 1979, and most agreed they had never felt as financially pressed as they did in the fall of 1980, with no apparent end in sight. Undoubtedly this pressure led almost one-third of the shrimpers to respond that, if they had it to do over again, they would choose another kind of work.

Income and education also explain shrimpers' answers to whether they would like their sons to follow in their footsteps as fishermen. A little more than half the respondents wanted their sons to be shrimpers. Many of these men also said, however, that they were encouraging their sons to get the education they, as fathers, did not have. They believed that their sons, armed with a degree, should not have to work as hard, as long, or in such dangerous surroundings as they did.

Combined with this feeling was a common response that their sons "should be something better than a shrimper." As one man said, "It was good work for me, but I want my son to have an education and not have to do this kind of work." Even those who did say they would like to have their sons become shrimpers qualified their remarks by adding that it all depended on what their sons wanted to do, although it was with some pride that many of these men told me their sons had learned or would learn to shrimp on their father's boat or the boat of another family member. Finally, a common attitude among many shrimpers was that "there's no future in shrimping anymore"; they had become disillusioned with shrimping as an occupation in the last few years.

When shrimpers were asked about what they did not like about their work at sea, they listed being away from home as the most important problem. Fuel prices, cleaning the boat, cleaning the nets, working in the ice hold during rough weather, storms and hurricanes, working with an inexperienced crew member, and working on a boat with equipment that was not properly maintained were also mentioned, but time and again shrimpers said that being away from their families and friends was the hardest part of being a shrimper.

Attitudes about the Importance of Work

Shrimpers are very much aware of the ways other members in the community react toward them because of their chosen occupation (see Table 4-10). A second set of questions was asked in the survey to determine shrimpers' attitudes toward the value placed upon their work by other members in the community and to define the shrimper's perceptions of the value of his work to the community and the general welfare of the country.

The first of these questions received more discussion from fishermen than did any other, except those dealing with declining wages and fuel prices. Opinion was divided on this issue; 54 percent of those interviewed believed that others in the community did not respect shrimpers, 41 percent said shrimpers were respected, and 5 percent were not sure. Many thought for a while before answering, then gave relatively elaborate answers to the question. Others launched into examples that proved their point.

Those who were in agreement that fishermen received little community respect most often explained the situation using the "rotten apple" theory. According to them there were a few wild, drunk, dangerous, or mean fishermen who made fools of themselves and gave all shrimpers a bad name. Often the respondent would list the names of shrimpers he had in mind as "rotten apples." (Interestingly, while these lists varied, naturally, from port to port, they also varied within ports; one man's rotten apple was another man's friend.)

Those who said they felt they received community respect sometimes qualified their statements by adding that, of course, there were a few shrimpers who made the others look bad—the rotten apply theory again. But these men said their friends knew, as they did, that "there are good shrimpers and bad just like everybody else." This is an important observation, suggesting that face-to-face contact with these fishermen results in the ability to make distinctions between the "good" and the "bad" shrimpers.

While a majority of shrimpers felt that their job did not earn them a place of respect in their towns, they did, nevertheless, see their work as important to the general welfare of the country. Eighty-one percent of the fishermen believed that they provided an important food source to the public, and 88 percent responded that shrimping was an impor-

TABLE 4-10. Shrimpers' Perceptions of Community Attitudes
toward Shrimpers

	Strongly Agree	Agree	Not Sure	Disagree	Strongly Disagree
Do most people in your community respect shrimpers?	1%	40%	5%	52%	2%
Do shrimpers provide Americans with an important part of their food?	0%	81%	5%	14%	0%
Is shrimping an important part of the American economy?	4%	84%	1%	11%	0%

NOTE: N = 100.

tant part of the American economy. In light of the fact that shrimp in
recent years has become a luxury-food item for middle- and upper-
income families, the answers of shrimpers thus may be seen as a necessary justification and legitimization of their work; given the risks and
dangers involved in fishing as an occupation, those who work as
shrimpers must believe not only that the economic rewards are worth-
while but also that their work provides Americans with a necessary
food and the economy with a needed boost.

Several of the shrimpers interviewed noted the irony in taking
risks so that "a few rich people could eat shrimp cocktail." These men,
in perceiving the irony, placed more importance on the money they
made and less on the value of their work to others. One shrimper said,
"Hell, I don't care who eats it [shrimp] as long as the price is right."

Particular demographic variables are less helpful here in understanding shrimpers' attitudes toward the importance of their work.
Age and income of shrimpers must be considered, however, when
viewing these men's responses to the question of whether most people
in the community respect shrimpers. Certainly, captains who earn
substantial annual wages are more able either to isolate themselves
from the hazards of negative status in the community or to come closer
to community acceptance than are other shrimpers. Headers, poorly

paid, often with few family or community ties, are much more likely to feel the brunt of community disapproval.

Attitudes toward the Impact of Work on Families

A set of questions also focused on the concern of these fishermen with the effects of shrimping as an occupation on their families. They were asked first whether they worried about their families when they were at sea (see Table 4-11). Seventy-eight percent answered that they did, 19 percent that they did not, and 3 percent were not sure. The most common response was, "Of course I worry, wouldn't you?" Shrimpers said that if an emergency arose, they knew their wives and families had to cope with it as best they could. While expressing confidence in their families' ability to handle any emergency, they said they would feel better if they were there to help them. They added, however, that if need be they could be contacted at sea by radio.

Even more revealing were the often-heard comments concerning the everyday family time missed while away from home. One shrimper said that his wife raised his kids; he was away too much to have much say in their upbringing. This worried him, because he felt he did not know his kids as well as he would have liked to. Another man ex-

TABLE 4-11. Shrimpers' Concerns with the Effects of Their Work on Their Families

	Strongly Agree	Agree	Not Sure	Disagree	Strongly Disagree
Do you worry about your family when you're fishing?	6%	72%	3%	19%	0%
Would you get along better with your family if you weren't a shrimper?	1%	44%	5%	49%	1%
Do you look forward to returning to port when fishing?	5%	80%	7%	8%	0%

NOTE: N = 100.

pressed his feelings this way: "If you're a shrimper you spend a lot of time away from your family. You don't get to see your kids grow up. You're not as close to them as you'd like to be. You have to count on your wife a lot. I know it's been hard on her, and it bothers me when I'm fishing sometimes."

Only a few men expressed concern over their wives' infidelity to them while they were at sea. A majority who were married were much more concerned about the general welfare of their families because of their own absence from home.

Interestingly, when shrimpers were asked further whether they would get along better with their families and friends if they worked at another job besides shrimping, a majority said they would not. Of this group, several said that, in effect, absence made the heart grow fonder. When they returned to port they could also look forward to an enthusiastic welcome from their families and friends. These men suggested that their marriages were more interesting because of their jobs, that their relationships with their wives did not fall into the same boring routines that others faced. Forty-five percent of the sample essentially disagreed with this opinion, however, affirming that major family problems could be solved if another occupation were chosen.

Only 8 percent of the sample said they did not look forward to returning to port. Of these men, the majority either had no friends or families to return to or had significant problems in port, so they actually preferred staying at sea, or simply liked being out at sea more than staying on land. Most shrimpers, as one would expect, looked forward to getting paid, seeing family and friends, and relaxing from their work.

Again, these responses are not as clear-cut as one might suppose, reflecting a general ambivalence about working as fishermen. That shrimpers feel time away from family is the major drawback to fishing as an occupation is at once evident. Less clear, however, is why so many men felt that changing jobs would not solve any problems. Joseba Zulaika offers perhaps the best analysis of this situation in his description of Spanish fishermen who must be absent from their families for long periods of time.[6] He suggests that the Spanish fishermen while at sea create active fantasy lives, which include an idealized con-

[6] Joseba Zulaika, *Terranova*, pp. 46–48.

ception of their own families, and that these men actually must stay away from their real families lest their idealized conceptions suffer.

Perhaps, although to a lesser extent, the responses of Texas shrimpers reflect a comparable situation. On the one hand, they miss their families and friends while out in the Gulf. On the other, they sometimes grow tired of the strain of land relationships when in port. Shrimping in the Gulf then becomes a needed respite before the realities of home can be tolerated.

Nevertheless, it is obvious that shrimping as an occupation and life-style can put strains on a marriage. One shrimper, for example, said he was looking for a woman who came from a fishing family. Already once divorced, he believed that such a woman would be far more capable of handling the problems that are common to families of shrimpers than had his first wife.

Attitudes toward Accidents and Safety in the Workplace

Data were collected on shrimpers' attitudes toward the hazards of their job and their on-the-job accidents. Comments were also collected on how shrimpers deal with their injuries sustained while working.

Texas shrimpers expressed mixed attitudes toward the risks and dangers in their work. Fifty-seven percent agreed that shrimping in the Gulf was dangerous, while 41 percent disagreed and 2 percent said they were not sure (see Table 4-9). Those who did agree, when asked to name specific dangerous situations on board, most often listed getting injured by the winch, burst lines, and falling as the most common kinds of accidents.

Many shrimpers pointed out, as suggested earlier, that greenhorn shrimpers, headers on their first trip or two, were accidents waiting to occur. Several of the captains and riggers told stories of how the greenhorns had gotten hurt because they did something stupid such as grab onto a line at the wrong time or get too near the winch, behavior that experienced fishermen would have avoided.

What is surprising in their responses here is that one might expect shrimpers to minimize their acknowledgment of the real dangers inherent in their work. By minimizing the risks, they could actively ignore some of the stress that comes from working in a hazardous oc-

cupation. Many of the shrimpers managed this real worry by acknowl-
edging that shrimping was dangerous, but "only if you make a stupid
mistake" or "do something that you shouldn't do because you're not
thinking." Captains, especially, said that even though they often were
exhausted by the end of their trips, they always stayed alert because
their experience had taught them always to be on the lookout for the
unexpected. Many men, when asked whether shrimping was dangerous work added that it was dangerous only "if you lost your concentration." Otherwise, they said, it was "no more dangerous than
driving on the freeway."

Shrimpers were asked whether they had ever had a serious accident while shrimping. A serious accident was operationally defined as
one requiring services from a medical doctor or other professional
health-care provider or hospitalization. Twenty-two percent of those
sampled answered that they had been seriously injured on the job as a
shrimper.

This response is particularly revealing for three reasons. First,
these men are much more likely to underplay their injuries than to
exaggerate them. Shrimpers, according to their own code of expectations, are supposed to be tough, and those who are tough do not talk
about their injuries. As a result, the response rate is probably less than
it would have been had I interviewed other white-collar or blue-collar
workers.

Second, only fishermen who were working at the time of the survey were interviewed. This sample bias, mentioned earlier, means
that those who possibly received injuries that kept them from fishing
simply did not show up in the sample. In effect, then, the sample of
shrimpers was far "healthier" than one including both working and
nonworking shrimpers.

Then, too, the age of the fishermen interviewed in the sample
suggests that shrimping as an occupation may selectively weed out the
older, and presumably less able, fishermen. Although a wide range of
ages was represented in the sample (see Table 4-6)—the youngest
shrimper was sixteen and the oldest sixty-nine—shrimping is a young
man's work.

Third, shrimpers are much less likely to seek medical care for
injuries sustained while working than are other kinds of workers. This
is first and foremost out of sheer necessity: there are no doctors at sea,

so if you cut yourself, sprain a shoulder, mash a finger, or rip a piece of skin from your face, you take care of it as best you can. Unless the injury is very serious or life-threatening, most captains will not return their trawlers to port. The captains weigh the cost and expense of returning against the seriousness of the injury sustained and how the injury may affect the work of the crew. The shared attitude among these fishermen is that most injuries either heal or do not heal, and in the latter case the shrimper can be examined for free by the doctor when he returns from his trip.

The shrimpers I interviewed had sustained a number of injuries, from minor facial cuts to bone fractures, that were not reflected in the responses. Common medical problems included back injuries that severely limited the kinds of work the fishermen could perform on board; cuts to hands, arms, and face that required but never received sutures; and variety of knee injuries and ankle sprains. Several shrimpers complained of still being bothered by blows to the head received from falling objects.

Shrimpers know that their job is at times dangerous, and when they do get hurt they are more psychologically prepared for it. They are much less likely to go to doctors than would others hurt on the job, even though their treatment is provided free of charge, because there is a commonly held attitude that a doctor is not seen unless absolutely necessary. Of equal importance, they want to keep on working to earn an income. They know that if the owner finds out they have been hurt he probably will not let them go out fishing. Shrimpers hide injuries that many of us would consider to be serious enough to keep us from working.

PART TWO

Landfall: When Shrimpers Come Home

5. When the Frenchmen Came: A Social History of Shrimpers in Texas Ports

"This town is a nice place to live. Only my wife had to raise the kids. I was gone most of the time."

"Shrimpers, well, they treat them like they were hippies or something."

While Galveston, Corpus Christi, Port Arthur, and Brownsville have their share of shrimpers, the majority live in or near the twenty or more small coastal communities that lie between Sabine Pass, which borders on Louisiana, and Brownsville, some four hundred miles to the south. With one or two exceptions, these small towns have escaped the rapid industrial growth common to the larger metropolitan coastal areas. They remain unique in Texas, resembling more the fishing communities of Louisiana, Mississippi, Alabama, and the west coast of Florida than they do other inland Texas towns not twenty miles away.

The social histories of shrimping ports along the Texas coast reflect parallel developments in the relationships between Gulf shrimpers and other community residents.[1] While each town possesses a unique history, taken as a whole the communities demonstrate similar patterns of social interaction between the commercial fishermen and those residents who do not fish for a living. That such is the case is in a large part a result of four characteristics these towns have in common: the towns maintained a relative geographic isolation from other metropolitan areas; they were, until the 1940s, homogeneous with regard to race; they relied on commercial fishing and related industries; and they faced the onslaught of the Gulf shrimping industry, with all the changes it portended, at about the same time, from 1946 to 1953.

[1] Data about the social history of these coastal towns are a composite of information gathered from the interviews with shrimpers and from those associated with the fishing industry, including lifelong residents of the towns. For an interesting description of Aransas Pass, for example, see Aransas Pass Chamber of Commerce, *Aransas Pass, Texas.*

Texas coastal towns are rural towns either lying at some distance from or with no direct access to major metropolitan areas. Port O'Connor, Port Lavaca, Seadrift, and Freeport, for example, all lie at considerable distances from Victoria to the south and west and the Houston metroplex to the north, and though Fulton, Rockport, and Aransas Pass are, on the map, less than thirty miles from Corpus Christi, yet by car the island topography requires an hour or more drive from Fulton, by way of a ferry at Aransas Pass, to South Padre Island and Corpus Christi. This physical isolation from urban areas contributes to a certain social rigidity. In these small towns, change, any change, is often suspect, as are newcomers to the area.

Until immediately after World War II these communities were relatively homogeneous with regard to race. Anglos predominated except in the extreme southern ports, where Mexican-Americans were in a clear majority. There were almost no blacks or other racial or ethnic groups. In addition, there prevailed a strong regionalism that reinforced the sociopolitical climate of these communities, especially in the northern third of the state, because Louisiana and other Gulf states were the homes of fishermen who competed for the same resource as did Texas fishermen. As a result, according to informants, those who were not from these towns were viewed as "foreigners," referring to those from other Gulf states and points north, or "outsiders," meaning weekenders or summer residents from around the state who were drawn to the Texas coast to fish its bays, beaches, passes, and offshore reefs. The decision-making structures, the small-town elites, remained stable over the years. There was no significant population shift, since the bay fishery and its subsidiary industries could support only a limited population.

The geographical isolation and racial homogeneity reinforced a political and social isolation. These towns have historically oriented themselves to commerce and trade along the Gulf. Their residents until recently have been in closer contact with the coastal communities farther up the line, all the way to Louisiana and beyond, or down the line, to Port Isabel on the Mexican border and farther south to Tampico and Veracruz. Consequently, as suggested earlier, these fishing communities bear more resemblance to coastal communities in Louisiana or Alabama, for instance, than to agricultural centers like Refugio or Odem less than fifty miles inland from the Gulf.

The majority of these communities gained a subsistence from the bay fishery, although a few, like Freeport, always had some other limited industrial development. Trout, redfish, shrimp, oysters, crabs, and clams provided commercial bay fishermen a living, and during certain seasons charter boats, fish camps, bait stands, and marinas provided additional income to residents. Several communities also boasted processing plants and packing sheds for the wide assortment of fish products. All in all, it was the bay fishery that kept the small towns going; there were no shrimpers per se in these towns, only fishermen who seasonally fished for shrimp.

Bay shrimping, according to several old-timers interviewed, was first accomplished by hand-carried throwing nets. Later, in the teens, twenties, and early thirties, sailboats, with a large net between, hauled in tons of shrimp and other fish in season from Texas bays. The sailboats dragged the net for a short time, then crossed paths, at which time the crews jumped out into the waist-high water to begin the tedious process of gathering in the nets and unloading the fish and shellfish into one of the sailboats. Sometimes a motor-powered boat or a rowboat was used to transport the shrimp and fish from the sailboats to the dock.

Shrimping took place during daylight hours and only when the weather permitted, which limited the effort to summer and early fall. There was no ice on board and no mechanical winches, and, as one older shrimper put it, "it was hardly worth all the work for what you got sometimes." Shrimp were headed and iced at the dock, packed in 125-pound barrels, and sent to urban markets. One former shrimper, now retired, said that as a boy he used to earn two cents per barrel as a deckhand on the sailboats.

In the middle 1930s and early 1940s, gasoline-powered skiffs came into use. According to interviews with lifelong residents of the coastal communities, the engines were often car motors that had been overhauled and adapted for fishing. Occasionally the bigger skiffs would venture out to the mouths of the passes and cuts and, even more rarely, fish offshore. They always stayed within sight of land on these trips, however, and returned to shore by nightfall.

Up until the war years, fishing as an industry could support only a small work force. Men who could not find work as fishermen or tour guides, in the canneries, or on nearby farms and ranches most often had to move elsewhere. Thus, the populations of these towns remained small, from never more than several thousand in the largest to a few hundred or fewer in the smallest. Tourists from the larger nearby cities appeared on the weekends, and some built weekend and summer cottage homes along the bay shore, but few outsiders came to stay the year around.

Very little is in fact known about today's bay shrimper and his impact on the industry. It is estimated that bay shrimpers harvest about 18 percent of the landings each year in Texas, not an insignificant amount.[2] Their real impact on the fishery remains unknown, however, in light of the paucity of research.

From my interviews with shrimpers in Aransas Pass, some of whom had close family who were bay shrimpers, a brief profile of the Texas bay shrimper did emerge. In general, the shrimper owns his own boat, which ranges in size from eighteen to forty feet or longer. The larger boats fish the Gulf when possible but stay close in to shore. The bay boats are run by a captain-owner and, sometimes, an all-purpose deckhand; sometimes the smaller boats are operated by just one man.

Bay shrimpers are up in the dark hours before morning and home by evening. They probably earn less from their shrimpfishing than do captains of Gulf boats, in the $15,000-to-$25,000 range. The work demands the same kind of fishing skills, but the pressures of isolation and distance from family and friends are considerably reduced. The weather is often extreme, as most Texas sport fishermen know, and can get every bit as rough and dangerous as in Gulf waters.

Demographic characteristics of bay shrimpers are little different from those of Gulf shrimpers, with several notable exceptions. First, since citizenship is required for shrimp and boat licenses, there are far fewer Mexican bay shrimpers in Texas than Mexican Gulf shrimpers. Second, there are a growing number of Vietnamese bay shrimpers in several Texas coastal communities, whereas as of this writing there are no Vietnamese Gulf shrimpers. (Local experts in the shrimping industry expect the Vietnamese to enter Gulf fishing when, in the next several years, they have earned their U.S. citizenship and can qualify to own and run Gulf boats.) Third, there are very few black bay shrimpers, although the reasons for this remain unclear. With these excep-

[2] See Wade L. Griffin, "Economics of Production and Marketing in the Commercial Fish Industry," in *Sea Grant College Proposal, 1979–81*, vol. 2, pp. f-1-16–f-1-20.

tions, the bay shrimpers come from the same work force as do the Gulf shrimpers.

Life in the coastal towns and villages changed abruptly in the late 1940s, when, as one respondent said in some dismay, "the Frenchmen came." The "Frenchmen" were in fact Louisiana-based trawler owners who had heard by word of mouth that large quantities of brown shrimp could be netted off the Texas coast and Mexico. One man interviewed said he remembered as a boy the time he first saw one of the French boats, in 1947. "It was the biggest boat I ever saw," he said, "much bigger than anything we had around here." The French boats were oceangoing trawlers similar to the modern design. They ranged in size from thirty-five to fifty feet, small by today's standards but quite impressive when compared to the local Texas boats of those days.

Compared to today's boats, the French trawlers seem primitive. Lacking, among other things, adequate crew accommodations, bathrooms, showers, and tables, the men slept in the pilothouse in closely stacked bunks and kept warm in the winter the best way they could—with small heaters, on some boats, or sometimes by sleeping in the engine room. The boats did carry a limited supply of ice, however, and could venture out much farther than the Texas bay shrimpers had ever dared, for they had been designed to fish for the nocturnal brown shrimp, which, during certain seasons, are to be found in the deeper waters of the Gulf.

The Louisiana boats required both immediate access to the Gulf and adequate dock space with services and supplies. The Cajuns, and the others to follow, settled where such access was available. Soon some of the towns began to grow, backed by the impetus of a new Gulf fishing industry, while others remained the same. The skylines of those towns with easy access to the Gulf changed radically as port facilities were enlarged and enhanced.

Many of the owners were Cajuns who came from Louisiana, especially from around the Morgan City area, bringing two or three trawlers on the average. They were successful boat owners looking for better fishing grounds and for higher profits. Some had fished off Texas before, some not. Some had extensive fishing experience south into Mexico, while others had never crossed the Rio Grande. In any case, they knew that if the shrimp did not last off Texas waters, they could always return to Louisiana. A few of the owners interviewed, in fact, were among those who had previously migrated from the west coast of Florida to Louisiana; for them the move was less of a risk than for others, since they knew the problems associated with picking up your business in one place and putting it down among strangers in another. These men were ambitious entrepreneurs, a few of whom had already made sizable fortunes, and they were willing to risk losing a season or more of fishing off Louisiana in order to resettle and fish new, and more profitable, grounds.

Often the boat captains and crew came with Cajun boat owners. These fishermen included Anglos from Louisiana, Mississippi, and the other Gulf states and blacks from small fishing towns in Georgia, North Carolina, and South Carolina. Many of the new Gulf boats, however, did not bring complete crews, or the men returned home because they did not like living among strangers in Texas. In these cases crews were drawn from the local supply of bay fishermen and others in the communities.

Some of these same Texas headers and riggers eventually became captains and owners in their own right. Several of these men were interviewed. They learned the business on a Cajun boat and then, when they could afford to, bought into a boat and captained it themselves. In this way, over the last thirty years, native Texans, members of these small fishing towns, have become an important part of the Gulf shrimping industry.

In the beginning, the new shrimpers were neither warmly nor uniformly accepted into all the fishing communities. In Aransas Pass, for example, local bay fishermen invoked a court injunction that prohibited Cajun shrimpers and others from fishing by limiting trawler licenses to state residents. The Cajun shrimpers fought the injunction for several years in court and eventually won, but they were threatened with violence, on occasion, over the use of the Gulf shrimp fishery, which caused some of them to move south to Port Isabel and Port Brownsville in the late 1940s and early 1950s. Their initial acceptance in these two new communities was mixed, at best: while the Cajuns had jobs to offer the local work force, they were looked upon by the dominant Mexican-American majority as strangers who even spoke a foreign language (French). Port Isabel's older residents still speak of their surprise when the large boats appeared from the north.

Residents of the communities in which the Frenchmen settled

viewed the Gulf fishery as a limited resource that belonged to them by right. Although they could not, except in a few rare cases, as in Aransas Pass, afford the large trawlers that were capable of fishing the Gulf, they saw little reason to let the Frenchmen from the north exploit what they viewed as belonging to Texans. That Cajuns, southern blacks, and the other men who later followed "talked funny" and ate different foods—in short, were often of a different culture, class, and, in many cases, race—intensified the struggle over the fishing resources.

The small fishing communities lacked statewide political influence, so their legal battle to protect "Texas" shrimp from the "foreign" Gulf shrimpers was relatively short-lived, though the feelings of hostility and antagonism did not die out so quickly. In any event, the new Gulf shrimpers settled into the bay communities that were their new homes and went about the business of earning a living from the sea.

While local bay fishermen were incorporated into the work force of the Texas Gulf shrimp-fishing industry, other ethnic American fishermen were also attracted, in the years that followed, to the abundant shrimp fishery and the substantial profits to be made. First- and second-generation Americans of Greek, Italian, and East European descent, some of whom had extensive fishing experience from their countries of origin, found new homes in Texas fishing towns. Central Americans, including an especially successful group of Hondurans, were similarly drawn to the Texas shrimp industry. Some came with no financial resources, starting out as headers, while others brought enough cash to buy fishing boats. Thirty years later, when I interviewed shrimpers, owners, brokers, and others closely tied to the industry, I found a rich diversity of ethnic and racial groups represented.

Men from various parts of the United States also were attracted to the Texas fishery. Many had experience in the Navy, as merchant marines, or as deckhands on tugs and barges along the Mississippi River and other Gulf Coast states. Like the other groups mentioned, these men sought what they had heard was good money for hard work. Others just "fell into it," with no related experience on vessels or in commercial fishing.

Shrimpers who migrated to Texas towns found themselves initially in a precarious position vis-á-vis others in the community. On the one hand, many of the new owners and captains were relatively affluent in comparison to the local townspeople. In any other circumstance they might have joined with the other community leaders who comprised the decision-making elites in each community. On the other hand, because of prevailing small-town attitudes, the newcomers were not easily accepted but were instead regarded as "foreigners." Then, too, trawler owners often had very little time at first to devote to any affairs but those of the fishing business, and captains and crews had even less time to spend while in port except with family and close friends. Thus, the Gulf shrimpers were not as quick to make friends and social contacts with others of similar rank and prestige. Additional ethnic, racial, and ethnocentric attitudes inhibited closer interaction between the newcomers and the locals. Lacking the time to participate in community affairs, missing the social contacts, and being seen as different, Gulf shrimpers from the beginning lacked influence in the towns' political structure.

Antagonism between shrimpers and others in the community was exacerbated by differences in visible life-styles. Shrimpers were often stereotyped as heavy drinkers. Drunken comportment by a lifelong friend and neighbor is more easily forgiven or ignored than are similar excesses exhibited by a "foreigner." As a result, local law enforcement in the 1940s and 1950s was too often randomly and unequally applied.

In general, then, shrimpers were increasingly tolerated but not socially approved in some fishing ports. Their wage dollars and the dollars that the industry generated were in demand, were indeed a tremendous boost to the local economies, but shrimpers and those who associated with them were often roughly and unfairly treated.

The lines between shrimpers and the towns in which they lived were established by the early 1950s. While it was not impossible for a owner or, more rarely, a captain to cross these social lines of community acceptance, the physical setting of many shrimping ports clearly inhibited communication and understanding between shrimpers and nonshrimpers. As in countless American communities, the railroad tracks and yards that ran through town often were a symbol of the physical separation of the rich and the middle class from all others, so the ports and their immediate environs became known, whether in truth or in fiction, as the undesirable homes and workplaces of shrimpers.[3] In the 1980s the physical distancing of these small-town ports

[3] See Arthur J. Rubel, *Across the Tracks: Mexican Americans in a Texas City*, p. 8.

from the main residential and industrial areas of the seaside towns represents, in concrete, wood, and tin, the social distancing of community members from shrimpers and their families. This distancing, this view of shrimpers as deviants, is far from universal; yet a shrimper today may still be welcomed in one port and arrested with little provocation in another.

The Ports

The ports are made up of stinking docks, refuse, rusted equipment, and almost always the sunken hull of a trawler still tied to the dock, almost a ritualistic warning symbol to the other boats and men who pass by daily. Except in one case, they include rotten timbers, abandoned toolsheds, and huge mud parking lots complete with potholes. An oil sheen muffles the ripples in the water, and shrimpers periodically throw beer cans into it over the sides of their boats; in spring and summer mullet swarm in schools near the surface. The ports are as seedy as the boats they periodically spit out to sea and welcome back a few weeks later with their frozen catch.

The ports are also excitingly alive, exuding man-made noises that reaffirm the shrimper's land senses when he returns from his trip with only the sound of the sea in his ear. Metal parts grind against each other; welder's torches pop; radios blare rock and roll, *cumbias*, soul, and fiddle tunes; and men yell at, through, and around each other, striving to make themselves heard. The languages and dialects are English and Spanish; the accents are a mix of Cajun, the American South, the Southwest, and Mexico, both rural and urban.

Shrimpers who return with their catches after the fishhouses have closed often spend the night on their boats and unload the following morning. They celebrate their returns with onboard parties or with trips to the nearby bars. Many, with their families in tow, head for home. Often the headers, having no home or place to which to return, spend the night at the dock on their boats. They sleep as late as they can until the port noise, generated by the men who work nine to five at the welding shops, freezers, ship stores, net shops, marine yards, and fishhouses, begins.

The port noises begin about 7:00 A.M., sometimes earlier, depending on the season. By eight the day is in full swing: boats are unloading, repairs are being made, and business is being conducted in the owners' offices. The service workers quit for lunch at twelve, along with the secretaries. By three the ports have grown quieter, as the majority of the boats have long since been unloaded, usually before lunchtime. Trawlers leave for the Gulf by 4:00 P.M. after making last-minute repairs, taking on supplies, or waiting around for a crew member who does not show up on time. Wives, girlfriends, and children say their goodbyes, wave, and drive away. Owners and boat managers loose huge sighs of relief; their worries are over until the boat either breaks down or returns with its catch.

Other boats come and go. Occasionally oil-supply boats venture into the shrimp ports, along with the weekday fisherman in his outboard. A few tourists find their way to the docks looking for fantastically low fish prices, which, of course, they never find. Male tourists stand at the fishhouses and stare at the boats while their wives wait patiently in their cars. The conveyor belts spray their slacks and shoes with salty brine. They ask me whether I want to sell them some fish.

The working day at the ports is over for everyone but the fishermen by 4:30 P.M. By then a few shrimpers are still scrambling around their boats trying to get organized so they can leave for the night's fishing. Others, usually headers, sit in the pilothouse drinking beer or coffee, socializing with crewmen from other boats, enjoying the day, or listening to music. Lone tourist fishermen stand or sit on the docks, their lines disappearing below the polluted waters. The gulls begin working the channels as the sun sets.

Each of the ports represents a slightly different spatial configuration in relation to the community; this configuration is a function of the constraints of the local topography as well as of the history of the growth and development of the particular town. With one or two notable exceptions, however, a common pattern is at once evident in Texas ports. The immediate port area is a cluster of bars, pool halls, restaurants, inexpensive motels and hotels, vacant lots, and decaying or empty buildings, which all serve as a physical and social barrier between the men at the port and the rest of the community.

In Aransas Pass, for example, the port facilities are six blocks from the main downtown businesses. The area between the central business district and the port lies vacant except for a few bars and nightclubs, low-rent motels, a large fishhouse, several net shops, and an occasional single-family residence in disrepair. Filled with junked cars and dilapidated structures, this land stands in marked contrast to the docks and other port facilities, which are in excellent shape.

Freeport, Port Isabel, and the majority of other shrimping ports visited have a similar "no-man's-land" that surrounds the ports and physically separates them from other commercial or residential areas. To varying degrees, these areas are filled with small businesses serving the port, bars, nightclubs, small restaurants, and occasionally motels or hotels. These businesses cater almost exclusively to shrimpers; few nonshrimpers venture into them.

Shrimpers in ports other than their home find it far easier to stay within the immediate port area than to venture into town. Those without a car at the port must either find a ride, call a cab, hitchhike, or walk into town. Besides, many shrimpers believe it is safer not to venture out of "their" territory. A common complaint heard from many fishermen was that they often were harassed by local police and were likely to be stopped by local law enforcers even if seen only walking to and from the downtown area. As a result, they said that they stayed either on their boats or around the dock area to avoid trouble.

This no-man's-land and the appearance of the ports themselves discourage all but the most curious nonshrimpers from exploring further. As noted above, the ports are smelly, ugly places. Some of them are, in addition, visually disorienting at first glance. All one sees is the backs of large sheds, junked boat parts lying on the ground, and deep ruts in the mud parking lots. These places are not the scenic tourist ports sometimes found on the East Coast and West Coast, but working ports with little regard for any architectural aesthetic. There are no picturesque restaurants overlooking the trawlers, no quaint bars with large plate-glass windows through which one can see the sun set over the harbor. Tourists in search of scenery or bargain fish prices rarely return.

Nonshrimping community residents also contribute to the separation between port and town. As far as they are concerned, there is little reason to visit the port or the docks where the trawlers tie up. Those who work in the fishhouses drive directly to them, work their shifts, and return to the communities. Secretaries, clerks, and office workers rarely go out to the boats that are tied up at the docks where the shrimpers are; their contact with the fishermen remains minimal.

The People

Those in closest contact with the shrimpers are the welders, electricians, mechanics, supply clerks, and general dockhands, some of whom are likely to be former shrimpers. These blue-collar workers work daily alongside shrimpers, especially captains and riggers, to maintain and repair the boats so that the fishermen can return to sea as quickly as possible. The consensus of these men, when interviewed, was that shrimpers were little different from any other men who work for a living. The dockside workers seemed to have an accurate view of the hardships at sea, a certain respect for the men who fished the boats, and not a little envy for the incomes of some of the captains. These men perhaps know shrimpers better than any others in the community.

The women at the ports work as secretaries, office workers, and fishhouse employees; I interviewed only three who worked as shrimpers. Other women in the port are the wives and girlfriends of shrimpers.

The women in the fishhouses are a segregated population, encapsulated in their fish factories, and have little in common with others in the port.[4] They spend all day inside the plant, taking their lunch breaks together in their cars in the parking lots or often on the back loading docks. Very few have direct ties to the shrimpers or the other men who work on the docks. They are a marginal labor supply that comes and goes; they usually have no interest in the other activities of the port, nor are the other port workers interested in them.

The women in the offices may be directly contrasted with the women on the docks, shrimpers' wives and girlfriends, only fifty yards away. The women office workers function as extensions of the fleet owners; for them shrimping is a business in which the weakest link, the most unpredictable factor, is the fisherman. While these women are in daily contact with the shrimpers, they would never think of socializing with them or their wives on an equal basis. Shrimpers are employees of the company who may earn substantially more than the secretaries but who do not enjoy an equal status.

[4]See Michael V. Miller, "Industrial Development and an Expanding Labor Force in Brownsville," *Texas Business Review* 55 (November–December, 1981): 258–261.

The secretaries bring with them an air of decorum, of officiousness, of community values—a reminder that, at least inside the owners' offices, the business world thrives on the bureaucratic tradition. I have often sat in the waiting room of an owner's office when the shrimpers charged through. The captain usually leads the charge, most often searching for that last piece of equipment he needs so he can leave the dock or, after the trip, looking for his advance or paycheck. The rigger and header follow more tentatively, looking clumsy, a little awed by the fact that they are inside a permanent land structure. It is the owner's secretary, most often a middle-aged female, who serves as buffer to the shrimpers' ambience, which often hangs over the fishermen like a cloud. It is a clash between land and sea, office and boat. Shrimpers soon become uncomfortable under the challenging gaze of the secretary behind her desk, and they retreat back out to the docks, their territory.

The owners, depending on whether their boats are at the dock or out fishing, come to the port early, often in pickup trucks or four-wheel-drive vehicles. Like the secretaries, they bring with them the business values and attitudes that link fishing as business to the community financial centers headquartered in the downtown areas. Few in number, they are, besides the shrimpers, the most pervasive influence at the ports. On the docks and boats, however, they are less visible and less impressive than in their offices.

In relating to their fishermen employees, owners are constantly frustrated because of the nature of the fishing enterprise and the traditional work relationships between shrimper and owner. This frustration is situational, based on the owner's inability to control his employees once they leave the dock. The owner can plead, he can cajole, he can advise, he can yell, or he can threaten, but, when it comes right down to it, shrimpers are going to take his three-hundred-thousand-dollar investment and do what they want with it. Maybe they will return with a large catch and maybe not. There is always the possibility that when they return the boat will have suffered extensive damage.

On a daily basis, then, owners confront the fact that they must trust their men implicitly with the very future of their business, knowing that chance carelessness or inexperience can cost them thousands of dollars. Despite this situation, some owners never trust their shrimpers. Instead they seem to view them as tangential to the whole fishing effort. They talk to them as if they were children. These owners, then, face continual, insurmountable frustrations in their daily contact with their employees.

Those owners who have, for a variety of reasons, selected men in whom they have some confidence have entirely different attitudes toward shrimpers. The shrimpers are seen less as employees and more as coworkers who share in the profits. Problems that develop are attributed less to the inadequacies of the shrimpers and more to the nature of the work itself. Pay advances and loans are given to shrimpers when they need them because these owners see this as a reasonable, humane, and businesslike thing to do. They know that sometimes, especially in the winter, their workers will need extra money to get by, and they know they will get their money back in the spring when the shrimpers return to fishing. Unfortunately, a few owners view pay advances to shrimpers as a way to ensure their continual employment. These owners run operations, reminiscent of a coal company store, in which shrimpers must keep working just to get out of debt.

Owners are much more tolerant of shrimpers at sea than they are of them on land. Various character or personality traits, even if overtly manifested, tend to be overlooked when a shrimper is fishing. In part this is because, as suggested earlier, shrimpers at sea are judged by their production, not necessarily by how they go about netting the catch, running the boat, and handling their crew.

But from the owner's perspective the rules for the shrimper change when he hits the dock. Although a captain is most likely to get fired because of low production, the next most common reason is his inability to get along with the owner. The same qualities of personality and character that allow a particular shrimper to produce regularly for an owner may be, on land, the very qualities that get him fired. Thus, owners are very likely to observe that one of their captains is a good shrimper but is "hard to get along with," meaning that he is too independent or authoritarian to be a good employee. Other owners take the position that they do not care what the shrimpers are like; if they produce, then they remain valued workers. These owners are more likely to have an assistant or boat manager who acts as a buffer for them.

These men, then, have been identified by the community as

"businessmen in the fishing business" rather than as Gulf shrimp boat owners. They do not see themselves as tied to the shrimpers who actually do the fishing; they leave that to the shrimpers. They see themselves as the men who are the brains and the financial brawn behind the trawlers.

Time and Its Social Consequences

The development of strong ties between shrimpers and the communities in which they reside has been inhibited not only by physical barriers but also by the fact that shrimpers spend relatively little time on land. For seven to ten months out of each year shrimpers regularly work at sea two to three weeks or more at a time, spend two to four days in port, and then return to sea for another lengthy trip.

The shrimper's work schedule contrasts vividly with that of the average American worker, who works approximately thirty-five hours a week, plus commuting time, a total of approximately forty hours. For the average worker, the eight-hour-a-day work schedule and time away from home leaves eight hours to spend as he chooses, assuming eight hours for sleep. This time may be spent running errands, perhaps pursuing a hobby, taking care of children, and so forth. In contrast, even though shrimpers do have some time on board to relax, read, listen to the radio, watch television, and talk with one another, the dominant characteristic of their work remains their isolation from family, from friends, and from their most important social relationships on land. A final comparison will underscore this point: shrimpers spend as many total hours away from home and family in the first two days at sea of an eighteen-day trip, forty-eight hours, as the average American worker spends away from home in his entire workweek.

As a result, during this precious time on land, shrimpers have a tremendous amount of living to do—all the living that could not be done at sea. They want to spend time with their wives or girlfriends, give some care and attention to their children, and see that their household is maintained; there are repairs to be made, children to be punished or praised, and loved ones for whom affections must be reaffirmed. If there is any time left over, it may be devoted to community concerns, but there seldom is.

While the shrimper is away, his wife acts as the head of the household. During her husband's absence, the shrimper's wife is both mother and father for her family. This means she not only must carry out the traditional role of housewife but also must respond to the daily demands that her husband, were he at home, would handle. As one captain said, a shrimper expects his wife to cope with emergencies on her own, filling in for him when he is gone. This particular shrimper said that his wife was liberated long before the feminist movement. He was proud that his wife could, if necessary, mow the lawn, do minor repairs on the car, and pay the bills—all traditional male roles—and also cook the meals, clean the house, and raise the children.[5]

Shrimpers as a group are aware of the tremendous expectations and pressures placed upon their wives. One shrimper, twice married, said that the second time around he chose a woman who came from a shrimping family because she knew what to expect—how to handle the extra demands required by being married to a shrimper. He recommended that other shrimpers marry the same kind of women or, at the very least, explain to their potential wives what their marriage would be like.

A shrimper's wife also has to be a good money manager. Usually, the shrimper will leave a certain amount of money with her to cover foreseeable expenses. If she runs out, she can borrow from their savings or, in some cases, get an advance against his pay from the boat owner. The major problem is that a shrimper's monthly income is extremely inconsistent, since on some trips he may net many shrimp, which bring a high price, while on others he may not do as well. Thus, while shrimpers and their wives know more or less what they will earn on an annual basis, they cannot predict when the money will come in.

This income problem of shrimpers and their families contrasts sharply with the situation of workers who are paid either by the hour or by a weekly, monthly, or annual salary. In either case, the worker can adjust his costs of living to what he expects to earn. Granted that unexpected expenses often occur, most workers still have a reasonable possibility of balancing their expenses with their incomes because, barring unforeseen circumstances, their incomes are assured.

Shrimpers and their wives are in no such situation. They may

[5] See Fran Danowski, *Fishermen's Wives: Coping with an Extraordinary Occupation*, University of Rhode Island Marine Bulletin No. 37, for an excellent discussion of the important role of the fisherman's wife.

have several thousand dollars in cash from one trip and two hundred from another. If there is a lot of money around, the human tendency is to go on a spending binge. The point here is that it is often the wife who, in addition to all her other responsibilities, must manage her husband's fluctuating income as best she knows how. She is the one who must face the bill collectors and the creditors. She is the one who must tell them that they will get their money as soon as her husband returns from the sea.

Prudent families can avoid such financial problems by saving their money, resisting the temptation to buy additional material goods before paying off previous debts, and allocating money to pay for new debts that will accrue before the fisherman's return from the next trip. Even in the good years, though, it can be touch and go, because the shrimpers and their wives know that they always have to save for the lean winter months. Now that the catch has fallen off, now that the price is low, the crew share has diminished, and double-digit inflation bites into the buying power of the money that they do earn, the financial pressure on many shrimpers and their families is acute. Even a captain who earns forty thousand dollars annually must be clever with his money; he must save everything he can for expenses, plus he must have money to pay taxes and Social Security at the end of the year. Shrimpers' wives share the burden of these financial concerns.

In many respects, shrimpers' families really have two lives, one when the shrimper is away at sea and one when he is at home. While the shrimper is at sea, his wife and children must accommodate themselves as best they can to the long absence of their husband and father. When the shrimper returns, he steps into his role as head of the household. This sometimes creates problems. As one shrimper told me, he constantly has to remind his wife of twenty years that the role of head of the household is, in fact, his. He then tries to lead what he and his family consider to be a "normal" life before his next trip.

The wonder is, to some degree, that shrimpers and their families manage to do as well as they do under these conditions. Most of the shrimpers I interviewed seemed relatively satisfied with everything about their lives, from family to job, except the recent inflationary squeeze they all have felt. While it is the binge drinkers and, to a lesser extent, the heavy drinkers who are the most visible and get the most publicity, on land the majority of shrimpers and their families lead relatively stable, quiet, even mundane lives, little different, with the exceptions noted, from the lives of those around them. I found no evidence, such as an unusually high divorce rate, that would suggest that most shrimpers and their families lead their lives or conduct their daily affairs any differently than anyone else in the community.

Shrimpers are, however, much less likely to belong to voluntary associations, such as men's clubs, political parties, Little League, and church groups, than are nonshrimpers. Moreover, although 89 percent of those sampled identified themselves as belonging to some form of organized religion, their attendance and participation were severely limited. Again, it is a question of finding the time. Wife and kids come first, then close relatives and friends. There is seldom much time for the shrimper to spend doing much else. Occasionally his wife may be active in the community, but this is very rare.

Thus, when shrimpers were asked in the survey whether it was hard to keep up with what was going on in their communities while they were at sea, 73 percent of those who responded said they strongly agreed or agreed. Most shrimpers have radios, and some have televisions on their boats, so they can keep abreast of world, national, and local news if they so choose. But many shrimpers said, as an aside to the question, that it was not hard to follow what happened in their communities because either they did not care that much what happened or nothing ever happened that was of interest to them. Both these kinds of comments reflect little real participation by these fishermen in the general social life of their respective towns.

Shrimpers find it difficult to attend meetings on a regular basis, even meetings that have directly to do with their occupations. Their irregular schedule precludes attending the weekly or monthly meetings that are the hub of social activity. They know, before each trip, approximately when they will return, but they never know to the day when they will be back. When they are out at sea, if the fishing is good they will not return just to make a scheduled meeting. The shrimp do not wait.

Shrimpers as a work group are in part, then, politically impotent because of their inability to participate fully in their communities as full-time members. They do not have the full set of social relationships that others who work scheduled forty-hour weeks are likely to have. They put first things first. Participation in community-wide affairs,

even attendance at high-school football games in which their sons may be the team's star players, is severely limited. Participation in town affairs, whether in an informal capacity such as a Little League coach or in a more formal function such as an officer in a service club, is virtually impossible. There are shrimpers in these communities who are mayors and councilmen and who are active in church, school, and other social and political affairs, but they are always retired shrimpers who now have the time they never had when they fished for a living.

Social Distancing

Gulf shrimpers initially were not wholeheartedly welcomed into the communities they came to. Today those social barriers still exist, symbolically embodied in the spatial separation of port from town and reified by shrimpers' lack of time to involve themselves in their community and thereby dispel the negative image townspeople sometimes have of them.

There is, however, one exception to this general trend. Shrimp boat owners, though initially treated as pariahs in their new homes, have gradually come to be regarded less as shrimpers per se and more and more as businessmen who, through their day-to-day efforts, have brought jobs and dollars to the community. Although the Cajun and other Louisianan owners, for example, spoke differently and possessed somewhat different customs, they were eventually accepted as legitimate businessmen, not only because they could afford the expensive trawlers in the first place but also because throughout the 1950s and 1960s and into the middle 1970s, they had become even wealthier by their enterprise. Relative to other entrepreneurs in the small towns, the owners often possessed considerable financial resources. Money, financial status, began to speak louder than ethnicity, race, and ethnocentrism.

These shrimpboat owners raised families, bought expensive homes in the best neighborhoods, and sent their children to local schools and colleges. They developed close ties with local bankers, with whom they were naturally in contact as their businesses grew, and other local businessmen. The smartest and the most successful diversified their investments; local bankers served as advisors and sometimes were partners in other business ventures. The wives of owners mixed freely with the wives of other influential men in the community. Business and social ties brought the Gulf trawler owners eventual acceptance into the towns' elites and, thus, into the towns as a whole.

In addition, over the last thirty years, Texas trawler owners have come to include not only those owners who were born and raised in Texas coastal towns but also local businessmen who have purchased shares in Gulf boats. Both these groups of men have helped to bring legitimacy to the status of the original trawler owners. If a local accountant, for instance, or a lawyer or liquor store owner, owns a boat, then shrimping becomes a business venture, not dirty, smelly work fit only for outcasts. Shrimping as fishing has retained its undesirable association, while shrimping as a business has been cleaned up and reshaped and is now a legitimate activity in which local businessmen as investors can be involved.

As trawler owners became increasingly accepted, they typically distanced themselves from their captains and crews. As attitudes in the communities (and certainly there was some degree of variance from one community to another) rigidified against shrimpers as "deviants," owners jumped one way or the other. The majority sought the relative social comfort of men, women, and families of similar income and class. While at first owners had felt closer to each other, and many still maintain close family ties, they developed new friends and acquaintances. They found that personal contact broke down barriers, especially if they downplayed their own cultural differences and, most important, the unique characteristics of shrimping as an occupation. They maintained to others that shrimping was just another business, that fishing for shrimp was like any other work, and that, by implication, as boat owners they were little different from any other businessmen.

The more boats the owner had, the more likely he was to maintain social distance between himself and shrimpers. Such distancing is brought on both by the demands of running a larger and larger operation and by the consequential rise in status that produces in some owners the need to identify with those in the community of similar income, life-style, and values.

Boat owners have had more opportunity to modify their community image than have shrimpers. Although owners work longer hours than the average American, they can attend meetings, join clubs, and participate in church groups. They can function in step with the rest of the town because they have a land job that, although demanding long hours in the office and at the docks, gives them time with family, friends, and neighbors. The owner's wife can, similarly, donate her time to voluntary activities in the town, if she so chooses, because she has the time and the financial resources to do so. More important, she now also has the social acceptance to participate in community affairs.

The way in which one dresses often reflects identification with a particular class and its corresponding set of values. With one exception, the boat owners I talked with dressed substantially differently from the shrimpers, even though the owners might work on the docks with the fishermen. If the owners stayed in their offices, they dressed in expensive slacks, cowboy boots or loafers, and open sport shirts. If they were in daily contact with shrimpers on the dock, they wore more functional clothes. In either case, it was very easy to tell just by dress who was an owner, who a shrimper.

I witnessed one particular case that illustrates this social distancing when I was in a downtown store in one of the port towns. While I was looking at several items next to the cash register, a very well dressed woman drove up in a new Cadillac. She purchased several items and paid with a check. The woman behind the counter, looking at the check, asked whether she was Mrs. Blank, the wife of a well-known shrimper. The woman replied that she was but that her husband was not a shrimper, he was a boat owner.

Others associated with the shrimping industry at a local level similarly distance themselves from the shrimpers and the actual fishing. These men and women often are in daily contact with shrimpers but, at the same time, have developed attitudes that preclude an acceptance of them. Like many owners, they could provide the other townspeople with a more accurate description and understanding of the nature of the work. On the contrary, however, these individuals often wholeheartedly accept the prevalent deviant stereotype, regardless of whether their own direct observations contradict these notions.

For instance, one man who worked with shrimpers in his capacity as foreman for a fishhouse maintained that all shrimpers were lazy, stating that anyone could do the work on boats that shrimpers do. He also said that shrimpers made so much money they did not know how to spend it all. He ended by saying that shrimpers had an easy life and were fools to complain.

Another woman I talked with, again someone in daily contact with shrimpers, dogmatically stated that shrimpers not only made twice as much money as other people in town but would steal owners blind if given half a chance. When I suggested that fishing was often dangerous, and certainly not easy work, she said, "All they do is throw the nets out, sit around on deck, then haul them in." She did go on to say that being away from home for so long was hard, but she added that the money to be made should compensate them.

The shared attitudes of these community members reflect the opinions of those who should have a good idea of shrimpers and their work but do not. Again, this is because they do not see the shrimpers work at sea; they see them only leave port, return, collect their paychecks, and go home. Thus they not only distance themselves from shrimpers because of the fishermen's acquired negative status but often perpetuate the negative stereotypes at the same time.

Community residents who do not have close ties to shrimpers know very little about the demands, the dangers, and the isolation from family that are all a part of shrimping. Instead they see shrimpers' visible drinking, the ready cash, the fact that shrimpers appear to have thousands of dollars after every trip.

They see, also, that the owners can afford big houses, custom-built homes, expensive cars for their wives, vacations in what are perceived as exotic places, and all the other material goods that represent wealth. They see that the owners hobnob with bankers, lawyers, accountants, doctors, store owners, and the town's elite, and they make the logical assumption that if the owners are so rich, the shrimpers they have seen flashing their money must be rich too.

Owners and others close to the industry who have shrimped for a living, or even gone out for a few short days, are more likely to hold views opposing those suggested above. They are more likely to serve as social mitigators for shrimpers; their experience in shrimping means they are more likely not to believe negative stereotypes. Thus they are more likely to disagree in a conversation if a negative attitude toward these fishermen is expressed and to challenge statements that allude to shrimpers as being different from others. They remain a minority, however.

Fleet owners are in a difficult situation vis-à-vis their men and the community. They are often caught between the community hostility toward the shrimper, based on a stereotype that they often know to be misleading, and the sometimes unreasonable demands of their fishermen. Added to this is the owners' increasingly precarious financial burden, which is exacerbated by fixed wholesale prices. Owners would like to pay their shrimpers good wages and also clear a profit on their investment. In the past they have been able to do this. Now, though, they are having to choose between the two, and, naturally enough, their own pocketbooks speak louder than do those of the men who work for them.

6. At the Dock: Drinking and Deviance

"What I want to do is get paid, get drunk, and get laid."

"I want to get as far away from the boat as I can and spend time with my family."

When shrimpers leave the dock, it is with the hope that many shrimp will be netted, the weather will hold, the price will rise, and perhaps the problems left behind will find solutions while they are gone. When they return, they know how many boxes they have netted, what the weather did or did not do to them, and, within a few cents, the price they will receive for their catch. They also know at some level that their problems with family and friends, problems most of us have, probably have not gone away; many realize that they more than likely have new ones.

But the hardest thing for many shrimpers is not the backbreaking work at sea, or even the emotions and feelings that must be confronted when they finally settle into their homes. The hardest thing for many shrimpers is the coming back, the returning from sea to land, the transition from being "out of civilization" to having to respond to obligations of family, friends, and community.

The same social behavior of shrimpers that works so well at sea, when they must constantly respond to the demands of fishing in an alien environment, is not easily tolerated by those who have remained on land. This is especially the case when that behavior is viewed within the context of the social relationships that have developed over time between shrimpers and the communities in which they reside. The rules of a shrimper's workplace are very different from the expectations that begin at the dock when he returns. The same man who is known by other shrimpers as the best fisherman in port may be seen by his community as someone to be neither admired nor respected; he may even, perhaps, be seen as a social outcast.

Texans who live and work on land usually have little if any idea of what a shrimper's work is really like. We see the trawlers enter and leave the harbor. Perhaps, if we are sport fishermen, we encounter the trawlers at sea in the early morning hours when the final catch has been boarded and the crew is heading the last pile of shrimp. Our view of shrimpers and their work remains severely limited to what we can imagine or what others tell us. If we have any expectations at all of shrimpers when they return from the sea, we expect them to act as if they were returning from a day at the office or an eight-hour shift at the construction site.

At the dock the shrimper has not yet returned completely to his home, yet he has left the sea. The rules quickly change. Upon docking, the captain is no longer in complete control of his boat. Three or four men jump on board to begin the unloading process. They are strangers, even if known well by the crew. After two weeks at sea in a space defined by the size of the boat, the sight of others walking around the boat can be a shock. The new men on board have done nothing to net the shrimp, yet they are unloading it and, occasionally, even looking for a chance to steal it; some have been known to stuff it down their boots or to try to make deals with the crew.

During the unloading the owner of the boat more than likely sits in his paneled office somewhere along the dock, waiting to see how many boxes will be taken off the boat. Regardless of anything that might have happened to crew and boat at sea, what counts most to him is how many boxes were harvested. Excuses are meaningless; in the long run, production per boat per annum is what matters.

Owners' attitudes toward their boats and their crews do differ, of course, depending on their own experiences in the shrimping business. Men who have worked their way up to boat ownership, who once may have started off as headers, are more sympathetic to the captain when he explains particular conditions on the trip that may have limited the number of boxes that were caught.

One owner, who had started as a header and, through the years, had come to own five boats, said that he could understand how crews felt when they first got back because he had felt the same way. If a captain yelled at him after the captain had been at sea for three weeks, he did not take it as a big deal. "What do you expect, after they've been away from their wives and families for so long?" this owner said. The next day, he went on, that same man would be back at the dock shooting the breeze with him and the dock workers as if nothing had happened. The owner said that he expected his crews to show the strain of the work and that when they did he took it for what it was worth and nothing more.

Many owners interviewed, however, had little or no experience in actual fishing. Surprisingly, very few had been captains of their own boats. As a group, they were aware of the numerous problems that could develop, but as managers of their businesses they saw the problems in terms of downtime of equipment and dollar loss. They viewed the harvesting of shrimp from the perspective of the dock rather than the wheelhouse.

The owner's response to the catch is just part of the intense pressure and change shrimpers may feel. Family members often meet them at the dock. Wives and children have three weeks of living that they want to communicate to their husbands and fathers, while the fishermen themselves have emotions and experiences that they must share with their families.

The fishermen are quickly confronted with the demands and needs of their families and friends whom they left behind. At the same time that they must worry about the owner's assessment of their trip, their wives and girlfriends are demanding attention. Fatigue, in addition, befuddles this time of transition, in which social relationships with those on land are once more renewed, sometimes after long examination by the shrimper in his thoughts at sea and, perhaps, by his family members and friends at home.

I have observed the effects of a two- or three-week trip on the faces of the shrimp crews. The stress, the tensions, the anxiety, all clearly show in their behavior at the dock when shrimpers face both the reality of what they are going to be paid for their work and the reality of their most important personal relationships. The perceptions of some crews are distorted by the hard and long work, and in some their anxieties about returning are heightened.

Two examples of the effects upon shrimpers of this transition from sea to land particularly stick in my mind. In the first, the shrimpers had just docked after a twenty-day trip. By the time I arrived at the docks and got the owner's permission to talk to the crew, their boat had chugged around to the other side of the harbor to unload at the fishhouse. I finally found the boat, but the captain, said the header, was inside the fishhouse office. I went inside. The captain sat in a chair talking to his wife on the phone. More accurately, he was sprawled in the chair, and the chair was taking his whole weight. He was so tired that he could barely sit up.

The captain wore stained brown pants with a tear in the rear and a pair of shrimper boots that were falling apart. An old leather belt was tied around his waist. Shirtless, he had a twenty days' growth of beard, bags under his eyes that seemed to sink to the corners of his mouth, and curly black hair that gave him a slightly crazed look. Two beer cans were at his feet, a third in his hand.

At first the captain was more suspicious than friendly, but once he learned that I was not from the government and that I was a sympathetic listener, he spoke for some time of his twenty-two years of experience as a shrimper. While his body remained slumped in the chair, his face took on a liveliness that reflected his pride in his knowledge of shrimping and his ability to provide his family with an income so that they were, in his words, "living very well." Another captain walked in, and the interview turned into a discussion.

The first captain spoke so long and well that when he had finished, the crew had been paid their advances and were anxious to leave. I told the captain that I still wanted a chance to talk to the rest of the crew, and we agreed to meet the next morning, when the crew would finish cleaning the boat and get their full paychecks for the trip.

The next morning I had driven out to the harbor and parked my car and was walking to the boat when a man said, in a friendly voice in Spanish, "Hello, how are you doing this morning?" I looked over at him, said hello back, then started to walk on. He did look vaguely familiar. I looked back over my shoulder. It was the captain from the day before, but he was not the same man. This man was dressed in sixty-dollar slacks, expensive shoes, and an attractive shirt, open at the collar and exposing a thick gold choker chain. The beard was gone, the hair was in place, and his eyes were covered by prescription sunglasses. It was the captain, but he had changed bodies.

I quickly told him that I had not recognized him, that he looked like a different man. I did not want to insult him, to tell him outright that he had looked like a bum before but that now he was dressed like one of the community's finest, but I think he understood my confusion. He shook my hand and smiled, and we walked over to the boat and completed the interviews with the rigger and header.

The second example of the point I wish to make involves a rigger who, when I interviewed him, was very friendly and helpful in the information he provided but was obviously leaving out something important about himself. The boat we were on had unloaded its shrimp, and the crew were waiting around for their advances. The rigger was answering the questions as I went through the interview, but when we got to the section on health he got visibly upset. I skipped that section, seeing his reaction, and went on to some other apparently less threatening questions.

The rigger himself was a Cajun, originally from a small town near Morgan City, Louisiana, about forty, and considerably overweight. He had already changed from his fishing clothes and now looked more like a clerk in department store than a fisherman. The captain, whom I had just finished interviewing, came in every five minutes and made comments to the effect that the rigger was very experienced, was a hard worker, and had been a captain on his own boat for many years. The captain by his behavior seemed to want to deny any bad impressions I might be getting from the rigger.

I never did complete the interview. A friend of the rigger came by, their advances were completed at the office, and the men wanted to leave. I set up a time the following day to complete the interview. I waited the next morning at the boat, then finally went inside to the owner's office to get out of the summer sun, which, although it was only 9:30, was pushing the thermometer up to ninety-five degrees.

The secretary told me that the rigger would probably not be back that day. He and his friend had had some problems getting back to their families. The rigger had passed out in the back seat of his car from drinking more than a case of beer, and his friend and his wife had carried him into the house. But then his friend, who also had had a lot to drink since he left the boat, ran into a parked car. The police had let him go but had confiscated the car because they did not want him driving it in his condition. The rigger was at home sleeping it off.

At this point the owner came in and, when told by the secretary about what happened to the rigger, commented that the rigger was a drunk and that it was only a matter of time before his drinking problem would catch up with him.

In these two examples, both the captain and the rigger were trying to cope with the initial impact of coming home—with returning

from the sea to the demands of land society. Both used alcohol to varying degrees to help in their transition to the known social setting of the
land they had left behind. The captain, however, would in all likelihood be judged by most in the community to have made his landfall
more successfully. Appearing the next morning, he looked ready to
play a little golf or make some important decisions; in short, he was in
control of himself and his situation. On the other hand, the rigger
passed out in the back seat of his car, never showed up for work the
next day, and acted, as one social-service worker once told me, "like
most shrimpers act."

Community expectations and standards of alcohol use are predicated on the habits of men and women who work, or are seen to work,
five days out of the week. If these community members drink in public, they do so at predictable times and in predictable ways—after
work, in the evenings, and during the weekends. They are very unlikely, as contrasted to shrimpers, to be seen drinking in a bar at 9:30
on a Tuesday morning.

How a particular public perceives the use and abuse of alcohol by
shrimpers, as defined within the context of established social relationships, is an important factor in determining a community's continuing
acceptance or rejection of all shrimpers, regardless of individual behavior.[1] It is, in sum, this interaction between the real behavior of
shrimpers and their behavior as perceived by residents of a community
and, finally, the effects of the established stereotype on both fishermen
and nonfishermen that has determined the negative status of Texas
shrimpers in many Texas coastal communities.

[1] For a complete discussion of the importance of a community's perception of drink-
ing, see, for example, Ralph E. Tarter and Dorothea U. Schneider, "Models and
Theories of Alcoholism" in *Alcoholism: Interdisciplinary Approaches to an Enduring
Problem*, ed. Ralph E. Tarter and Arthur A. Sugerman, pp. 6–30. R. T. Trotter II and
J. A. Chavira, in *El Uso de Alcohol: A Resource Book for Spanish-Speaking Commu-
nities*, discuss the impact of different cultural values on consumption. See also R. Jessor,
T. D. Graves, and S. L. Jessor, *Society, Personality, and Deviant Behavior: A Study of a
Tri-ethnic Community*; H. J. Paine, "Attitudes and Patterns of Alcohol Use among Mexican Americans: Implications for Service Delivery," *Journal of Studies on Alcohol* 38
(1977): 544–553; L. V. Johnson and M. Maitre, "Anomie and Alcohol Use: Drinking
Patterns in Mexican-American and Anglo Neighborhoods, *Journal of Studies on Alcohol*
39 (1978): 894–902; and Robert Lee Maril and Anthony N. Zavaleta, "Drinking Patterns
of Low-Income Mexican-American Women," *Journal of Studies on Alcohol* 40 (1979):
480–484.

When I think back to how I felt when I returned from my first trip out on a shrimp boat, I find myself sympathizing with both the captain and the rigger. The day before we hit port, as we sat around the galley table after dinner talking about what we were going to do when we returned, the crew began to shrink back to normal size. The young header was going to get drunk and find a prostitute. The rigger had some friends he would go see and was going to have big fish fry with all the fish he had caught. The captain was not sure, but he missed his kids and he would probably buy them presents with his pay advance. When they asked me, I said I was not sure, but I missed my wife and thought I would take her out to dinner and a movie.

The rigger and I had gotten to be good friends on the trip and planned to get together a few days after we got back and before he went out on his next trip. I gave him my phone number. He looked smaller than he had just the day before, and he also began to look wilder to me, even a little crazy.

The boat motored up the ship channel to the port. Men and boys sat fishing on either bank. It was only a Friday afternoon, but already many people were starting the weekend. It was the first time in two and a half weeks I had seen other people. I looked closely at them. Although they were less than a hundred yards away, I got out the binoculars and stared at them, their clothes, their fishing gear, and, behind them, their cars. The colors of the objects particularly attracted my eye. The reds, oranges, and greens looked very bright, almost garish. The header yanked the glasses away from me and focused on a female. We both took turns looking at her.

The boat docked, and I stepped out on the wooden pier. The pier moved. It began swinging back and forth, so I walked back to the boat, jumped on, and told the rigger what happened. He laughed and said that sometimes, when he was sitting at his favorite bar, the room would start to rock back and forth too. Then he would grab onto the bar for dear life until the motion stopped; usually it did.

I was seasick at the dock. Not as badly as during the first few days on the trip, but I did not feel very good. I staggered up to a pay phone, called my wife, and told her to come get me as soon as she could.

I went over to the owner's office to thank him for letting me go out. He had not really known me very well, and he had taken a chance on my being in the way of the crew. It had worked out well, and I knew the captain would tell him so, but I wanted at least to let him know I appreciated his favor. He was busy in his inner office, so I went outside and sat down in the gravel parking lot. Later, I realized that I do not normally go around sitting in parking lots.

Eventually he came out of his office and started to get in his truck. I walked up to him and said hello; he looked at me in a funny way, recognized me, and asked me how I had liked going out on the boat.

Later, hanging onto the sink in my bathroom against the roll of my own house, I looked at myself in the mirror. I had changed. I looked wilder, more like I thought the rigger looked. My hair had grown enough to cross the line between respectable and questionable, the red bandanna I had used to hold it in place and as a sweatband making me look like a younger Willie Nelson. The sun had turned my face and arms a darker brown, my beard was ragged where I'd trimmed it down to stubble with the scissors from my Swiss Army knife, and the T-shirt and cut-offs I wore should have been buried at sea. I looked ominous and was proud of it.

What is more, I felt like getting drunk. Not just because the house, like the highway coming home, would not stop rocking, but also because when I sat down to talk with my wife, I found there was just too much to say, too many experiences, too many feelings. It was hard to adapt. For one thing, my house seemed like a palace compared to the way I had lived on the boat. Also, I found other people's faces incredibly interesting. I noticed small things I would not normally pay attention to. I felt as if I did not fit, that everything around me was very different from what I remembered. Everything was out of focus.

The way I felt is, to a lesser degree, perhaps, similar to the way many shrimpers feel when they return. Since it was my first trip out, I was affected more by some things that happened, less by others. Certainly some of my responses were attributable to feelings I had upon returning to my own culture after completing fieldwork in another. But inherent in those feelings was also frustration at not being able to talk to special people about all that I had experienced. I wanted to tell them that I had seen things I never had expected, had worked hard and taken some risks, had been depressed and elated, had lived a lot in a very short time. I was different; I had changed. But how could you tell people these things when they did not know the difference between a try net and a lazy line, or when their preconceived notions of shrimping automatically assumed that a person was crazy even to go out on a shrimp boat?

There is so much to explain in terms of the situation—what the boat is like, the gear, how shrimp are caught, the encompassing sea—that finally the whole point of the individual experience is lost in the context of all that was intended to give it meaning. I stopped talking to people about it.

And, finally, how can you listen patiently as those closest to you describe three weeks out of their lives? Even though I did not have to face the economic pressures with which shrimpers must contend, I still found the social pressures of readjustment to family and community disorienting. Several of the shrimpers I interviewed spoke of living on trawlers at sea as "being in jail" and the time spent in the Gulf as "dead time." Those statements I take as extreme; the point here is that coming back home after three weeks at sea bears no resemblance to returning from the job after "a hard day's work."

I am not trying to make excuses for why many shrimpers, especially in this transition stage, use alcohol to smooth out their lives. Yet I also feel that many people, given similar circumstances, would do the same thing, would find and use alcohol as many shrimpers do. Shrimping as an occupation creates a situation for the shrimper, a set of circumstances, in which drinking upon return to land serves a definite purpose.

The real questions here, however, are tied not only to why many shrimpers begin drinking at the dock but also to the ways some continue their drinking to the point that it interferes, to a greater or lesser degree, with their jobs, their families, their friends, and the places in which they live. A concern of equal importance is how the community interprets this drinking: how the public accepts or rejects it as "normal" drinking behavior. First we will look at several patterns of drinking that are established in this transition stage. Then we will observe how the public responds to its perceptions of shrimpers as drinkers, which is the central issue in determining how community members interpret the behavior of all shrimpers on land.

Patterns of Alcohol Consumption

There is a variety of methodological approaches to gathering data on patterns of alcohol use.[2] Perhaps the strongest among these is information gathered in the context of the structured interview about the quantity of alcohol consumed, the frequency of consumption, beverage preference, and the social setting in which drinking takes place. From these data one could, ideally, construct categories of drinkers based on patterns of consumption and substantiate the findings with interviews with other family and community members.

Although this approach was approximated in the present study, it was not possible to replicate it for several reasons. First, it was important to gather not only other demographic characteristics but other data as well, including attitudes toward work and safety. In consequence, it was very difficult, at times, to gather just these use data alone. Second, time was a major constraint, as was circumstance: shrimpers were interviewed on the boat or at the dock just before going out for a trip, in which case they were always anxious to leave, or just after returning, in which case they were anxious to finish unloading, get their checks, and go home.

The final constraint was the problem of confidence and rapport between the interviewer and the respondent and the important issue of privacy. Drinking is considered by many to be one's own business, best kept to oneself and one's close relations.[3] Shrimpers, in addition, are particularly sensitive to questions about alcohol use because they feel that they have all been unjustly labeled, as one shrimper said, "wild drunks." After careful consideration, then, the following approach, an adaptation of the usual methodology, was employed.

Shrimpers at the end of the regular interview questions were asked, instead of laborious quantity, frequency, and other alcohol questions, what they most wanted to do upon returning to the dock and to land. Time and again they said that all they really wanted to do when

[2] See Tarter and Schneider, "Models and Theories of Alcoholism," pp. 6–30.

[3] Interviewing respondents about what may be their most private concerns is a sensitive issue in the social and behavioral sciences that, in practice, is all too often ignored. Sissela Bok, in *Lying*, has observed and commented on this insensitivity to personal privacy.

they landed was to get out of their dirty clothes, clean up, see their families, and relax with "a few beers."

The fishermen then were asked, if it seemed appropriate, whether or not they continued drinking and, if so, for how long and in general how much. Some shrimpers, in fact, volunteered this information during the course of the interview. In order to protect the privacy of the respondents, those who were interviewed in front of other men were not asked this follow-up question, nor were fishermen whose wives or other family members were on board.

This method of questioning led to approximately a 50 percent response rate. Some data collected were, in addition, validated in conversations or interviews with family members, employees, or friends. For example, in talking with the wife of a shrimper after all the interviews of the crew had been completed, she might say, as an aside to the conversation, "Did Jim tell you he drinks too much? Well, he does, even though he won't say it." Data from this approach were thus "messier"—some would say less accurate—but this was the more appropriate methodology and, at the same time, did respect the privacy of the fishermen interviewed.

Keeping in mind that the community attitudes toward shrimpers are constructed not necessarily on the real patterns of alcohol use but rather on what the public perceives these patterns to be, we now turn to an examination of the results of the question on alcohol use.

The majority of all shrimpers who responded to the drinking questions were either nondrinkers or light and medium drinkers (see Table 6-1). Seventeen percent of those interviewed said they rarely drank or did not drink at all; these respondents were operationally defined as nondrinkers. About another quarter of the respondents could be classified as light drinkers, those drinking one or two beers daily. (When questioned further, many of the men who at first said they did not drink at all admitted they did have one or two beers when they first return to port but added that they rarely consumed any additional alcohol. These nondrinkers were more likely to be younger males, often of Mexican-American or Mexican descent,[4] or older Anglo males who did not drink because of strongly held religious values. Light

[4]Maril and Zavaleta, "Drinking Patterns," p. 481.

TABLE 6-1. Drinking Patterns of Texas Shrimpers

Type of Drinker	Frequency*
Nondrinker	17% (12)
Light drinker	24% (17)
Medium drinker	33% (23)
Heavy drinker	12% (8)
Binge drinker	14% (10)

*N = 70.

drinkers were represented by a diversity of men of different age, ethnicity, and job position.)

Medium drinkers were fishermen who consumed less than one six-pack a day on a regular basis. These men tended to drink slightly more than the nondrinkers and light drinkers upon returning from a trip; then they would go either to their own house or to friends' homes, where beer drinking would continue for a short while. These men, like the light drinkers, were not distinguished by any particular demographic characteristics.

Heavy drinkers, for the purposes of these remarks, are fishermen who may drink just as much as binge drinkers when they first return— two six-packs of beer or more. They do not, however, stay drunk all the time they are in port. After an initial bout of drinking, they cut down their alcohol use. Although they continue to consume on the average one to two six-packs a day, in general they are not "out of control" in their drinking by any means. They drink at home and in their bars; their drinking is more public than that of light or medium drinkers.

Heavy drinkers represented a cross section of all shrimpers about whom drinking data were collected. They were, however, somewhat less likely to be married and to have families than were other drinkers. They were also less likely to own their own homes, although they did not appear to have any less income than those who were not heavy drinkers, as one might have expected.

For purposes of this study, binge drinkers are those who stay drunk from the time the boat docks to the time it leaves again. They are contrasted to the heavy drinkers not necessarily in the amount of alcohol they consume, but rather in their reaction to the consumption of this alcohol. Yet, although binge drinkers represent a small minority of all the shrimpers who responded to the drinking questions, their pattern of alcohol consumption is the basis for the deviant stereotype of shrimpers that is commonly found in port communities—that is, although the binge-drinking shrimper is numerically in a minority, his typical behavior is taken to represent that of all shrimpers and of those who have anything to do with the industry.

Binge drinkers, like all other shrimpers, rarely drink on the boat while at sea. This is because captains usually do not allow any significant drinking, not even a few beers, on a trip. Almost all the owners and captains I talked with were adamant about the "no drinking" policy on the boats. The risks in shrimping were too great, they felt, without drinking's compounding the problems.

Shrimpers with reputations for drinking problems find it difficult to get work. Those who have been known to drink while on a trip often do not get rehired. The very few exceptions to this observation I heard of were captains who drank at sea and did not care whether the crew did also. They were considered very good captains who produced a lot of shrimp, so their drinking was ignored.

The typical binge drinker begins drinking as soon as the boat docks. He usually finds a convenience store near the dock or a bar where he can buy a couple of six-packs to go. Then he returns to the boat and sneaks beers, unless the captain does not mind. While the shrimp are being off-loaded he sips beer and does the necessary cleanup work. (The crews will go to some lengths not to drink in front of the owner. Since many owners rarely venture onto their own boats when they come in, however, this is not a big problem for the crew.)

As soon as the advances are paid out, a binge drinker hits the bars and cantinas or buys a case of beer and goes home to his family. If he hits the bars, which is more likely, it is almost always with friends who are shrimpers, other male family members, or girlfriends. Certain bars in all the communities selected were known by all as "shrimpers' bars." Often these bars are located directly across the street from where the shrimpers dock. When this is not possible, because of legal codes or the isolation of the port facilities from populated areas, certain sections of town are known as places that welcome shrimpers. While shrimpers are encouraged as patrons of these bars, nonshrimpers are not. Community members who are nonshrimpers know which bars are for them and which for shrimpers only.

Restaurants, bars, and motels in general give indifferent service to shrimpers and those often falsely identified as shrimpers. I have observed this behavior on a number of occasions. One time I watched as two shrimpers were given a table at the very back, near the exit, of an expensive tourist restaurant that had a reputation for good food. They were virtually ignored, were finally served, and left loud and angry at the inferior service. The prophecy thus self-fulfilled, the waitress and restaurant host also seemed relieved they had gone.

In any case, the binge drinkers who hit the bars drink excessively in a very short time. One rigger, when asked how much he usually drank when he returned to port, said, "It takes a case of beer to get me off. Then I usually need half a bottle of Scotch. That usually does it."

Individual responses to this large intake of alcohol vary and are consistent with those of binge drinkers in other occupations. Some shrimpers get quiet and eventually pass out; some are loud and abusive; some seem to feel mellow and relaxed. Drinking usually occurs in more than one bar, and often a small group of shrimpers, friends, or acquaintances winds up at someone's house or checks into a motel room, where the drinking may continue.

Many binge drinkers eventually pass out or fall asleep. When they wake up, the effects of the large amount of alcohol are still with them. They continue their drinking but usually do not consume as much in one time as they originally did when they first got off the boat.

Some stop drinking the night before their boat is to go out on its next trip. Others drink right up to the time the boat leaves the dock. Hangovers are common complaints among this small group well into fishing trips.

Family members, especially wives and girlfriends, are usually confronted after the binge-drinking shrimper is drunk. Wives and families of binge drinkers often expect the drinking behavior and are not surprised by it, although they do not like it. Wives do not usually join their husbands in drinking. Girlfriends, on the other hand, often participate in the heavy drinking.

Many married binge drinkers regularly divide their money into drinking money and money for their families. Often the wives do it for their husbands. In this way the hard drinking stops when the money runs out, although that is the time when drinking friends become important as sources of extra money. Single men, especially those without permanent girlfriends, are less likely to divide their money in this way and more likely to spend almost all their money on drinking and other entertainment.

The heavily patronized bars generally run tabs because binge-drinking shrimpers are such good customers. These tabs, which may be as high as several hundred dollars, must be paid off at least in part before the binge drinker is given more credit. A few binge drinkers leave port in debt to the bars, but most of the experienced shrimpers find ways to pay off their bar debts, plus any other loans from friends, so that they come out with enough money to last them until the next trip.

Binge drinkers during this transition stage are much more likely to get arrested for their drunken behavior than at any other time. They are also more likely to get arrested than are other shrimpers. Fights, arguments, and public displays of frustrations and emotions are much more likely to occur among bingers. One former captain put it thus: "Who wouldn't raise a little hell when you've been out there for two or three weeks?" Binge drinkers, and heavy drinkers, are more likely to "raise a little hell," and get caught, than are other drinking and non-drinking shrimpers. Binge drinkers are most commonly arrested for driving while intoxicated, public intoxication, and simple assault.

Binge drinkers, as is the case with the other drinking categories, exhibit no outstanding characteristics that immediately differentiate them from other shrimpers or the population in general. There are, however, more headers in this group than captains or riggers. Headers are a more marginal population than riggers and captains; binge-drinking headers are most probably selected out, because of the demands and responsibilities of the work, and rarely achieve the status of trawler captain.

It is quite possible that because of the sample size and bias in response to questions concerning drinking behavior, major intragroup differences between drinkers are not apparent. Too, the sample is quite diverse in regard to ethnicity, race, job status, income, and age. Further research would be needed to assure that the results did not reflect these biases.

Although these patterns of alcohol use among shrimpers are rather broad, and the data more suggestive than definitive, nevertheless they do point out important real intergroup differences. First and foremost, shrimpers rarely drink at sea. Most shrimpers do drink upon returning, even those who rarely drink at any other times, but only a significant minority then go on to consume relatively large amounts of alcohol, most often beer. By far the majority of shrimpers consume less than do the heavy and the binge drinkers among them.

Shrimpers are still seen by many in their communities as "wild drunks." Comparisons to Cahalan and Room's national survey of drinking behavior,[5] however, do little to clarify the discrepancy between shrimpers' actual drinking behavior and the public perception of their drinking behavior. In a word, shrimpers do not consume that much more alcohol than do other similar work groups.[6]

Further comparisons belie the major behavioral differences in alcohol use between shrimpers and other occupational groups. It is not that shrimpers on an annual basis necessarily drink significantly more than do other working men; it is, rather, a question of timing, of when they drink and how much they drink in a relatively short period. What is distinctive is that, as suggested, little drinking occurs at sea, even among heavy and binge drinkers. The vast majority of drinking takes

[5] Don Cahalan and Robin Room, *Problem Drinking among American Men*.

[6] Categories of abstainer, light drinker, moderate drinker, heavy drinker, and binge drinker have been operationally defined for shrimpers and are similar to, but not entirely consistent with, Cahalan's usages. Cahalan has five major categories of drinkers which include, besides abstainers, "infrequent drinkers [who] drink at least once a year, but less than once a month; light drinkers [who] drink at least once a month but typically only one or two drinks on a single occasion; moderate drinkers [who] drink at least once a month, typically several times, but usually with no more than three or four drinks per occasion; and heavy drinkers [who] drink nearly every day with five or more per occasion at least once in a while, or about once weekly with usually five or more per occasion" (Don Cahalan, Ira H. Cisin, and Helen M. Crossley, *American Drinking Practices*, p. 19). The category of "abstainer" among shrimpers includes Cahalan's categories of "abstainer" and "infrequent drinker," while Cahalan's "heavy drinker" has been broadened among shrimpers to "heavy drinker" and "binge drinker."

In general, comparisons of patterns of drinking between shrimpers and other similar occupational categories in Cahalan's study, including "craftsman," "foreman," "operative," "service worker," and "laborer," broadly suggest that these fishermen do not differ substantially in their patterns of alcohol use from other work groups. There appears to be a lower number of heavy and binge drinkers among shrimpers as compared to other occupational groups (16 percent of all shrimpers, as against 19 percent of all craftsmen and foremen, 26 percent of all operatives, 21 percent of all service workers, and 20 percent of all laborers). Shrimpers also appear to have a higher representation of moderate and light drinkers (57 percent, as compared to rates of 44, 35, 54, and 39 percent, respectively, for craftsmen and foremen, operatives, service workers, and laborers). There are significantly fewer abstainers among shrimpers than there are abstainers and infrequent drinkers in the national survey.

place on land—either between trips or during the winter season, when there is often little fishing. It is the timing of shrimpers' drinking, and its visibility, that distinguish their patterns of alcohol use.

Public Drinking: The Visible and the Invisible Drinker

> "You ain't going to find no shrimpers in the AA meetings. That's for executives. But you'll find 'um drunk in the gutter over there on the street."

While most other men and women at 10:00 on a weekday morning have a solid start on their workday, some shrimpers returning after a two-week or three-week trip are ready to "blow it all out and raise some hell," as one shrimper told me. Other shrimpers, the majority, return to their families and friends, relax, sleep, and spend time with their kids. These shrimpers, from the public's perspective, are often invisible. The hell-raisers are the ones the communities see.

A number of social scientists have noted that there are acceptable and unacceptable ways, as judged by society, in which to consume alcohol.[7] We all learn when to drink, how to drink, and what to do if we drink too much. To some degree social class determines that which is defined as acceptable and that which is not. All communities have norms of alcohol use; shrimpers break many of these rules and expectations.

Shrimpers have their own bars. They also go to other bars and public places. They often hang around other shrimpers, as cops hang around with other cops, social workers with social workers, doctors with doctors. But whereas nonshrimpers may drink just as much as, if not more than, shrimpers, their behavior as drinkers is judged less on their total consumption than on how they handle themselves when drinking.

Some few shrimpers, particularly the binge drinkers, after three weeks at sea do not seem to care much how they handle themselves.

---

[7] See, for example, Leonard V. Blumberg, Thomas F. Shipley, Jr., and Stephen F. Barsky, *Liquor and Poverty*; and Harry F. Wolcott, *The African Beer Gardens of Bulawayo*, in which the role of state government is stressed. See also Norman R. Layne and George D. Lowe, "The Impact of Loss of Career Continuity on the Later Occupational Adjustment of Problem Drinkers," *Journal of Health and Social Behavior* 20 (1979): 187–193.

All they want is to forget for a while what they have been doing. Their public display of drinking often breaks the unspoken rules of acceptable drinking and sometimes, though more rarely, the legal rules as well.

The shrimpers who break the rules are too loud, sometimes obnoxious, sometimes aggressive, and often rowdy. As long as they stay in shrimpers' bars, there are no real problems. But when they exhibit the same behavior in other bars, restaurants, movies, and shopping malls, they reinforce an existing stereotype, in some communities, of shrimpers, all shrimpers, as drunks.

Interestingly, men who are not shrimpers but "act like shrimpers" are often mistaken for them. Thus, in port towns longshoremen, men who work in the fishhouses, merchant marines, sailors from other countries, and Coast Guard and Navy men, as well as drifters, winos, and bums, are all sometimes identified as shrimpers, and their behavior consequently is attributed to shrimpers.

This labeling by occupation is rather unusual. If, for instance, we were to happen by a bar filled with trial lawyers in three-piece suits, all, let us say, celebrating a court decision, most of us would not then assume from that point on that all lawyers were necessarily drunks, or even that only lawyers wore three-piece suits. Yet this is, to a degree, what has happened to shrimpers.

Most people in the communities under study felt they could easily identify shrimpers. Their descriptions included, in general, a man in worn out, smelly clothes needing a shave and flashing his money as he drinks large amounts of alcohol. He is loud and obnoxious and "acts like a shrimper."

There are some shrimpers who do, indeed, fit this description, just as there are some lawyers who are drunks. But the majority of shrimpers, once they are off the boat, seek to distance themselves from the grime and the smell of their chosen occupation by dressing as neatly and as expensively as possible; some, in fact, overcompensate in this regard. On land they become "invisible" shrimpers.

One former captain told me the following story. He was at a discount store buying a part for his car. He had been back in port for several days. While he was standing in line at the checkout counter, a loud and obnoxious man, who said he was a shrimper, made a scene with the clerk. The captain said he felt extremely frustrated as he observed how others around him reacted to the shrimper. He said that he wanted to tell everyone that he was a shrimper, too, and that all shrimpers were not like the man in front of him.

The captain is one of the majority of shrimpers who are invisible. They are the shrimpers who use alcohol "successfully" to ease the transition from sea to land, from work to family, and who in most ways are indistinguishable from other members of the community. They, as well as those shrimpers who do not drink, are invisible because their behavior is not judged by other members of the community as representative of shrimpers in general.

Two Communities

Community attitudes that have developed toward shrimpers are less a product of the fishermen's own actions than of the interaction of the shrimpers' real behavior and the perceptions of community residents within a historical context. As with any stereotype, there is a grain of truth that gives it weight, that helps to perpetuate it. A minority of shrimpers, as suggested, have drinking problems, brag about their paychecks, and are loud and obnoxious. So do a minority of truck drivers, policemen, psychologists, and doctors. But those who realize that the stereotype is misleading are unable or unwilling to do anything about it, and the fishermen themselves lack the time and the political clout to do much to change or promote their public image.

The stereotype persists, but it is certainly subject to variation depending on the particular community. Inland, for example, the stereotype is far less pervasive. One shrimper told me he vacationed in Austin although he lived in Aransas Pass because he felt people respected him more in the capital city than at home. Attitudes toward shrimpers also vary from port to port: the size of the community, its reliance on the fishing industry, and its relative isolation from major metropolitan areas are structural variables that influence the strength of the shrimper stereotype. A closer examination of two Texas shrimping communities emphasizes these observations.

Brownsville is located at the southern tip of Texas on the Mexican border. It lies approximately twenty miles inland from the Gulf and is the home for many Texas shrimpers who fish out of Port Brownsville, some ten miles north and east of the city. The port is located on a deepwater channel that leads to the Gulf of Mexico.

The city had in 1980 a resident population of approximately eighty thousand, of whom about 90 percent were Mexican-American, 10 percent Anglo, and less than 1 percent black, with a "shadow" population of Mexicans that was uncounted. It lies directly across the Rio Grande from Matamoros, Tamaulipas, Mexico, a city of three hundred thousand. Brownsville is best characterized by its poverty (figures for per-capita income are among the lowest in the United States), its high unemployment rates, and its recent economic development during the last decade.[8]

As a city Brownsville sustained a relatively rapid economic growth in the 1970s. It is now the home for a variety of industries that employ a growing labor force. *Maquiladoras*, or twin-plants, have stimulated development on both sides of the border, attracting new industries to the area. As a result, while wages remain low for the majority and unemployment is still a serious problem, the total number of jobs in the last ten years has substantially increased. On the other hand, employment has not kept in stride with the growth of the indigenous population and the influx of Mexicans seeking work, and, because of this recent rapid industrialization, the shrimping industry, once one of the only industries in the area, is now of limited importance to Brownsville.

As a port Brownsville has attracted a number of heavy manufacturers in the last several years, including five oil refineries, while the shrimp fleet has remained about the same size.[9] The port has planned for a number of incoming industries by providing additional facilities, including dredging the ship channel to handle larger vessels and constructing new rail lines and a new international bridge. There are no plans on the drawing board for additional dock space or services for the shrimp fleet.

Port Brownsville is distinctive because it is totally isolated from any residential communities. This isolation means that most Brownsville residents' only contact with shrimpers in their place of work is limited to their occasionally seeing fishermen hitchhike back and forth to their boats along a major highway. Those who do drive by the shrimp basin are limited to what they can see from their cars—only

[8] Michael V. Miller, "Industrial Development and an Expanding Labor Force in Brownsville," *Texas Business Review* 55 (November–December, 1981): 258–261.

[9] For an informative, though superficial, history of Port Brownsville, see Henry N. Ferguson, *The Port of Brownsville*.

the backs of sheds, fishhouses, and other metal buildings, between which they may catch a glimpse of the boats. A guard at the gate discourages the curious from driving around the small port, and on the weekends visitors are not allowed. I have talked with many Brownsville residents who have never visited the port and in fact do not know where the trawlers are docked.

Attitudes toward shrimpers in this city are uniformly negative. Strong deviant stereotypes are prevalent and are sustained by local media, which continuously identify shrimpers and emphasize their run-ins with the law.[10] Whereas other occupations and professions, such as welder, electrician, teacher, or doctor, are usually not identified in newspaper headlines by their generic job title, such is always the case with shrimpers.

The word *shrimper* is used in the headlines because its connotations are well understood by both the reporters and their readership. Just by using "shrimper," the reporter conveys a presumption of a certain life-style. This kind of reporter bias would be out of place if the meanings were not shared by a majority in the community. But these connotations are shared by many; "shrimper" in Brownsville means someone who is often violent, drinks too much, and is likely to commit a crime and be written about in the newspaper. The newspaper and other media not only perpetuate the stereotypes but also in fact reflect dominant community attitudes about shrimpers.

These strong, shared attitudes among nonshrimpers in Brownsville have remained unchanged since the 1940s, when shrimpers first moved their operations to Port Brownsville. They have, in part, also been sustained because the actual number of shrimpers, in relation to nonshrimpers, is small. No more than several hundred fishermen and their families live among Brownsville's residents; hence, the chances of other community members' coming into close personal contact with the fishermen are small. Limited contact means that the stereotypes are never challenged by the personal experiences and understanding one gets from knowing shrimpers and their families as friends and neighbors.

Regardless of the infrequency of social contacts between shrimp-

[10] Some mention of shrimp fishermen in a negative context appears regularly in the *Brownsville Herald* (for example, "Shrimper Shot in JP Lounge," October 12, 1980, and "Shrimper Pleads Guilty to Charges of Murder," January 6, 1981). There are few stories or articles that emphasize any positive aspects of shrimpers or the industry.

ers and nonshrimpers, I found that many people with whom I talked said they knew all about shrimpers and their fishing. When the conversation progressed further, most often it turned out that the nonshrimper knew someone else who said he knew a shrimper. Information about shrimpers' supposed life-styles and other important characteristics thus was passed around in an informal network based on facts received from friends of friends. Not surprisingly, strong negative stereotypes prevailed; stories were recounted in which shrimpers demonstrated or acted out the negative characteristics attributed to them. These stories were validated by reference to the friend of a friend.

Another source of information upon which rest the prevalent stereotypes of shrimpers is those who have limited work experience as shrimpers. Most often these men worked briefly as headers, perhaps only for one trip while in high school or summers during college or between other jobs. Their perspective of shrimping is limited, then, not only by their work experience but also by their status as headers. They remember the most negative aspects of the work; time and limited experience have dulled what perspective, if any, they had. They know that shrimping is difficult work and, because they have not known any shrimpers very well, assume that shrimpers, in order to do the kind of work that they do, must be crazy or stupid.

Those few residents I met who either lived in the same neighborhood as did a shrimping family or for some other reason had close ties with shrimpers saw the fishermen as little different from anyone else. One neighbor of a shrimping family observed, "They're just like everybody else except he's gone all the time."

There are two areas of the city commonly associated with shrimpers. One is a strip of highway within the city limits but only a short ride from Port Brownsville. It consists of a few bars and low-rent motels scattered in between welding shops, automotive paint shops, bait stores, and vacant lots. It is also the temporary home for some shrimpers, mostly headers and riggers, who need a place to stay between trips.

Shrimpers without a permanent residence in Brownsville or the surrounding area find this strip of highway convenient to the port and to the rest of Brownsville, especially if they do not have a car. They can be seen walking back and forth between their residences and the bars, small grocery stores, and bait stands in their work clothes.

The bars in this location are identified by other community members as shrimpers' bars. Shrimpers who are binge drinkers and heavy drinkers, as well as other shrimpers who consume considerably less, regularly congregate in these bars to talk about their trips, how many pounds they brought back, and the prices they were paid. They go to the bars to drink, to relax from their work, to spend money, to talk with their friends. The police regularly patrol these bars, which have a reputation for being "rough places."

Interestingly, my impression of the bars is that they do not differ from other town bars and nightclubs except that often the majority of the patrons are fishermen. Fights, stabbings, and occasional shootings are just as likely to occur at a variety of other bars and clubs, including local discos patronized by college-aged adults and the country-and-western bars that saturate the city.

The other area in Brownsville commonly associated with shrimpers is a central downtown square. The area is filled with old and decaying buildings, secondhand-clothing stores, used-furniture stores, and bars. Winos and bums often stand or sit on the street corners or in doorways. At night, fights in the bars are likely to take place. Men dressed in old, tattered clothes and with unkept beards are commonly identified by community members as shrimpers or former shrimpers.

There seems, in fact, to be a very small, highly mobile subculture of midwestern hobos and bums who annually winter in Brownsville, enjoying the warm climate before heading north again after the winter months have passed. These men have no background in commercial fishing. In addition to this group there is a larger, year-round population of area residents who live in the upstairs apartments and hotels over the stores or in tiny back-alley houses. This population is unusually poor, even by Brownsville standards, and is overrepresented by the elderly and by female heads of households. Shrimpers do visit a few of the downtown bars, but, in general, all but the binge and heavy drinkers of limited incomes avoid this area, which is considered by most shrimpers to be undesirable. If shrimpers are going to spend their hard-earned money, they will pick the best bars and restaurants in town, not the worst. Their taste in restaurants and bars is no different from that of the rest of the population.

Why, then, is this particular town square associated with shrimpers? Since many residents feel they know about shrimpers, their work, their habits, and their appearance, this area is presumed to be their hangout because so many of its inhabitants look like shrimpers are supposed to look—that is, they look like what residents *believe* shrimpers should look like. In any case, shrimpers who do drink heavily, the "visible" shrimpers, are much more likely to do their drinking in the first area described than go all the way downtown.

In spite of two locations commonly held to be the hangouts and residences of all shrimpers, most shrimpers in Brownsville are dispersed throughout the residential neighborhoods. A number of the captains live in the most exclusive suburban areas of the city. They own moderately expensive homes that are well maintained. The homes are filled with the accumulation of material goods associated with those in the upper income brackets. Headers and riggers, who earn substantially less, live throughout the lower-income sections of town. The poorest headers, of course, live in the poorest parts of town.

The point is that the vast majority of fishermen do not live in the places considered by most residents to be their homes. These fishermen, the "invisible" shrimpers, do not fit the dominant stereotype and thus are not recognized as such. There is no single neighborhood where shrimpers live, despite local beliefs.

A factor that did help to give substance to the shrimper stereotype in this city was the practice, discontinued some years ago, in which a captain visited the county or local jail when in need of a crew. In return for paying a jailed shrimper's fine, the captain expected the man, most often a header, to work his debt off at sea. This practice gave credence to the negative status of all shrimpers. What is overlooked is that a captain who must hit the jail to find a crew most probably is not a very good fisherman in the first place; if he were, he would not have difficulty hiring legitimate headers and riggers. This is to suggest that the worst captains were the ones who most often had to spring a potential crew member. In any case, this common practice, which also took place in other coastal communities, is now an occupational artifact that gives fu.ther credibility, however misinformed, to the shrimper stereotype.

Brownsville residents have little reason to change their attitudes toward shrimpers. The port is unknown to most. The only shrimpers they see or hear about are in the two areas described. There are so few shrimpers in Brownsville in relation to the size of the community that the chances of personal contact are small. Residents who are in fact shrimpers are often not identified as such because they do not look or act like shrimpers. The media, in particular the local newspaper, continuously reify the shrimper's negative image. Finally, because the shrimping industry is one among others in Brownsville, knowledge of it and respect for it are not automatically forthcoming from the community. Few residents, for example, have as much knowledge of the patterns of fishing that occur annually as they do even of the large migrant farm-labor population that lives in Brownsville and the surrounding areas.

In marked contrast to Brownsville is Port Isabel, twenty-five miles to the northeast. A majority of its population of approximately three thousand either are shrimpers or are associated with some aspect of the shrimping industry as workers in the local shipyard, fishhouses, or bait stands. While stereotypes of shrimpers pervade Port Isabel, the strength of those stereotypes is far less than in Brownsville.

Keeping in mind the social-historical factors suggested above, structural variables of size and of industrial development play an important role in the pervasiveness of the stereotypes of shrimpers. The nonshrimping members of Port Isabel are much more likely to have firsthand knowledge of shrimpers, and this personal experience is likely to militate against the stronger stereotypes found in Brownsville. While there is an area close to the town's harbor that is known as a tough place where shrimpers drink, many around town will also tell you of the rich shrimpers who live in the best parts of the community in the same breath that they show displeasure with the area immediately surrounding the port.

A major difference in Port Isabel, as contrasted to Brownsville, is that residents in this small community make distinctions in status among shrimpers depending on whether the fishermen are captains, ..ggers, or headers. Such is rarely the case in Brownsville, where a shrimper is a shrimper. In Port Isabel a man may be known as a shrimper *and* a rigger.

This knowledge of shrimpers and the industry in Port Isabel derives from the fact that shrimping is one of the only businesses in town. Tourism in this community plays an important role, especially in recent years with the growth and development of South Padre Island across the bay, but since 1948 it has been Gulf shrimpers and their industry that have generated the dollars and the jobs. While nonshrimpers may have little need for shrimpers themselves, they do need the income that the industry generates in the community.

In recent years the Chamber of Commerce has been quite adept at using the shrimp fleet as a commercial asset to the community. In the construction of several new housing developments and trailer parks, shrimp trawlers have been used in sophisticated advertisements to promote the uniqueness of the community to potential buyers. Indeed, the trawlers are becoming an advertising motif for the town, a background to the selling of the community as a desirable place in which to live. The use of fishing fleets as items of curiosity to tourists is of course not unique to this town,[11] but it does note the recognition on the part of some community entrepreneurs that the trawlers can make Port Isabel "quaint," and thus considered by some a better place to live than other towns that do not have a shrimp fleet.

The local newspaper is particularly geared to news about shrimpers and about the industry. It closely follows news affecting commercial shrimpers in other parts of the state. While it does, like the Brownsville paper, identify shrimpers by occupation, it also is likely to present shrimpers in a positive light, or at least in circumstances other than run-ins with the law. For instance, when the present survey was initiated in Port Isabel, the newspaper ran a front-page story describing the project.

The status of shrimpers remains relatively high in Port Isabel compared to other communities, like Brownsville, in part because nonshrimpers are much less aware that shrimpers only a few miles away are treated worse. The physical isolation of Port Isabel from nearby urban areas allows shrimpers there to enjoy a relatively higher status. They are still seen by many as deviant, just not as deviant as shrimpers are seen in Brownsville.

Deviance?

> "Deviance is not a quality of the act the person commits, but rather a consequence of the applications by others of rules and sanctions to an offender." (Howard S. Becker)

Many members of the communities in this study treat and think of shrimpers as if they were deviants. Others do not; fishermen are viewed just like any other working men. One young captain, describ-

[11] M. Estellie Smith, "Sociocultural Continuity: The Role of Tourism."

ing how he handles the opinions of the former group, said: "I went out with this girl for a while. I never tell them I'm a shrimper. If I did they wouldn't let me in their house. That's just how it is, so I never tell a girl what I do."

Are shrimpers really deviant? Clearly the meanings that the public attributes to the social behavior of "visible" shrimpers in some of the communities studied are interpreted as deviant and, occasionally, even as "perverted," as stated by several members of one community.

Shrimpers appear not to follow the rules from the time they return from a trip to the time they leave again. But the appearance of the "visible" shrimper belies the reality of the "invisible" shrimper. The demands of shrimping as an occupation, which include the necessity of a transition period from sea to land, make difficult the appearance of an acceptable middle-class existence for many shrimpers and their families. Notwithstanding these difficulties, which are discussed further in the following chapters, the "invisible" shrimpers and their families do, in fact, accommodate themselves to the occupational set of circumstances that defines their lives.

Many shrimpers, especially riggers and captains, possess both the values and the accoutrements of the American middle-class. Their so-called deviancy is predicated on the demands of their work and on their "visible" counterparts. It is grounded as well in the social histories of the communities in which they reside, their political powerlessness, and their fragile economic position as harvesters of a variable fishery. Their labels as deviants are far from uniform, depending to some degree on the particular characteristics of the coastal communities in which they live.

PART THREE

In the Marketplace: Shrimpers, Big Business, Big Government, and Unions

7. Economic Risks

> "It's not as good as it used to be. Used to be a man could
> make a real good living from it. I'm doing okay now, but
> not like I used to."

Texas shrimpers want the best price they can get for their shrimp.
They go to unusual lengths to ensure that the shrimp are returned to
the dock undamaged and unspoiled. They want to catch the large
shrimp that bring the highest price, and they want to do it as quickly as
possible to save fuel and prevent possible injury to crew and damage to
equipment. The captain incorporates these goals into his fishing strategy. To some degree, he has control over the factors that directly affect
price. He has little or no control, however, over seasonality of catch,
rising operating costs, rising capital investment, short-term fluctuations in the abundance of the fishery, imports, and inflation.

Seasonality of Catch

Griffin has noted that seasonality of catch is an important economic constraint in annual shrimp production.[1] Seasonality of catch is,
of course, a universal limitation to fisheries and is most often directly
influenced by legal restrictions on the fishing effort, migration patterns
of the species, adverse weather conditions, and cultural beliefs and
rituals that prohibit or otherwise limit fishing.[2]

Adult shrimp are found in abundance off Texas shores only during

[1] See Wade L. Griffin, Melvin L. Cross, and George W. Ryan, *Seasonal Movement
Patterns in the Gulf of Mexico Shrimp Fishery*, Department Technical Report No. 74-4;
and John P. Warren and Wade L. Griffin, *Costs and Return Trends for Gulf of Mexico
Shrimp Vessels*, Department Information Report 78-1, SP-4.

[2] See especially Patrick B. Mullen's two works: "The Function of Magic Folk Belief
among Texas Coastal Fishermen," *Journal of American Folklore*, 1969, pp. 214–225, and
I Heard the Old Fishermen Say: Folklore of the Texas Gulf Coast. See also John J.
Poggie, Jr., "Ritual Adaptation to Risk and Development in Ocean Fisheries: A New
England Case."

certain times of the year. The six-member Texas Parks and Wildlife Commission, which has the authority to regulate fishing seasons in the bays and estuaries and up to ten miles into the Gulf, closed in recent years the shrimp fishery within this ten-mile limit during certain seasons.[3] In theory, the closed seasons allow the juvenile shrimp and migratory shrimp to grow to full size and market value, at which time they can be legally netted.

In May, 1981, under the recommendation of the Gulf of Mexico Fisheries Management Council, the Fisheries Conservation Zone, the area that extends from ten to two hundred miles out into the Gulf off Texas waters, was closed to shrimpers at the same time as the ten-mile limit was closed by the Texas Parks and Wildlife Commission, from June 1 to July 15. Most owners and captains agreed with this change, noting that it was in fact long overdue. As they saw it, the ten-mile limit had never stopped shrimpers from going out. Once out, many fished within the ten-mile limit because the chances of being caught were negligible and fines minimal. In fact, the law was counterproductive, since even shrimpers who agreed with the intent of the law regularly fished in restricted waters because they could not afford to stand by and watch their friends haul in shrimp.

A few captains I interviewed were outraged by the state of affairs that had allowed blatant disregard of the law in recent years. In their views they represented many other captains I met. Most shrimpers will obey the law if it makes economic sense to do so and if the punishment for not doing so is quick and just. Shrimpers are like most other citizens; ineffective or nonenforceable laws increase their distrust of and disregard for all laws. A few shrimpers did say they would not follow any restrictions, regardless of what they were and who enforced them, but I believe this was just bragging on their part.

The majority of shrimpers felt that the new law, which in effect assures that all boats are tied up at the dock from June 1 to July 15 of each year, was a fair law because it could be readily enforced and applied equally to everyone. The law can be enforced because boats will have no reason to be out in the Gulf, few if any choosing to travel two

[3] For a discussion of these issues and related topics, see Gulf of Mexico Fishery Management Council, *Draft Environmental Impact Statement and Fishery Management Plan for the Shrimp Fishery of the Gulf of Mexico, United States Waters.*

hundred miles offshore, and fishhouses can be watched to ensure that no quantities of illegal shrimp are unloaded.

What worried many shrimpers about the new legal restriction was its direct effect on their income. Many, especially riggers and headers, were concerned about what they would do during the long off-season. Normally they might expect to be idle for two to four months out of the year; now they feared that an additional fixed time (forty-five days) of unemployment in the summer would necessitate their finding other jobs to supplement their incomes.

Many shrimpers, especially captains, spend up to two months during the winter in boat maintenance and repair. They are paid a nominal amount by the boat owners to ready the vessels for the coming fishing season. Often they hire on their riggers to help them. While the money they earn during this time does not meet all their bills, when it is supplemented with past savings and pay advances, these shrimpers manage to get by during the "hard months."

The new legal limit on fishing may mean that many fishermen, especially riggers and headers, will be forced to seek alternative full-time employment. A few shrimpers already do so on a regular basis. One particularly ambitious captain said that, although he earned $35,000 in 1979 from fishing, he regularly worked as a construction foreman during the winter months when the fishing was at its worst and the weather severe. From his job as foreman, a special arrangement he had with a friend who was a builder, he earned in 1979 a salary of $250 a week.

Most captains, because of their relatively high salaries, do not find it necessary to supplement their fishing incomes. This is certainly not the case with riggers and headers, who earn considerably less and whose incomes are more marginal, as is certainly true of headers. The average header, whose median income was $6,400 in 1979, was much more likely to work other jobs during the two, three, or four months or more that many boats stay tied up to the docks. Most often riggers and headers worked at semiskilled or unskilled jobs—as carpenter's helpers, apprentice welders, service station attendants, journeymen electricians on nonunion job sites, and restaurant workers. In South Texas several headers said they worked as farm laborers in Michigan and Illinois during 1979.

The wives of riggers and headers are much more likely to work as compared to those of captains. They worked, as did their husbands, in predominantly semiskilled and unskilled jobs that paid the minimum wage. They were part-time secretaries, waitresses, clerks, and saleswomen. In general their husbands preferred that they did not work, but the wife's income, averaging less than five thousand dollars in 1979, was seen as vital to the family.

The effects of an additional six weeks' closed season on these men and their families thus is predicted to be considerable. Undoubtedly the overall production will increase, all things being equal, but economic pressures on some fishermen will intensify. For example, many riggers and headers received unemployment and food stamps in 1979, a particularly bad year for crew wages though a good year in terms of production.

Unemployment payments are only a partial answer to the new legal restrictions affecting seasonality of catch. Men who cannot earn what they judge to be a reasonable salary will, if the alternatives are there, turn to other work. The salaries of captains and captain-owners are such that the earnings from seven to nine months of good shrimping can be made to last, with prudence, for a full year. Riggers and headers, however, often lack both the real income and the money-management skills to stretch their earnings over a whole year. Increasingly their new incomes have not carried them through even if they have had the required management skills. This was certainly true in 1979. Some will most probably seek other full-time jobs and be replaced by men more marginal to the work force, in particular Mexican illegals.

Louisiana trawler owners sought an injunction against the new law, fearing Texas shrimpers would flock to Louisiana waters when the waters off Texas were closed. They failed to obtain the injunction, however. The total effects of the two-hundred-mile ban are not yet evident, although initial response from Texas boat owners has been, not unexpectedly, enthusiastic.

Migration patterns of shrimp in the Gulf, the second major component affecting seasonality of catch, remain in general something of a mystery, although extensive research has been undertaken.[4] Shrimp-

[4] For example, see Griffin, Cross, and Ryan, *Seasonal Movement Patterns.*

ers have their own theories about where the shrimp are likely to be during certain times of the year under certain weather conditions. They do not read the scientific reports, nor would they believe them if they did read them. They trust the "hang book" because experience has shown it helps,[5] but they put little faith in general in any kinds of suggestions that periodically are made to them, such as the recent list of safety tips.[6]

Shrimpers believe that the shrimp migrate in Texas waters from north to south and, eventually, wind up off Mexico. Until recently many Texas shrimpers would catch the good fishing off Louisiana through the summer months and then, depending on their success, gradually work their way down along the Texas coast, following the shrimp into Mexico. Since Mexico's shrimp fishing was banned to American shrimpers in 1976, there has been a significant, if under-played, impact on Texas shrimpers.[7] According to Griffin and Beattie, before the ban 17 percent of the entire catch of Texas shrimpers, and 19 percent of their revenues, were from Mexican waters. They note that in Port Brownsville and Port Isabel "fifty-eight percent of the land-ing [came] from U.S. waters and forty-two percent from Mexican wa-ters."[8] Griffin and Beattie demonstrate, however, that expanded and redirected shrimping efforts in U.S. waters will, given current price trends, offset any expected losses. Moreover, they go on to argue that few companies will go under from loss of revenue attributable to in-ability to fish in Mexican waters.

Again, as is the case with the new legal restrictions, the real im-pact on the crews has been ignored. In this particular case, the impact is measurable in terms of reduced incomes, especially for South Texas shrimpers, and a growing reliance on unemployment and food stamps during the winter months of 1978 and 1979. For South Texas shrimpers the effects of inflation and fuel have been less, all things considered, than the effect of the ban on fishing in Mexico. One Port Isabel

---

[5] Gary Graham and Jim Buckner, *Hangs and Bottom Obstructions of the Texas/ Louisiana Gulf: Loran-C.*

[6] Dewayne Hollin, "Fishing Vessel Safety Tips."

[7] Wade L. Griffin and Bruce Beattie, "Economic Impact of Mexico's 200-Mile Off-shore Fishing Zone on the United States Gulf of Mexico Shrimp Fishery," *Land Economics* 54 (February, 1978): 27–38.

[8] Ibid., p. 31.

shrimper who fished off Campeche for years during the winter months said, "Mexico was my gravy. I'd make $5,000 down there every winter. The Mexican trips got me through the hard months."

A third and universal factor affecting seasonality of catch is weather. Northers in the summer and fall not only can make the shrimpers cold and miserable but also can jeopardize the safety of the crews and cause damage to vessels and equipment. Many shrimpers fish regardless of the weather, and, to some degree, these shrimpers are the ones most likely to earn higher incomes than the average. They stay out the longest during the good weather, spend the least time in port when they unload, and offer few excuses when their luck is bad. Northers and other Gulf storms are carefully watched, and captains share information and firsthand experience with each other. Many captains tie up to ride out a norther, winds of which may exceed sixty knots, while others head for port if they can make it.

During the worst winter months of December through February, the price for shrimp is often at its highest. The hardest-working, most determined captains are out fishing in spite of the freezing temperatures, the height of the seas, or the unwillingness of their crews to leave the dock. A majority of the shrimpers tie their boats to the dock during these months and either live off savings they may have put away during the good months or work at other part-time jobs. Some around the Aransas Pass–Rockport area turn to other kinds of commercial fishing, while those along the border find alternative employment harder to find and less remunerative. But the most adventurous, ambitious, daring, and, some would say, foolhardy risk the bitter weather and the increased hazards at sea for the high price they will receive for their shrimp at the dock.

When the seasonal hurricanes appear in the Gulf in the late summer and early fall, all the captains head for the nearest ports as fast as they can. Yet the hurricanes can be a blessing in disguise. A shrimper may conceivably lose his boat and thus his job, but he also stands to net more shrimp after the hurricane than he may see in three months of the regular season. After Hurricane Allen in August, 1980, one bank officer I interviewed reported that shrimpers were paying off loans that were six months due and putting the rest of their considerable profits into their depleted savings accounts. In two good weeks some shrimpers netted more than they had over the last several months.

Hurricanes are exceptional occurrences and are of minor importance to shrimpers in the general course of things, although, of course, of great concern when they do appear. What is a more important limitation to fishing is that three months out of the year (over four months, since the new closed season began in 1981) the boats are tied up because the weather is judged by most to be not worth the fishing effort. Who goes out and who stays in during the regular season also depends on a number of factors, including how well the shrimpers are doing at that particular time. For example, if it has been a bad year, if the average captain has been getting two to three boxes a night or less, then he will ignore the weather and fish in spite of it. If, on the other hand, it has been a good year to date, more captains are less likely to stay out should bad weather appear.

Traditional beliefs and values play an important role in the decision whether to fish or not and therefore directly influence the seasonality of catch.[9] The larger Gulf boats could conceivably fish all year around, with time set aside for routine maintenance. Although the weather often does make fishing impractical during the winter months, there are many days when shrimping is possible and the dock price is very high.

What is more to the point is that shrimpers would refuse to fish year-round even if the weather was good. There is a general feeling that one of the best things about being a shrimper is that, despite the fact that a shrimper works long hours, every year he can look forward to several months of slack time. During the winter months a shrimper can take it easier, even if he must work at another job; he can spend time with the family, catch up on household chores and repairs, and enjoy the fruits of his hard labor. Several shrimpers compared their winter months to the summertime vacation for teachers. They said that they worked hard for a living and deserved some time to enjoy their money and get away from their boats.

Thus "bad weather" for some is fishing weather for others. Slack time in January for some is time to get another temporary job because no Gulf boats are available until midsummer. For others it is a time to fish for the extra money that will make a considerable difference in life-

[9] See Mullen, "Function of Magic Folk Belief," pp. 214–220; and Mullen, *I Heard the Old Fishermen Say*, p. 13.

style or financial security. In any case, most shrimpers welcome the winter months as a change, as a time to do something different.

Cultural values and attitudes toward work also strongly affect the number of days shrimpers spend at the dock in preparation for fishing. Justifications for not going fishing, in addition to bad weather, include additional repairs to boat and equipment, the inability to get the repairs done because of incompetent service men, family illness or problems, crews not showing up, and other reasons that are a part of the complex feelings all men have about the work they do.

Operating Costs and Real Profits

Warren and Griffin have detailed rising variable and fixed operating costs of Gulf shrimp trawlers in recent years (see Table 7-1). These increased costs directly influence the price of shrimp the crew receives, say the owners. Rising variable and fixed costs are the reasons most owners give for an apparent reduction in their own profits and, therefore, for the need to decrease the boat's share for the crew.

There is no question that operating costs have increased dramatically in the last few years. There is, however, a question as to the effects of these increases on owners' profits. A brief examination of the figures presented for the years 1971 through 1977 demonstrates the trends. Costs for ice, nets and net repairs, supplies, groceries, packing, and payroll all showed significant increases. In fact, costs for ice had roughly doubled; fuel had jumped by 1977 more than 30 percent; nets, supplies, and groceries were up to 600 percent; salaries had doubled; and costs for packing were up approximately 50 percent. Repair and maintenance had, almost unbelievably, remained about the same, even a little less in 1977 than in 1971. Payroll taxes, after a high of $1,815 in 1975, were considerably reduced in 1977 to $257. This was a result of the fact that owners no longer paid Social Security or unemployment insurance on shrimp crews, a topic discussed in detail in the following chapter.

According to interviews with owners in 1980, the picture since 1977 has considerably worsened. While inflation is certainly the major cause of most of these operating increases, the energy crisis has substantially increased diesel fuel prices. One owner put it this way: "Three years ago I was paying thirty cents a gallon. It takes ten thou-

TABLE 7-1. Average Annual Costs and Returns for Gulf of Mexico Shrimp
Vessels, Fifty to Eighty Feet in Length, All Types of Construction, 1971–77

	1971	1973	1974	1975	1977
Receipts, shrimp sales	60,742	74,135	78,864	101,324	135,216
Variable costs					
Ice	1,387	1,579	1,541	1,766	2,788
Fuel	6,561	9,539	18,976	19,144	20,194
Net, supplies, groceries	2,358	6,747	9,885	11,211	13,131
Repair and maintenance	11,708	9,593	9,337	11,643	11,143
Crew shares	19,437	23,723	26,593	32,422	43,320
Payroll taxes	388	474	1,547	1,815	257
Packing	2,411	1,899	2,428	2,905	3,852
Subtotal	44,250	53,554	70,307	80,876	94,685
Returns above variable costs	16,492	20,581	8,557	20,448	40,531
Fixed costs					
Insurance	3,532	4,291	4,306	4,840	5,677
Depreciation	6,333	8,177	11,228	12,607	14,623
Overhead	0	2,415	3,201	3,073	3,194
Interest	2,256	2,611	5,604	6,984	6,880
Subtotal	12,221	17,494	24,339	27,504	30,374
Total operating costs	56,471	71,048	94,646	108,380	125,059
Profit or loss	4,271	3,087	−15,782	−7,056	10,157
Required return to equity	2,636	3,155	16,590	12,587	5,399
Return to owner management	1,635	−68	−32,372	−19,643	4,758
Vessels in sample	25	103	109	101	81
Average shrimp price	1.20	1.85	1.70	2.30	2.39
Cost of new vessel	77,949	100,641	138,188	155,168	179,981
Percentage financed	67.00	67.00	67.00	67.00	80.00
Depreciable life (years)	8	8	8	8	8
Salvage value (percent)	35	35	35	35	35
Required return rate**	10.25	9.50	13.00	14.00	15.00

SOURCE: Reprinted exactly from John P. Warren and Wade L. Griffin, *Costs and
Return Trends for Gulf of Mexico Shrimp Vessels*, DIR 78-1, SP-4 (College Station:
Texas Agricultural Experiment Station, Texas A&M University, 1978), p. 11.
    *Reflects a base rate, determined by bond yields, plus a financial-risk premium.

sand gallons to fill my boats for a trip. Now I'm paying over ninety cents a gallon. You figure it out. It costs me almost ten thousand dollars just to get that boat out where it can start fishing."

Operating costs for the average Gulf vessel more than doubled from 1971 to 1977. Rapidly rising fuel prices since that time suggest even greater operating increases in addition to inflation. All owners and captains said that fuel was their biggest economic problem. While some felt that fuel prices had leveled off and, they hoped, would remain about the same, most were extremely pessimistic about the long-term costs of fuel and their effects on the industry as a whole. Fuel prices were most often given as the owner's reason for reducing wage-share arrangements with their captains. Captains, and to a lesser extent riggers and headers, explained reduced salaries as directly attributable to skyrocketing fuel prices.

Wage-share arrangements have historically differed from one Gulf port to the next. This has certainly been the case in Texas. Until 1973, for example, Port Brownsville and Port Isabel for many years had a 60–40 agreement, the boat owner receiving 60 percent and the captain and the crew the remainder. Other ports surveyed offered less to the shrimpers, usually 70–30 (although a few owners did pay 65–35), or 75–25 in the fall of 1980.

Differences in wage-share arrangements seem to a degree grounded in the particular historical circumstances of the shrimping industry in a certain port. Even more important, there is a direct relationship between wages and the ratio of large companies to independent boat owners in ports. The more independent operators, all things being equal, the higher the wages for everyone. This is another way of saying that the more competitive the port is, the higher the wages. In an extreme case, for example, one Texas port's shrimping fleet is essentially controlled by one large company, which pays, relative to other ports, lower wages to shrimpers.

A general leveling and lowering of the boat's-share agreements has taken place in Texas in the last three years, although, as noted above, there do remain some differences. The majority of shrimpers interviewed were, in 1980, earning some variation of the 70–30 split. In Port Brownsville, for instance, many shrimpers were getting 65–35 but were paying 20 percent of the total fuel bill, which, in effect, reduced the arrangement to approximately a 70–30 cut, depending on the trip and the catch. In Port Isabel many shrimpers said that they received a 75–25 cut, but, again, they did not have to pay fuel, ice, or any other but small costs. Thus it was an "honest" 25 percent, meaning that no additional costs were subtracted from their incomes.

It is important to remember that, although the percentage share that crews receive has decreased in recent years, incomes, until recently, have substantially increased. Many shrimpers in 1980 were saying, however, that their salaries were not keeping pace with inflation. Most owners, on the other hand, reported that their crews, in their opinion, were getting paid quite well for the work that they did. The owners said that even if they wanted to pay more they could not afford to do so and keep their operations in the black. Crews said that 1979 was their first really bad year in several years. Although production was high, many shrimpers went into greater debt than usual during the off-season and were still paying off their personal and bank loans well into 1980. Fishermen who said they had never received either unemployment or food stamps reported that they were forced to seek these government subsidies for the first time.

Fixed costs to boat owners also increased dramatically from 1971 to 1977, as evidenced in Table 7-1. Insurance was up 60 percent, overhead 75 percent, and interest payments more than 300 percent. Increases in insurance payments were particularly irritating to boat owners. Most said they paid approximately seven thousand dollars a year per boat in insurance premiums in 1979. Many found fault with the insurance companies' willingness to settle out of court on personal-injury suits. It was the general opinion of the owners that the insurance companies would rather settle, regardless of costs, than take the case to court.

Several owners, in fact, expressed outrage at their insurance companies, citing specific cases in which a crew member was hurt on their boat and given what they considered an excessive settlement. The owners felt the insurance companies were less interested in paying for honest injuries to boat and crew than they were in collecting their premiums, which continued to rise annually. All owners did not oppose just compensation for injured crew members, but many said that fishermen had sometimes taken advantage of the situation and, with willing insurance companies, received settlements one year that drove up the premiums the next.

There seems to be a very large variation in lawsuits from one company to the other, although I did not record figures for all the owners of companies whom I interviewed. One owner said that he had been sued only once in the last ten years and that that suit was fairly brought against him. The kind of operation that a company ran directly affected whether or not it was likely to be sued; corporations that paid relatively high wages, offered other benefits to fishermen (including off-year, part-time employment and pay advances), hired and promoted from within, and were seen as "looking after their men" seemed much less likely to get sued than those that followed few or none of these practices. The single most important characteristic determining the likelihood of being sued by a fisherman seemed to be the attitude a company had toward its employees, rather than the actual occurrence of an accident in and of itself. Those companies that were seen by shrimpers as not caring about their crews' general welfare, both on and off the boat, seemed to be sued more.

There are a few lawsuits brought by shrimpers that are most probably fraudulent; there do appear to be a few individuals who go from one boat to the other over the years and create accidents in order to collect a settlement. One owner told me about a header one of his captains took on at the last minute who mysteriously injured his back on the first trip out. Another captain said that he had hired a header who he felt wanted to get a minor injury in order to avoid working for as long as possible while he lived off the settlement.

What is most remarkable about lawsuits that shrimpers bring against owners is their infrequency. While insurance rates have jumped, lawsuits among the men I interviewed were very rare. Of the 142 men who responded to the question, "Have you ever settled out of court or gone to trial over an injury you had while shrimping?", only 6 percent answered in the affirmative. If one considers the dangers of the job and the possibilities of getting seriously hurt, then what is impressive is how few suits are brought against the companies by the men. This is particularly true when one considers that many boats are not always maintained with the safety of the crew in mind. Infrequency of lawsuits is tied to the complex attitudes fishermen have about their work. If anything, they seem to want to avoid suits unless the corporation is seen as unjust or the injury is so serious that they need the money to get by until they can work again.

There is a possibility that the men interviewed reflect a strongly biased sample with regard to legal suits and settlements. It may be that many of those who did bring suits were no longer working as shrimpers because of the seriousness of their injuries or the unwillingness of owners or captains to hire them after they had sued. Based on my experience and knowledge of the industry, however, I do not believe this to be the case.

Warren and Griffin report that profits from 1971 to 1977 were marginal, as a result of rising operating costs, losses per vessel being suffered in 1974 and 1975. When profits were returned to equity, losses accrued in 1973 as well. Profits in 1971 and 1977 were minimal when all costs were met—$1,635 and $4,758, respectively. Therefore, it is logical to assume that, because inflation has by no means subsided since 1977 and because, in addition, fuel prices have taken astronomical leaps, the profit-loss figures, according to Warren and Griffin, for 1978 to the present reflect in general the trends established by the 1971–77 figures.[10]

Since 1978 the picture for owners has undoubtedly worsened. When interviewed, owners said that rising fuel costs have put a huge dent in their profits. In order to maintain a viable margin of profit they have been forced to decrease the percentage share to their men from 65–35 in the early seventies to a more recent 70–30 or lower. The key to their comments is "margin of profit," for, according to Warren and Griffin, there has not been a consistent margin of profit for some years.

If taken at face value, these figures raise a number of serious questions. How can the shrimping industry maintain itself on presumed consistent losses in the last ten years? Surely it is a rare industry that on a per-unit basis can afford to lose on its investments in 1973, 1974, and 1975 an average of $17,361, particularly when fleets of eight or more boats are not at all unusual; in that case, losses for an owner with ten boats would be well over $175,000 per year. And in the "good" years of 1971 and 1977, vessels on the average made only $3,196, so a company with ten boats would have earned little more than $30,000. Clearly either Warren and Griffin's figures are misleading or Texas fleet

[10]The figures of Warren and Griffin can be interestingly compared with those in M. E. Sass and K. J. Roberts, *Characteristics of the Louisiana Shrimp Fleet, 1978*, Sea Grant Publication No. LSU-TL-79-006, for Louisiana shrimp trawlers. The return on investment of the Louisiana boats is similar to the findings in the present study.

owners are fools, willing to invest up to $300,000 on new trawlers when in the "good" year of 1977 returns were $4,758, or a return on investment of their trawlers alone of less than 2 percent.

Depreciation and tax credits may be a partial answer to this seeming paradox. It may be that by using them, owners can offset the rising operating and fixed costs and turn a profit that can justify their large capital investments. Warren and Griffin report in their findings that depreciation rose from $6,333 in 1971 to $14,623 in 1977, a substantial rise but certainly not enough to excite most accountants.

Tax credits do seem to be a partial answer to increased investment in new trawlers. "Investor" boats, bought primarily as a tax write-off, do in fact turn over a considerable tax credit the first year to those seeking just such advantages. Boats that are managed are also seen as a good return if they are sold three or four years later. Given that the costs of new vessels have risen considerably, money could be made in reselling the trawler in a few years. Investors, then, would be conceivably less interested in yearly production profits than in tax credits and earnings after the vessel was resold.

But what of the owners of the vast majority of boats that are not "managed" but are owned outright by companies or individuals? According to the figures, they should long since have declared bankruptcy or, at the very least, shown some signs of the disturbing losses in the last ten years. What is troubling is that the owners I interviewed did not seem like men who had taken or were taking financial beatings; they were by no means desperate. They did not act or talk like men who were barely holding on. They did complain loudly, especially about rising fuel costs, but they did not appear on the brink of financial ruin. Undoubtedly the industry is hurting, especially since 1978 and the abrupt rise in fuel prices, but it certainly cannot be in the fiscal state reflected by Warren and Griffin's figures, or the owners I talked with would have shown it.

A final consideration in viewing these figures is that they include all real short-term and long-term costs, which may or may not be apparent to the owners on an annual basis. Certainly this is true in considering depreciation of equipment, in which there are large investments. This consideration notwithstanding, owners have, despite their public complaints, earned substantial profits since 1970. These complaints, similar to those of many businessmen, belie the real earnings accrued over the years. Owners did quite well from 1970 to 1977, contrary to the figures suggested, although some, perhaps because of poor management skills, did not do as well as they did in the 1950s and 1960s. All told, then, the economic picture began to change in 1978, but, to date, it is the shrimpers, not the owners, who have been affected most by recent economic trends.

How much are the boat owners really making? The evidence suggests that while the glory days of shrimping are at least temporarily over, shrimping remains a viable industry. I have not collected data from all the owners, as have Warren and Griffin, but I have caught more than a glimpse of some of the ways in which owners are coping with rising costs and turning a reasonable profit.

If we divide boat owners into those who own one boat, those who own two to five, those who own six to fifteen, and those who own sixteen or more, we may note that the fiscal problems they face are quite different. Each group has adapted somewhat different strategies that make sense for the owners and their operations. They are not stupid; they are not sitting back and doing nothing while rising costs eat away at their profits. They have reacted, as all good businessmen do, in the best ways they can to a changing economy. While some economists would have them dead and buried by now, my impression, to the contrary, is that they have been doing quite well, all things considered. If nothing else, their political effectiveness at swaying votes in both the state legislature and the Congress is a clue to their ability to survive. The future, however, is another matter.

The individual boat owner is enormously envied by many fleet owners. Time and again multiboat trawler owners told me they would give anything to return to the days when they owned only one boat. And for good reason: the captain-owner has a double income but costs over which he can personally act as watchdog. As stated earlier, he receives the captain's share of the profits plus the boat owner's share. Thus he can make 85 percent or more of the total profit from the sale of shrimp. Out of this profit he must, of course, pay all bills and also maintain the boat. Yet captain-owners all told me the same thing: it takes a lot of work but they are making good money.

Also, captain-owners have less capital invested in their operations, so they can take their profits and put them into other places; they are not overcapitalized. As a group, inflation and fuel prices have affected them the least. They have very few problems hiring and keeping crew and no difficulties with losses because of theft. My estimate is that these men are earning forty thousand to ninety thousand dollars or more per year before taxes, depending on their skills as captains and money managers.

Owners of small fleets, from two to five boats, were unanimous in their views. All said that if they could sell their boats for a reasonable price, they would do so immediately. But it is no longer a seller's market, as had been the case up until recently. These men would love to reduce their capital expenditures and get back to the basics—one boat or two, captained by themselves and a dependable in-law or close friend.

In the meantime, these small fleet owners are doing all they know how to be more cost effective. If they can, they have purchased fuel-efficient devices, such as the Kort nozzle, for their trawlers. They have tried to educate their captains in the advantages of running their engines at more efficient speeds. They keep a much tighter rein on supplies and have tried to reduce stealing of shrimp and equipment. They live or die by their accountants' recommendations. They will never buy another boat under current market conditions; they say that they would not even take one for free. They are struggling because all their capital is tied up in their boats and they cannot make some of the adjustments the larger owners can. Some are overextended. They bought vessels in the early and middle 1970s with their excess profits, and now they are hard put to make the payments to the bank. Those who purchased boats in the late seventies are paying back, at high interest rates, loans on inflated purchase prices.

As a result, this group is probably the hardest hit of any boat owners. But though they are not getting what they were accustomed to in the past, they are surviving. Although these men were gloomy, it was evident in conversations with them that they were keeping their heads above water. My estimate is that these men are clearing ten to fifteen thousand dollars per vessel per year before taxes, depending to some degree on whether or not they have joined a co-op. Their gloom is based on relative need, because they are used to making much more. And, given the changes since 1978, it could get much worse for them.

Fleet owners with from six to fifteen boats are doing much better than the smaller boat owners because of the economy of scale. They can afford to make large purchases of fuel, for instance, because of the size of their operations. They are less affected by rising costs for supplies and services, too, because their boats are maintained by their own company men.

Even more to the point, these owners indirectly pass on increased costs to their crews in addition to the decreased wage rates everyone is now paying. Since captains and crews on many boats now must pay a percentage of fuel, some companies are essentially buying fuel "cheap" and selling it "high" to their own captains, clearing a few cents a gallon. In a similar fashion crews are debited various supplies and equipment, especially ice, from which the company makes a profit. These companies profit handsomely from their business with other small-fleet boats and the independent captain-owner by supplying fuel and ice. One informant put it this way: "The bigger companies don't have to make a lot off their boats. They are doing fine just on fuel, ice, and supplies." Perhaps the observation is exaggerated, but the point is well taken: the larger companies profit considerably from their services to shrimp trawlers.

Profits per vessel are down since the energy crunch, but these owners are still doing quite well. My estimate is that the larger companies are clearing twenty thousand dollars per vessel, plus, as suggested, making additional profits from ice, fuel, supplies, and other services that they offer. Large companies are not as likely to be as overextended as the smaller companies. Their boats are more likely to be free from the banks. Some of the owners of larger companies, more skilled in money management than smaller owners, have taken their profits and invested them in "inflation-proof" industries. They have minimized their losses by diversifying their investments; unlike the smaller boat owners, they do not have all their eggs in one basket.

The trends evident in these companies hold tenfold for the largest companies, those with sixteen to thirty or more boats. These large fleet owners, only a handful in number, are able to turn a handsome profit by selling gas, ice, and other services to their captains and others in port. One informant said that even if these owners were to take actual losses on their vessels they could come out ahead at the end of the year on their other businesses. Return on their boats is probably not outstanding, but it does not have to be; yearly profit cleared per vessel is most likely in the fifteen- to twenty-thousand-dollar range. These companies profit less from their trawlers than do some of the smaller companies because they are less efficient. On the other hand, they do much better in profits from service to boats. These men know the industry better than anyone else and know how to manage their money.

These observations emphasize the necessity of differentiating between companies by size as well as by expertise in resource management. The figures from previous studies would show the shrimping industry in the 1970s in total financial disarray, which was simply not the case. Looking at the annual costs and returns in 1980 (see Table 7-2), one must remember the ways in which smart owners of some companies pay far less than the figures suggest. For example, the catch varies dramatically, as suggested, depending on the proficiency and motivation of captain and crew. The best boats with the best crews, as argued below, could have netted as much as 75,000 pounds to as little as 30,000 pounds, with earnings ranging from $90,000 to $225,000.

Figures for fixed costs in 1980, again, fail to reflect considerable differences in companies. A company with ten boats, for example, usually has its own icehouse, fuel depot, net repair shop, and general boat repair and maintenance facilities. Thus, considerable costs are moved from the ledger sheets of one company to those of another firm with the same owners. As suggested earlier, most larger companies pay less than the going price for fuel; in this case, according to informants, ninety cents per gallon would be much closer to the real price paid by many companies in 1980 than one dollar. The companies then turn around and sell the fuel to themselves and others for the figure shown in Table 7-2.

The crew share in the 1980 figures is reported at 35 percent of the gross poundage price. As suggested, a 35 percent boat's-share arrangement is the most common arrangement, according to respondents in the sample, but certainly not the only one. A not insignificant 37 percent of those interviewed had a lower cut, a 30 percent share, while 10 percent had a greater cut. The range in crew shares would run, then, from $45,000 to $75,000, assuming the figures for pounds landed are credible. Again, remembering that it was the larger companies that tended to pay less to their crews than the smaller ones, one can see that the size of the company certainly affects profits. Also, costs for gro-

TABLE 7-2. Annual Costs and Returns
for a Typical Seventy-five-foot Gulf Shrimp Vessel

	$/Unit	Amount
Returns		
Pounds	50,000	
Price per pound	$3.00	
Gross returns		$150,000
Variable costs		
Gallons	36,170	
Fuel	$1.00	36,170
Ice		$ 4,552
Nets and groceries		22,612
Repair and maintenance		16,378
Crew share	35%	52,500
Backing	.04668	2,334
Total variable costs		$134,546
Fixed costs		
Vessel cost	$250,000	
Down payment	46,380	
Insurance		$ 7,073
Depreciation		26,563
Overhead		5,896
Interest		12,217
Total fixed costs		$51,749
Profit		−$36,295

SOURCE: John P. Nichols, Correspondence to Ed Wolfe, National Shrimp
Congress, June 11, 1980.

ceries are listed here; this is surely a mistake, since groceries are always paid for by the crew.

If fixed costs are considered, one must question the figures for
depreciation. Such figures are more a function of a good accountant's
attempts at legally manipulating the regulations of the Internal Revenue Service than a real business cost. In truth, shrimp boats have appreciated over the years, especially in the middle 1970s. Finally, many
boat owners do not pay any interest, or certainly less than the figure
given here; they have long since paid off any bank loan on their boat.

Thus, while the reported figures suggest a net loss of more than

$36,000 per boat, if consideration is given to even a few of the factors suggested this net loss is seen to obtain only in the specific cases in which the owners through their companies have not employed the business strategies commonly used by those interviewed.

Rising Capital Investment Costs and Investor Boats

Warren and Griffin correctly note the dramatic rise in new-vessel costs from 1971 to 1977 from an average of $77,949 to $179,981. In 1980 it was not unusual for a newly built trawler to cost $300,000. Companies of all sizes now have tremendous capital investments in their vessels, as well as in their other equipment, buildings, and land.

The real question suggested by these prices in vessel costs is, Why have the boats appreciated considerably faster than can be explained by inflation? The answer, in part, is the "investor" boat.

Investment capital in these times of double-digit inflation has gone looking for someplace to hide. The investor-boat market has artificially driven up new-boat prices. As suggested, investors are less interested in annual returns, although of course they have heard about the fantastic profits of trawlers and expect a healthy payback on their money, than they are in tax credits and protecting their money.

Investors formerly were willing to pay a very high price for new trawlers, especially when the resale market was so favorable. This had the unfortunate effect of artificially driving up new-boat prices. Now prospects for a quick and profitable resale are not nearly so bright. In any case, investors, often encouraged by the fleet owners who managed their boats for them, until recently flocked to what has looked like a good tax break and return on their money.

On the other side of the coin, large companies that operate investor boats have done quite well. They turn a handsome profit on the boat-building end of the deal, since they often build the boat themselves or have a commission arrangement with the builder; then they operate the boat for the investor for a management fee off the top. The investor boat uses their facilities and is sold ice, fuel, and supplies. It all adds up, and, in addition, the large fleet owner himself has made no additional investment.

The impact of the investor boat on others in the industry is considerable. High vessel-purchase costs mean that the small guy—the independent, or the captain with years of experience—is closed out of the industry. In the 1950s and 1960s a captain who was prudent could buy a boat and pay it off in three to five good years. Now, say most boat owners, purchase of a vessel takes from eight to ten years—if the potential buyer can come up with the down payment.

Shrimpers themselves do not yet realize the effects of high vessel cost. Many captains and riggers still maintain ambitions of buying boats in the coming years, much as other shrimpers did in the last three decades. Few, however, will be able to manage the down payments. Small fleet owners are similarly affected; even if they wanted to buy new vessels, they could not. Those who bought boats in the late 1970s did so at inflated prices and high interest rates, and they are now suffering because of the monthly payments.

The other major impact of investor boats is that the overall net increase of Gulf trawlers in the last five years has reduced production per vessel. As the owners put it, the more ways you slice the pie, the smaller the pieces for everyone. The investor boats are one reason the pie is getting smaller.

Overcapitalization

Fleet owners are, as a whole, overcapitalized. Many owners have continued to reinvest, until recently, in bigger and bigger boats, expensive electronic gear, and support facilities. Overcapitalization would not be such a critical problem, however, if the effects of monopoly did not continue to press the fleet owners in that direction. Many owners have overcapitalized in order to survive. They have poured more and more money into their businesses, believing that horizontal and vertical integration would stabilize and increase their profits, and have neglected other potential investments outside of commercial fishing for lack of knowledge and expertise in anything but the fishing industry.

Overcapitalization in the Gulf fishing effort is particularly acute when compared to the financial situation of bay shrimp fishermen. Bay shrimp boats may be purchased from twenty to thirty thousand dollars, and maintenance is minimal compared to that for the larger trawlers. The bay boats are normally fished by two men, one of whom is almost always both captain and owner. Prerequisites are knowledge of the bay system and an ambition to fish as many days as possible, regardless of weather. Bay shrimp fishing is one of the best opportunities, then, for Texas commercial fishermen because it requires minimal capital investment.

Now that many Gulf fleet owners are overcapitalized, alternatives are limited. There are few trawler buyers these days, although some owners have suggested that one solution would be for the government to buy their boats at a reasonable price and then perhaps sell them to foreign governments. A large part of the fleet owners' loud response to their current problems is based on their investments in their fishing businesses, the fact that they are overcapitalized. Many have their life earnings wrapped up in their boats and service operations; they are very afraid of losing it all.

Short-Term Fluctuations in the Fishery

All fishermen are dependent on the annual abundance of the fishery. This is certainly the case with the shrimp industry. Shrimpers can never be sure from one year to the next just how many shrimp there are to catch. They have no control over short-term fluctuations.

A look at Table 7-3 does demonstrate that regardless of increased fishing effort, production per vessel has, in fact, decreased. Also, total production is subject to considerable variation from one year to the next. Even if the shrimpers are out doing their best, they have "bad" years. Bad years play havoc with a shrimper's income. In a bad year he will usually go into debt, and two bad years in a row can do him considerable harm. Some captain-owners have lost their boats because of a string of bad years.

Marine biologists believe that the salinity of the bays, determined to some extent by the spring rains, and the water temperatures both have an enormous effect on the annual shrimp harvest. Most shrimpers, based on their experience, concur, although other explanations of a good and bad year are given.

Fishermen are among the few remaining food producers who depend on a wild stock, as contrasted to domestic stock such as chicken or hogs. As long as shrimpers must depend on the annual variations in the abundance of the fishery, short-term fluctuations will directly affect their incomes and their life-styles.

TABLE 7-3. Total U.S. Gulf of Mexico Shrimp Landings: Volume, Value, Average Price, and Days Fished, 1956–77

Year	Volume (lb. millions)	Value ($ millions)	Average Price ($)	Days Fished (× 1000)	Percentage Increase/ Decrease in Price
1956	109.0	62.5	0.57	163.7	
1957	99.1	62.7	0.63	152.5	+12
1958	101.9	63.8	0.63	184.9	− 2
1959	114.7	50.3	0.44	175.8	−32
1960	122.2	57.5	0.47	186.3	+33
1961	79.5	43.4	0.55	164.7	− 2
1962	89.0	60.3	0.68	184.5	+23
1963	124.7	61.3	0.49	177.7	−29
1964	113.3	62.6	0.55	200.7	+14
1965	123.4	71.2	0.58	198.3	+ 4
1966	113.6	83.6	0.74	193.3	+28
1967	140.6	90.1	0.64	196.7	−14
1968	128.2	95.7	0.75	214.4	+17
1969	126.6	101.2	0.80	217.2	+ 7
1970	145.3	108.1	0.74	215.4	− 8
1971	143.1	136.1	0.95	219.7	+28
1972	143.8	163.7	1.14	245.6	+19
1973	114.8	171.0	1.49	255.7	+32
1974	117.1	137.5	1.17	241.4	−21
1975	107.0	178.2	1.67	228.0	+42
1976	132.2	275.2	2.08	273.6	+25
1977	163.4	206.4	1.26		−30

SOURCE: Reprinted with corrections from John P. Warren and Wade L. Griffin, *Costs and Return Trends for Gulf of Mexico Shrimp Vessels,* DIR 78-1, SP-4 (College Station: Texas Agricultural Experiment Station, 1978), p. 2.

Crew Efficiency and Production

A final factor directly affecting a shrimper's income and, indirectly, price is crew efficiency. The efficiency of the crew in harvesting and returning shrimp to the dock is one of the most important factors that day in and day out determine his annual earnings and total shrimp production. There is considerable variation in crew efficiency, as measured by production, which accounts in part for the wide range of salaries shrimpers earn. Individual captains can affect their own productivity but have, of course, no influence on the production of all crews in the industry. It is the general productivity of shrimpers that indirectly affects pricing and prices.

In recent years the number of experienced shrimpers has not kept pace with the number of new boats. Also, the chronic problem of unreliable supply of experienced headers has continued to plague the industry. Headers have traditionally been the weak link in the labor chain. Underpaid, they nevertheless perform a valuable function on the boat.

My own observations suggest that production, directly influenced by the efficiency of the crew, differs dramatically from one boat to another and is not necessarily dependent on the size of the boat, the condition of the equipment, or even the company that owns the boat. Much depends on the captain. A good captain hires good crew, makes the most of his equipment, and catches shrimp. A bad or inexperienced captain does just the opposite. Captains are the backbone of the entire industry.

One shrimper told me of a captain who had less than six months' experience on the boat as a header and a rigger. Promoted to captain because of the scarcity of experienced crew, his method of landing was to chug by the dock, throw a line to the pilings, and use the drag against the boat to come to a stop. It was the only way he knew how to do it. His productivity, not unsurprisingly, was extremely low.

Some crews, say captains, just seem to work well together. They complement each other well, the header helping the rigger when needed, all sharing the work that needs to be done. These kinds of crews are what all captains are looking for. Increasingly they are in short supply. In Aransas Pass, for instance, the growing offshore oil industry has attracted some shrimpers with offers of seven to eight dollars an hour, plus overtime, and a guarantee of a steady income. Owners and captains in Port Isabel and Port Brownsville complained much less of a labor shortage than did those to the north.

Imports

Imports of foreign shrimp in 1979 accounted for 267.1 million pounds (56 percent) of the available supply, not counting inventories, as contrasted to a catch by American shrimpers of 205.6 million pounds

TABLE 7-4. U.S. Supply of All Forms of Shrimp, 1970–79 (Heads-Off Weight, in Millions of Pounds)

Year	U.S. Commercial Landings	Imports	Total
1970	224.3	247.1	471.4
1971	238.1	215.0	453.1
1972	235.9	254.5	490.4
1973	228.6	230.8	459.4
1974	224.7	267.4	492.1
1975	209.1	231.0	440.1
1976	245.6	270.7	516.3
1977	288.4	270.4	558.8
1978	256.9	239.0	495.9
1979	205.6	267.1	472.7

SOURCE: Living Marine Resources, Inc., *Shrimp Market Report* (San Diego: Living Marine Resources, Inc., 1980).

(44 percent) for the same year (see Table 7-4). Although the import figures are somewhat higher than those for 1978, they are within the range of import averages, 215 to 270 million pounds, since 1970. Mexico is by far the most important single exporter of shrimp to the United States.

With the exception of fuel prices, foreign imports are most often blamed by most owners as the reason their businesses are suffering. Owners, especially in Texas, have responded to their perception of the problem by sponsoring a congressional bill designed to regulate imports.

Inflation, Luxury-Food Items, and Shrimp

Owners have focused on fuel prices, imports, and general effects of inflation on their operations as primary causes of dollar losses in the shrimping industry. Shrimpers have followed their lead; in the interviews, shrimpers most often cited fuel costs as the major reason for decreased profits. It is apparent, however, that a very important, but overlooked, factor is that, simply put, inflation has taken its toll on luxury items, including shrimp.

Almost 70 percent of all shrimp is consumed in restaurants. Eating shrimp is becoming more and more of an unattainable luxury for Americans. Total restaurant sales in 1979, for instance, were off 2.3 percent, when adjusted for inflation.[11] The average consumer visited restaurants less in 1979; not since the recession of 1974 did restaurant customer traffic suffer such a decline—9.2 percent during June, July, and August, 1979. The number of families who went to restaurants declined significantly in 1979 and was representative of all income brackets. Thus, fewer shrimp were eaten.

Prices for the shrimper in 1979 were low, and for the wholesaler not outstanding. In the restaurant, however, shrimp prices were very high. Rather than buy six fried shrimp for eight dollars or more, the consumer frequently chose something else on the menu. The shrimping industry viewed the problem as a supply problem—too many shrimp. But, on the demand side, it can be observed that the consumer was seeing less and less reason to pay so much money for a luxury-food commodity. Shrimp is not seen, nor has it ever been seen, by most Americans as a necessary food item. With inflation running at more than 10 percent a year, the demand for shrimp has decreased substantially since 1978.

[11] Living Marine Resources, Inc., *Spring Market Report*, p. 4.

8. The Structure of the Shrimping Industry: The Big Squeeze on the Owners

"Little dog got to do what the big dog say."

A variety of economic forces influence the shrimper, his fishing strategy, and the price he is paid for his catch. These forces, some of which the shrimper has control over, the majority of which he does not, only indirectly affect price at the two most important stages for the shrimper, the dockside price the shrimper is paid for his labors and the wholesale price the dealer is paid for a five-pound box of headless frozen shrimp.

No one complained much or in an organized fashion until recently. Although there have certainly been "good" and "bad" years for shrimpers, owners, and multinationals since Texas Gulf shrimping began over thirty years ago, in general pricing in the past has allowed the shrimper, excluding the header, a decent return for his work. Since 1978 these circumstances have changed for many companies. It has now become a question of who is going to have to pay for increasing dollar losses. It is like a game of hot potato, with the dollar losses being passed from the top, the very large multinational, to the bottom, the shrimper, by way of the owners. So far shrimpers have borne the impact of the recent economic changes; now it appears that owners, too, are beginning to feel the crunch.

To follow prices and pricing practices through the maze of owners, fishhouse dealers, brokers, wholesalers, retailers, processing plants, and market outlets is a formidable task and is outside the scope of this work.[1] What is of concern here is that monopolistic practices enter in at at least two separate stages and that these practices directly affect the incomes and the lives of shrimpers. In the ideal case, of course,

---

[1] For an excellent, encompassing view of a particular regional fishery, see Susan Peterson and Leah Smith, *New England Fishing, Processing, and Distribution*, Woods Hole Oceanographic Institute Technical Report No. WH-01-79-52.

supply and demand for the shrimp would, all things being equal, have a direct influence on price, with imports, fuel costs, the value of the dollar on the work market, and other economic variables all playing an important role.[2]

It is not argued here that these variables do not, in the long run, affect price, but rather that their effects are buffered by monopoly, so that the big multinationals suffer the least and the shrimpers the most. If the owners are indeed entering troubled times, then a realistic appraisal of how the industry functions, rather than a traditional market analysis that assumes classical, but rare, price-competitive arrangements, is in order.

Given their differing economic needs, shrimpers and owners naturally see prices from their respective positions in the industry. As in many other industries, shrimpers and owners find themselves on different sides of the same fence, each knowing that the other depends on it for its continued existence. Future solutions to recent economic difficulties, then, must be grounded in what is best for both shrimpers and owners. The owners alone are not the industry; neither are the shrimpers.

What Happens at the Dock: The Dockside Price

Economists have analyzed the shrimping industry in other states such as Louisiana and Florida in terms of traditional market structures.[3] In Fig. 8-1, one can follow the shrimp from the sources of supply—the American shrimper or the foreign fisherman—to dealer (primary wholesaler), broker, processors, secondary wholesalers, and retail outlets.

Such an analysis, however, makes too many assumptions based on

[2] Erwin S. Penn, in *Price Spreads of Fish Products among Producers and Distributors, Marine Fisheries Review* Paper 987, pp. 1–8, raises some critical issues, examination of which is not undertaken here, in comparing the wages that fishermen receive in various industries with the price that the consumer eventually pays in the supermarket.

[3] See, for example, M. E. Sass and K. J. Roberts, *Characteristics of the Louisiana Shrimp Fleet, 1978*, Sea Grant Publication No. LSU-TL-79-006; Fred J. Prochaska and James C. Cato, *An Economic Profile of Florida Commercial Fishing Firms: Fishermen, Commercial Activities, and Financial Considerations*, Florida State University System of Florida Sea Grant Program Report No. 19; and José Alvarez, Chris O. Andrew, and Fred J. Prochaska, *Economic Structure of the Florida Shrimp Processing Industry*, Florida State University System of Florida Sea Grant Program Report No. 9.

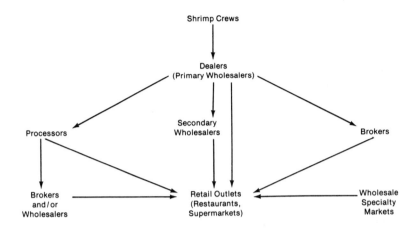

Fig. 8-1. Market channels for shrimp in the southeastern United States. (From D. R. Calder, ed., "Description of Industry: Economics," in *The Shrimp Fishery of the Southeastern United States: A Management Planning Profile*, Technical Report No. 5. Charleston: South Carolina Marine Resources Center, 1974.)

too few facts. In reality, price is set at the top through "bidding" by large multinational fish companies. The fleet owners and everyone else in the middle then struggle to make their own profits. A comparable argument could be made not just for Texas but for all the other shrimp-producing states along the Gulf coast.

The following scenario illustrates what actually happens. A captain unloads his shrimp at the dock. The daily price is usually on the wall just inside the fishhouse. The independent shrimper, if he does not like the price, does not take his shrimp somewhere else, however, because he knows that the price, within a penny or two, will be the same everywhere in port.

If the captain works for a company, then he must sell his shrimp at the price the owner offers; that is assumed when he goes to work for the owner. In effect, he has contracted to sell his shrimp to the owner before he has netted them. The captain, in order to earn good money, knows that he cannot do anything to increase the price he gets per pound for his shrimp, there being no competitive market system. All he can really do is try to catch as many shrimp as possible and hope to make up in quantity and quality what he loses in competitive pricing.

The situation becomes particularly acute for the captains who work for some of the largest companies, because these companies sometimes base their extra charges to the captain for fuel and repairs on the cash value of the shrimp he lands. Usually in this arrangement there is a value limit beyond which the captain has to pay little or none of the fuel or repairs to equipment. For instance, the company tells the captain that if he lands $17,000 worth of shrimp from his trip, he does not have to pay his 20 percent share of the fuel he has consumed while fishing; otherwise, he must pay a gradually rising fuel percentage based, again, on the value of his catch. One captain I interviewed told me the following story: While his boat was out fishing, the price of shrimp dropped eighty cents in one week. The captain returned, confident that he had easily netted more than the $17,000, only to find the value of his catch, because of the price change, well below the limit. He not only received less for his shrimp, in this case, but also had to pay 10 percent of the fuel bill.

The shrimp are then sorted and graded by the fishhouse, which, although a separate company, is usually owned by one of the larger shrimp owners or run by a board of directors who are owners. From this study it is clear that the owner of the fishhouse may sell the shrimp to a broker, sell it to a wholesaler himself, or wholesale and distribute it himself through his own marketing channels. What is important to remember is that the boat's owner, the fishhouse owner, the distributor, the wholesaler, and the broker are often the same man or men, although the companies and the operations go by an assortment of names. There are a few independent brokers and freezer operators, but they represent a relatively small part of the industry.

For their part, owners say that they base the prices they pay shrimpers at the dock on the bids for gross shrimp lots in Brownsville put in by the multinational fish companies. The owners must, in fact, base their prices to shrimpers less on their own real costs of harvesting and packaging the product than on the price in the "bidding" in Brownsville. What the owners do not say, but is clear if shrimp prices for all Texas ports are surveyed, is that the price they offer shrimpers is uniform. This practice is one major strategy that many owners have developed to combat the fixed prices in the Brownsville bidding. By eliminating price competition at the dockside level, some owners have erected partial economic barriers that allow them to squeeze in their necessary profits.

It could well be argued that in any market system the price tends to center at certain levels, some buyers offering a somewhat lower or higher price than others. What distinguishes dockside shrimp prices in Texas, however, is that they are rarely more than one or two cents, sometimes as much as five cents, apart on a three- to six-dollar product. Assuming a three-cents-per-pound difference at four dollars a pound, the price differential is less than 1 percent.

Shrimpers have no choice. They have to sell their shrimp at the

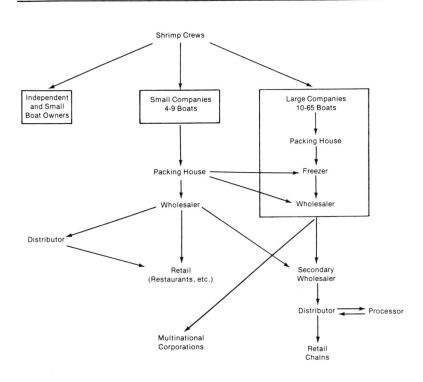

Fig. 8-2. Market channels for domestic shrimp in Texas.

offered price before it rots. Owners have little choice, either. They have to make a profit to stay in business. They could gamble, as a few do, and hold their shrimp in freezers until the Brownsville price goes up. But then they must pay freezer costs and face the possibility that prices might not go up enough to make their gamble profitable. A more appropriate model of the industry that incorporates the points raised is presented in Fig. 8-2.

Bidding in Brownsville: The Wholesale Price

Every Monday through Friday at 2:00 in the afternoon multinational fish companies put in their bids to shrimp brokers for gross lots of frozen shrimp. Bids are submitted over the telephone, and the highest bidders get the shrimp. Usually the bids are identical, varying by only a few cents per pound. The price the newly landed lots of shrimp bring in Brownsville then becomes the basis for the price bid for all shrimp in all Texas ports. Many ports in Louisiana and Florida follow Brownsville's prices.

In effect, the large multinationals decide daily what they are willing to pay for shrimp. This price is based on their own assessed needs, which include their costs and their profit margin. The smaller buyers, brokers, and owners and even the larger trawler companies follow the pricing line.

The large multinationals agree before they make the bids what the prices will be. They agree, in addition, to exchange with each other, at their own prices, the shrimp they do not need but buy anyway. For instance, one corporation might buy large quantities of various sizes of shrimp at a preferred price, then trade all the smaller shrimp it buys, and does not need, with another multinational for an equal value of large shrimp.

These multinationals are subject to various economic forces, some of which have been suggested. The point here is that the bids they put in are not price competitive; the fleet owner or the smaller company, like the shrimper, must pay the price offered or not sell his five-pound boxes of shrimp. The multinational price certainly is affected by inflation, world dollar values, and so forth, but the profit margin incorporated in the offered wholesale price to the dealer is fixed, is uniform, and does not necessarily reflect anything but the multinationals' own vested needs.

Boat owners do make money from their trawlers, only less than they might if a monopoly of multinationals were not at work. Since 1978, multinationals have passed on to the owners, through the offered wholesale price, the burden of increased fuel, imports, and so on. In an ideal market economy, these costs would be spread among wholesaler, harvester, and retailer. But owners cannot pass their costs on up, so they pass them down, to the shrimpers.

The Owners

It is difficult to generalize about the owners themselves because they are a diverse group who apply a variety of approaches, some of which have been mentioned, to running their businesses. After talking to owners in various ports, I have developed an appreciation for their work and efforts, especially for those who own the smaller fleets. Many of these men work long, hard hours when their boats are at the dock. Some actually do the repair and servicing themselves. They constantly move back and forth from the docks to their small offices. They often oversee the work from the tiniest detail to the building of a new trawler. As a group they impressed me with their drive, ambition, and business skills.

I talked with a number of Mexican-American, Mexican, and Latin American small fleet owners in Port Isabel and Port Brownsville. Many had come to the country *sin papeles* ("without papers"). Often they came with little money and no friends to help them. The Mexicans usually were from fishing families or were merchant mariners, as were many of the Hondurans. Many of the Mexicans had learned shrimping from their fathers in the waters off Campeche or in the extensive Mexican bays south of the Rio Grande. A majority had started shrimping in the United States because it was the only work they could find.

Mexican-Americans, Hondurans, and other Latin Americans are real-life examples of Horatio Alger's mythical hero of twentieth-century capitalism: they worked very hard, saved their money, and eventually bought their first boat. Not satisfied with one boat, they continued to save and work to buy other trawlers. Several owners told me fond memories of how their first boat had been a trawler that was bought for salvage, painstakingly worked on and repaired, and then finally fished in the Gulf. With the profits from this first boat, several owners said, they then bought their second and third boats, constantly striving to increase their new fleets through hard work and perseverance.

Most of these men reported that, besides the hard work of fishing, managing their operations was a challenge and often a headache. They all ran their businesses as seemed most natural to them, in a very personal, face-to-face way. They naturally knew all their captains, often having worked with them or trained them. Frequently the owner was related by ties of kinship to the captain; most often they were brothers-in-law, brothers, or cousins. These owners were more likely to understand the daily problems of shrimpers because they had extensive fishing experience themselves. They could offer advice based on their years of fishing and see that their boats were serviced the right way because they supervised the work.

The Honduran owners that I talked with worked very closely together, although each ran his own small fleet. Kinship ties were very strong among these owners and their captains and crews. The Hondurans seemed to stick together and were known, in Port Isabel, as owners who acted in each other's best interests.

The owners of fleets of from six to fifteen boats differed in several ways from the owners described above. These men represented two different generations. The first generation is represented by the original Cajun owners who migrated from Louisiana. Death and old age have taken their toll, but there are still a number of these original owners, who settled with their trawlers in Texas in the late 1940s and early 1950s.

These men, like the smaller fleet owners, have clearly prospered over the years, only to a greater extent because they have been around longer and have had more time to be successful. Their fleets have grown from two or three boats to eight, ten, or more, and their support facilities have also developed.

These men are now more money managers, company presidents, than boat managers, like the smaller fleet owners, although a few do still keep a close eye on their trawlers. By and large, they take much less of a part in the daily operation and maintenance of the boats, at least partially because of the size of their operations. They spend the

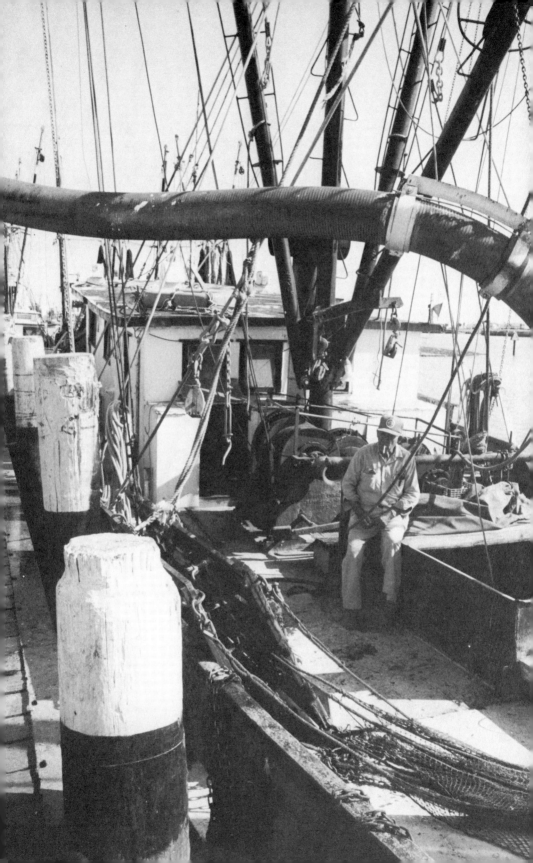

majority of their time running their companies, which often include icehouses, fuel suppliers, and, in some cases, ship construction yards.

The boat owners of this first generation have vertically integrated their business operations in order to make consistent profits to compensate for an uncontrollable wholesale price. They have found it more profitable to supply their own boats with what they require. They have formed subsidiary corporations, for tax purposes, that have purchased or built icehouses, fishhouses, freezers, and repair shops. They have a system of interdependent companies that provides everything they need to keep their trawlers fishing smoothly. This vertical integration is a response in part to fixed dockside prices. It is an attempt to gain more control over both the supply of shrimp and the subsidiary industries that support the trawlers.

The second generation of owners, the first Texas-born generation, is more likely to be college educated, to have little fishing experience, and to have inherited or married into the business. Many of these men have never worked on a shrimp boat. Although they may have gone out on a weekend trip, or possibly worked summers as a header, for the most part they have little firsthand experience. As sons, sons-in-law, or cousins of the first generation, these owners, especially the ones in Port Isabel and Port Brownsville, are much more management oriented. They spend most of their time in their offices behind their desks, in contrast to their fathers, fathers-in-law, or uncles. They are more likely to see shrimping only in terms of dollars and cents; their goal is to run a cost-effective operation. They work hard at the management side of the business; presumably they are better at it than their fathers and fathers-in-law because of their education and their business focus.

These differences in the two generations are emphasized because as the second generation begins to take over the businesses, one can, with a fair amount of certainty, make predictions about how the operations will change. In general, the companies are likely to become less personal, more cost effective, but more willing to venture into related fishing and nonfishing kinds of operations. They can, in general, be expected to be less sympathetic to shrimpers because the men who run them will have limited fishing experience and personal contact with shrimpers.

A critical point in the growth of a fleet is the time at which economy of scale demands either an end to the purchase of more trawlers or an involvement in companies that supply fuel, ice, and other necessities. Horizontal integration into the industry, accumulating more and more boats, necessitates vertical integration, buying into icehouses or fuel depots. An owner with five or six boats must make some important decisions if he wants to increase his fleet and still run an efficient operation. Either he must stop buying boats or he must look around to get his services and supplies at cheaper rates. There are two ways in which this can be done. An owner can go in on a small ice plant, for example, with other fleet owners, or, as is the case in Port Isabel and Aransas Pass, he has the theoretical option of joining a co-op.

In the first situation, the small owner with other investors builds a new facility or buys into an existing one. He keeps his companies separate but profits from each, as mentioned earlier, to the extent that he may eventually clear more from his icehouse, fuel depot, and repair shops than from his trawlers. In this way owners of four, five, or six boats have enlarged their fleets to ten to fifteen, which seems to be the next barrier to growth.

If the small fleet owner joins a co-op, he cuts down costs by splitting them with other members.[4] The Tarpon Seafoods Co-Operative in Port Isabel, for example, was founded by several small fleet owners who realized they could cut costs considerably if they pooled resources. Many small fleet owners and captain-owners have discovered a co-op to be just what they wanted to beat rising costs and to maximize profits. The co-op in Port Isabel has approximately forty boats, while the one in Aransas Pass has approximately eighty, and there are a few other much smaller co-ops. Joining a co-op means increased cost-effective trawler operations, but it also means that increased profits from other subsidiaries will be lacking. Horizontal growth stops: most co-op members own fewer than seven boats. Co-ops also suffer, in today's economy, from serious cash-flow problems.

---

[4]Carl Gersuny and John J. Poggie, Jr., in "A Fisherman's Co-operative: Open System Theory Applied," *Maritime Studies in Management* 1 (1974): 215–222, discuss in some detail the causes for and implications of fishermen's cooperatives. In a related piece, "Luddites and Fishermen: A Note on Response to Technological Change," *Maritime Studies in Management* 2 (1974): 38–47, they examine how East Coast fishermen have responded to technological and economic pressure.

The handful of owners of very large Texas fleets, from sixteen to sixty or more boats, have continued this process of both horizontal and vertical integration. As they have purchased more and more boats, their icehouses, fuel depots, and maintenance facilities have similarly grown. In Aransas Pass almost half the dock facilities appear to be taken up by one large company. In Port Isabel and in Freeport, one company's operations dominate the skyline of the docks. Some of these large fleet owners have purchased marine construction companies and fleets of trucks to distribute their shrimp to various retail markets, and they manage investor boats as well.

The owners of the largest companies have also diversified their interests and investments as their companies have grown. In at least one case a large fleet owner has purchased considerable local real estate. These and other money-management attempts to diversify are, of course, a protective business strategy to buffer these large trawler operations from the long history of fixed wholesale prices.

If running and maintaining five boats are quite a task, then, as one might imagine, the demands of owning and operating twenty, thirty, or more can be extreme. This job has been accomplished by dividing the work into paper work handling and direct management of the boats. In addition to the men who service, repair, and maintain the boats—the workers who run the ice, fuel, and supply operations—the very large shrimp companies require clerical staffs to keep track of the extensive paper work. On the dock, the general manager in charge of boat operations may have three or four assistants, whose task it is to keep the boats in good running shape.

According to the boat manager of one of the largest fleets, one big headache is theft of equipment. Equipment, especially expensive electronic gear, is regularly stolen directly off the boats or out of the buildings on the dock.

"Candy"

In addition to the ways in which some owners maximize their profits that have already been mentioned, "candy," or kickbacks, between owners, processors, fishhouse operators, and distributors, is common. In effect the shrimp are being sold at a lower price than the bidding price, with the owner and whoever else is involved profiting from the difference. The shrimper is the loser; he sees none of the candy.

It is impossible to assess how widespread the practice of paying "candy" is. My general impression, though, is that in many of the major Texas shrimping ports it is a common practice. I continually heard about candy from knowledgeable men in the industry all along the coast. Kickbacks are quite common in many American industries at the wholesale and retail levels.

Wage Cuts

A final business strategy that owners have employed, especially in the last three years, is a change in the traditional wage-share agreement with shrimpers, mentioned earlier. As noted, owners have, over the last three years, successfully lowered the percentage-share agreement from 65–35 to 70–30 or lower in many ports.

The owners have been quite successful in convincing shrimpers that, while they do not want to do so, they must decrease wages in order to stay in business. Their explanation of their current fiscal situation is that if they do not lower the percentage cut to shrimpers, they will simply go out of business and there will be no more jobs for any fishermen.

Fuel prices have been cited by the owners as the major villain. They say that increased fuel prices have driven their profits down the drain. In order to compensate for the beating they are supposedly taking, they must pass some of their losses on to the shrimpers. Even more recently, imports have been singled out as a chief contributor to owners' costs of operation.

The fuel explanation carries a lot of weight with some shrimpers because they can see that fuel prices have indeed gone up. Since they realize that a job at a reduced share is better than no job at all, many shrimpers have gone along with it. The owners' explanation of the need to decrease the share seems, however, at best a question of the degree to which they are really losing money because of fuel prices— or, for that matter, losing money for any other reason. It would be more correct to say that rising operating costs, a part of which is fuel costs, as well as other changes to the industry and the wholesale price squeeze, are hurting some of the owners. As discussed earlier, fuel prices affect the small fleet owner more than anyone else.

Whether or not the owners' claims are true, the point is that they have gotten away with them, at least temporarily. While some shrimpers threatened to quit, or to form unions and strike, at the beginning of the 1980 fishing season when a new decrease in the percentage share coupled with a crew fuel bill was suggested by many owners, most shrimpers did little but complain and grumble. The owners' strategy of blaming fuel prices has the extra advantage of putting the blame on an outside enemy, the OPEC nations. Many shrimpers are fiercely patriotic; by associating a decreased wage percentage with America's reliance on foreign fuel, the owners have neatly diverted attention away from their own business operations and profits.

Texas Shrimpers Association

The Texas Shrimpers Association (TSA), with headquarters in Austin, is the major lobbying force of fleet owners. Two federal bills in particular reflect its political clout and bias: the Tax Reform Act of 1976 and the Breaux and de la Garza bill initiated in the spring of 1981.

The TSA, along with the National Shrimp Congress (NSC), lobbied long and hard in Washington for a particular section of the Tax Reform Act of 1976. When the legislation passed, the TSA did its best to convince shrimpers of the act's immense benefit to them. In 1977, the executive director of the TSA said of the Tax Reform Act: "There are so many advantages to offset the cost. As private contractors, rather than employees, they can deduct up to $7,500 from their income for their retirement plan, and charge off on their income such things as pickup trucks, tools, equipment and home office space."[5]

Former U.S. Representative Al Ullman, then chairman of the House Committee on Ways and Means, wrote Representative Kika de la Garza of South Texas the following in regard to how those who lobbied for the act, the TSA and others, justified their efforts:

> Sponsors of the provision in the 1976 act contended that under the previous system it often *was difficult and impractical for the boat operator to calculate his tax obligations* as an employer, and that it was equally diffi-

[5] *Corpus Christi Caller*, May 7, 1977.

cult to withhold the appropriate taxes from the compensation of the crew members. They stated that the *boats frequently operated with "pick-up" crews* composed of individuals who worked for only a few voyages and were not paid a regular salary, but instead received a portion of the catch. They stated that the *crewmen should find it simpler and more convenient and report their own tax obligations.*[6]

Before the Tax Reform Act, shrimpers for tax purposes were "employees"; 5.85 percent of their paychecks was regularly deducted by the owner. This dollar amount was matched by the boat owner toward future Social Security paybacks at retirement. Under the act, shrimpers are required to pay 7.9 percent of their paychecks for Social Security; they have legally been reclassified as "self-employed." One tax consultant estimated that in 1977 the average shrimper would pay $300 more per year because of the change.[7] The owners, on the other hand, would save $900 a year per man, or $2,700 per vessel with a three-man crew.

The comments of the former executive director of the TSA on the new bill are interesting when one considers the money-management problems many shrimpers have. While his suggestions for tax write-offs might be appropriate for a white-collar, college-educated worker with a fixed monthly income, they show a definite insensitivity to and an ignorance of shrimpers as an occupational group. The idea that most shrimpers with their fluctuating monthly income should jump at the chance to sit down and figure out their Social Security taxes on each paycheck is at the very least ludicrous.

Shrimpers' reactions as recorded in the local newspapers and from my interviews with them four years later were consistent. They said then, and they said in 1980, that they would be, and have been, forced to hire accountants, at their own expense, to figure it all out for them.[8]

The justifications of the supporters of the reform, as cited by Ullman, are more ominous, calculating, and misleading. Most boat crews are not "pick-ups." Captains and riggers prefer to stick to a given boat,

---

[6] Ibid. (emphasis added).

[7] *Brownsville Herald*, May 15, 1979.

[8] To appreciate the extent of tax regulations with which commercial fishermen must contend, see U.S. Department of the Treasury, Internal Revenue Service, *Tax Guide for Commercial Fishermen*, Internal Revenue Service Publication No. 595.

unless of course the owner decides to shift them to another boat. Headers, though certainly more mobile, have been known to work for one boat for a year or more. In any case, the vast majority of shrimpers are certainly not men who go out on a boat only for several "voyages."

The TSA also had something else in mind when it successfully lobbied for the new section of the tax laws. By designating the crews as "self-employed" for tax purposes, the association intended to ensure that boat owners did not have to pay unemployment compensation for their employees. Thus owners would also save by not paying the extra money. Shrimpers at the time were quoted as saying that with the new tax law they would have nothing to count on but welfare if they were laid off.[9] Many shrimpers in Texas ports met informally; they were angry and confused, and they could not get a straight answer from some of the agencies involved. After much legal research and correspondence with the IRS, the Department of Labor, and state and congressional legislators, the decision was made that owners did not, after all, have to pay employment compensation.

A more recent example of the lobbying efforts of the TSA is a piece of legislation supported by John Breaux, Democrat from Louisiana, and Kika de la Garza, Democrat from South Texas and a primary supporter of the Tax Reform Act of 1976. The bill would impose quotas and tariffs on imported shrimp and, in addition, "would include tax incentives and investment credits for shrimpers; research and development to enhance fuel efficiency; possible creation of regional cooperatives to market U.S. shrimp, and profit making from other fish now discarded by shrimpers."[10]

A 20 percent ad valorem tax on all imported shrimp has been suggested most often. Owners believe that such a tax would "even things up" by giving domestic producers a break against what is seen as unfair foreign competition by foreign producers. Latin American countries, including one of the largest shrimp exporters to the United States, Mexico, have the American owners at an unfair market advantage. The Mexican government, for example, subsidizes fuel, so Mexican shrimpers pay considerably less for fuel than do American shrimp-

[9] *Corpus Christi Caller*, January 14, 1977.
[10] *Brownsville Herald*, March 13, 1981.

ers. In fact, in Mexico's case, the entire industry is subsidized by the government. The Mexican industry has seven trawler fleets with more than 450 vessels, plus extensive service, supply, and packing operations. Morover, the Mexican government even supports two fisheries research institutes as well as two importing corporations located in San Diego, California.[11] To protect its own industry, Mexico has prohibited any importation of foreign shrimp into Mexico. Other major exporters protect their country's shrimp industries with stiff duties.

McGoodwin, however, paints a broader picture of the Mexican shrimping industry that underscores the contradictory role it plays in the Mexican economy and, in the context of the current discussion, he suggests a variety of undesired effects from the 20 percent tariff.[12] Shrimp is Mexico's most important cash export—80 million dollars in 1972, surpassing the value of its oil, cotton, or sugar. Such wealth does not find its way down to the Mexican shrimpers, the *cooperativistas* (members of the Mexican fishing cooperatives), who earn less than seven hundred dollars a year.

What would be the impact of reduced Mexican imports of shrimp to the United States on Mexico's economy and government? In 1971 the United States levied a 10 percent tax on all imports. The 10 percent tax had, according to McGoodwin, a profound impact on the Mexican shrimp industry. Undoubtedly the additional import tax that has been suggested would greatly affect not only the *cooperativistas* but also the rest of the regional population, a population that is already economically marginal. The entire country would feel the economic effects of a substantial reduction in the number-one cash export.

The Mexican peso was devalued once in the spring of 1982 and again in the fall. At this writing the exchange rate is approximately one hundred pesos to one dollar. While the long-term impact of Mexico's financial crisis on its shrimping industry and on the American industry is difficult to assess, in the short term American shrimpers are noting both a decrease in Mexican production and the quality of the product. Both of these short-term effects would mean increased sales of Ameri-

[11] See James R. McGoodwin, "The Decline of Mexico's Pacific Inshore Fisheries," *Oceanus* 22 (1979): 52–59.

[12] Ibid., p. 54; James R. McGoodwin, "The Human Costs of Development," *Environment* 22 (1980): 25–42.

can shrimp. The immediate effects of the tax on imported shrimp from Mexico would be an increased instability in Mexico's national economy, with consequential effects on her ruling government. The American borderland could also expect an increase in the number of Mexican illegals seeking work, illegals directly hit by the short-term and long-term effects of an export tax.

Owners, of course, are unaware of this chain of events that might be set off by a simple raise of tariffs on shrimp coming into the United States. In an organized fashion, the TSA, under the leadership of a new national lobbying force called the Shrimp Harvesters Coalition of the Gulf and South Atlantic States (SHCGSAS), is lobbying the Federal Tariff Committee.

One of the other objectives of the legislation, namely to create regional marketing cooperatives, underscores the fleet owners' attempts to get out from under the thumb of the multinationals. In one newspaper account, Leigh Ratiner, a lawyer representing SHCGSAS, is quoted as saying the intent of the regional marketing cooperatives is that "they are trying to learn the marketing end of the business so they can cut out the middlemen."[13] In another newspaper report, Representative Breaux explained that possible creation of regional cooperatives or marketing boards might help shrimpers "make heftier profits."[14] Both accounts of the legislation emphasize the attempts by fleet owners to circumscribe the power of the multinationals over wholesale prices.

The chances of success for this particular piece of legislation under the Reagan administration are impossible to assess at this time. The potential effects of the bill have not been adequately studied, nor most probably will they be. It would seem that the TSA has chosen to focus on tariffs because this appears to the owners to be their best chance at increasing their profits. As suggested, however, fuel prices are just one of the several important factors affecting the shrimping industry in the 1980s.

Interestingly, the National Fish Congress, in the past a strong ally of the TSA, has not been supportive of import quotas and tariffs that

[13] *Houston Chronicle*, July 17, 1981.
[14] *Brownsville Herald*, March 13, 1981.

have been proposed. The impact of its influence on legislation will be sorely missed by the TSA in its legislative battle.

Fishhouse Workers

Almost nothing is known about the employees of the fishhouses, where shrimp landed in Texas are sorted, graded, processed, and packed in five-pound boxes.[15] Based on my own observations of four fishhouses I visited, workers were predominantly younger minority women who earned a minimum wage. The majority were married with families and worked as many hours a week as they were needed; there was very little opportunity for pay advancement. Safety and health conditions appeared reasonable. All of the fishhouse managers mentioned that their biggest problem was high turnover of their employees. Further research is required regarding this labor force and its role in the shrimping industry.

The Pickup Truck Shrimp Business

Roadside shrimp vendors represent a highly visible aspect of the shrimp industry with which many are familiar.[16] As with the fishhouse workers, there are no real data available on these small-time entrepreneurs. Owners seem ambivalent in their attitudes toward them; some point out that they are misleading potential buyers by advertising "Jumbo Shrimp" when in fact the "jumbo" shrimp are usually medium-sized shrimp.

Other owners discount any substantial impact of the pickup truck business on shrimping. They point out that the majority of the shrimp is sold to institutions, including restaurants, and that the consumer housewife is a relatively small part of the market. From this perspective the pickup truck business does fulfill a small demand yet does not to any serious degree affect the more established market routes.

There are no real data to substantiate the often-heard rumor that pickup truck shrimp is stolen shrimp. Although it is possible that some

[15] Michael V. Miller, personal correspondence, August 15, 1981.
[16] See "Tailgate Shrimp: What Are the Risks?," *The University and the Sea* 13, no. 3 (1980).

of this shrimp may occasionally be stolen, my impression is that most of it is bought directly from the fishhouses or from commercial bay-shrimpers. A simple survey of pickup truck shrimp is needed to assess its place in the industry.

9. Big Government

"Well, these people that never been on a boat, these
dignitaries, they try to make the laws. . . ."

Relative to other industries, the Texas shrimping industry has been left
alone by state and federal bureaucracies. This is just the way that most
shrimpers and many owners would like it to be. They have little use for
government intrusion into their livelihoods. Though often fiercely patriotic, shrimpers and owners remarked in their interviews that every
time the government sticks its nose into the fishing business it fouls
things up.

Shrimpers, as a rule, do not distinguish state and federal agencies
from each other. From their perspective the bureaucrats are all the
same, part of one huge bureaucracy. When shrimpers felt the impact of
the Tax Reform Act of 1976 they blamed it on the men in Washington,
the faceless ones, who were also responsible for other rules that either
gouged their paychecks or made their fishing more difficult.

While owners in general are always wary of government interven-
tion into the fishing industry, increasingly they are turning to state and
federal agencies as a last resort, as evidenced, for example, in the
Breaux and de la Garza bill. The owners are both more informed about
upcoming policies and decisions that may affect them and able, at the
same time, to make their opinions known where it counts. Nevertheless, the majority of Texas boat owners would prefer to be able to walk
that thin line between too much and too little government support and
regulation.

The View from the Boats

Shrimpers ignore some of the laws they are supposed to follow in
their fishing. They ignore them because the laws often make little
sense to them, were created without their advice and expertise, and, if

followed, would often make their work harder and less profitable. The closed season on fishing to ten miles in the Gulf was, until recently, one such example. In order to earn a living the shrimpers were forced to break a well-meaning, but unenforceable, law.

Some of the recent federal laws protecting certain species of sea turtles that border on extinction seem equally frivolous to these fishermen. Shrimpers make no special attempts to catch the turtles, but sometimes the turtles get caught in their nets. When the catch is boarded, the turtle very often has been injured, sometimes seriously. Some shrimpers enjoy turtle meat; they consider it a delicacy and have been eating it for years. So they cook the turtle and eat it, and they thereby break a federal law that would impose a heavy fine and imprisonment on them if they were discovered. This particularly irritates some South Texas shrimpers, who know that Mexicans, with the support of their government, regularly slaughter thousands of sea turtles and sell the meat to restaurants in Mexico and, more rarely, in the United States, although it remains illegal to import such turtle meat.

These two laws are examples of the contradiction between the intent of the lawmakers and its effect on those who must live with it on a daily basis. Many shrimpers have taken a job at sea to get away from just such rules and regulations. Their work emphasizes independence and self-sufficiency. They like the fact that they are their own men and that no one, not even the federal government, can make them do something they choose not to do. They realize that, unlike most land jobs, it is virtually impossible for the federal or state government to monitor their activities at sea.

Shrimpers were puzzled, then, when their government did not back them up and renegotiate a treaty with Mexico in 1980 so that they could continue to fish in Mexican waters. Those shrimpers who had shrimped for years off Campeche were particularly surprised that Washington did not do something in their behalf. American shrimpers agree that Mexican shrimpers should have first shot at harvesting shrimp in their own waters, but they remark that American trawlers, because they have fished for over thirty years in Mexican waters, know where the shrimp are that Mexican boats never find. American shrimpers believe, too, that there are enough shrimp in Mexican waters for everyone and that the shrimp, if not netted by them, will just die. Their assertions have been supported by research, but the Mexican government has not been receptive. As suggested in an earlier chapter, some shrimpers feel that when it counted, really counted, the government let them down.

During the course of this study the Coast Guard captured a Mexican trawler illegally fishing in American waters off Port Isabel. The boat, by chance, was tied to the dock just next to a boat on which I was interviewing. The American shrimpers were irate because they claimed the Mexican trawler and crew would be released in a short time with a minimum fine. Several days later the boat and crew were, in fact, released; the captain was fined approximately twenty-four thousand dollars, the price that his catch—presumably most of which had been netted in American waters—brought at the dock.

Several shrimpers interviewed told of being taken in by Mexican patrol boats in Campeche or other fishing towns, where they were released only through a series of expensive bribes. Shrimpers say that often their nets, doors, electronic equipment, and any other gear that could be carried off were taken by the Mexicans before they were released.

Shrimpers, then, are often on the wrong end of law or regulation. They see federal and state agencies as being on the outside looking in, noting that most of the legislators of laws that directly affect them have never been on a shrimp boat. The only representatives of a federal agency they may have some contact with are the National Marine Fisheries Service agent who fills out a report on their catch and, more rarely, the marine extension agent. With these exceptions, contact with the government is likely to be negative. Shrimpers do not see the government as working for them; they see it as policing their livelihood and making it harder for them to go about earning a living.

Thus shrimpers are fatalistic about obtaining any real help from any branch of the government that might aid them in their current dilemmas. The only shrimpers who felt that they could actually influence the political process were shrimpers in Port Isabel and Port Brownsville who belonged to a crewmen's association.

Texas shrimpers do not have a very high regard for the men who must enforce what the shrimpers often see as stupid laws. This feeling particularly extends to the Texas Parks and Wildlife Department, which is mandated to enforce much of the legislation concerning the uses of Texas bays. Gulf shrimpers, particularly those who also fished the bays in the winter or who supplemented their shrimping incomes with other commercial fishing over which Parks and Wildlife has control, saw the agents as rule enforcers infringing on the fishermen's right to perform their jobs.

Shrimpers' attitudes toward the Coast Guard, which patrols the Gulf, are more ambivalent. While they depend on the Coast Guard for any emergencies that might occur at sea, especially aid to an injured or lost shrimper or a trawler in serious trouble, at the same time the fishermen sometimes have little regard for what they perceive as the poor seamanship of the Coast Guard. Shrimpers are not critical of the Guardsmen's record at sea during disasters, but they view them at times as "boy scouts" lacking in real sea experience. Shrimpers say that the distinction is that fishermen are out on the sea trying to make a living, while the men in the Guard are there because they are forced to be there, not by their own choice. This attitude on the part of Gulf shrimpers reflects a professional chauvinism. Most shrimpers are proud both to be shrimpers and to have the seamanship skills that go along with it. They downplay the skills of others in order to promote their own.

The View from the Offices

Several very influential fleet owners increasingly see federal and state government as their only way to stay alive in the shrimp business. At the same time that they seek its help—in fuel subsidies, in tariffs, or as a friend to help in their fight with other commercial fishermen—they are sometimes critical of some of its past attempts to help the industry. For instance, some owners are critical of recent Small Business Administration (SBA) loans to trawler owners to keep them in business after a bad year. Owners in good financial condition believe the government is carrying on its back those marginal owners who, in time, would and should go under. They do not understand why their tax dollars should indirectly go toward increased competition in their industry.

Congressional involvement in the shrimp industry goes back at least as far as 1957, when Congress initiated the Fisheries Loan Fund. This program was designed to provide "direct loans for the building, equipping, and repairing of craft, to craftowners and operators who could not obtain funds from any other sources on reasonable terms."[1] Gillespie notes that immediately after the loan program began, there was a sharp decline in the average income earned per vessel.

Again, in 1960 Congress initiated another program designed to help the industry—the Fishing Vessel Mortgage and Loan Program. This program, according to Gillespie, provided funds for insurance on mortgages undertaken to finance the building and repairing of fishing vessels and, like the previous loan program, stimulated increased entry of new vessels into the industry, decreasing, again, the average revenue per vessel of those already fishing. It is interesting to note that some of the same owners, now successful businessmen, who are critical of SBA loans to other boat owners were recipients of earlier government loans.

From interviews with several of the owners who did receive SBA loans to keep from going out of business, it does seem to be the case that the SBA has sometimes handed out loans, as one captain put it, "like they were fried chicken." That is to say, some SBA loans to owners of one or two boats are merely prolonging their financial agony. One owner in particular impressed me with his lack of sound business skills and practices. He had purchased a trawler with a bank loan at a high interest rate, having no experience in fishing or in running a business. The first year, the boat had been fished approximately three weeks before it was discovered to have serious engine problems that required expensive repairs. The second year, the boat spent most of its time at the dock because the owner could not find a responsible crew. On one occasion the newly hired captain had taken the boat out, had fished for a week, and had then off-loaded the catch at another port, taking the money from the catch with him when he and the crew abandoned the boat.

This owner had received an SBA loan to get him through the second year. Now, in his third year, he was faced with interest on two

---

[1] See William C. Gillespie, James C. Hite, and John S. Lytle, *An Econometric Analysis of the U.S. Shrimp Industry*, Economics of Marine Resources, No. 2.

loans, the bank loan and the SBA loan, which came to a considerable monthly sum. The boat was still not being fished regularly, and maintenance costs were considerable. This one example is not representative of all SBA loans to the owners, but it does emphasize how, notwithstanding the government's best intentions, the loan program can be abused. It is also the kind of example that other shrimpers and boat owners hear about and that gives the program a bad name. SBA loans do serve, in a broader perspective, to keep afloat more marginal business operations, much as did the government's loan programs in the late 1950s and early 1960s, but, at the same time, they have allowed many competent shrimpers to purchase their own trawlers.

Most owners' only direct contact with any governmental agencies is through the National Marine Fisheries Service agents and marine extension agents, whom they run into by chance on the docks or around town, and through the lobbying efforts of the TSA. They are much more likely to have personal contact with these agents than are shrimpers. The majority of owners I talked to had a limited awareness of the ways in which governmental policy affecting owners and the industry were implemented. They depended on their trade association, the TSA, to keep them informed. Many owners were much too busy with the day-to-day operations of their businesses to follow the machinations of big government, although, in general, their understanding of the industry and its relationship to state and federal agencies was much more comprehensive than that of the shrimp fishermen.

As some of the more astute owners have faced increased industry problems, they have, as suggested, looked to the federal government to help them out. At this time, however, the majority of owners along the Texas coast remain unconvinced that the industry is undergoing hard times in the present and will face even tougher going in the future and that the federal government is the answer to their problems.

Gulf of Mexico Fishery Management Council

Under the Fishery Conservation and Management Act of 1976, management councils were mandated to develop fisheries management plans for their respective regions. The councils fall under the U.S. Department of Commerce. The Gulf of Mexico Fishery Management Council, located in Tampa, Florida, has developed a management plan for the Gulf shrimp fishery that involves the states of Texas, Louisiana, Florida, Alabama, and Mississippi.[2]

Much time and effort has been spent on the part of the council in developing the shrimp fishery plan. A series of public hearings was held before the plan was put into effect in order to incorporate as many divergent opinions and interests as possible. Since none of the shrimpers I interviewed had any idea of what the Gulf of Mexico Fishery Management Council even was, however, it is likely that the final plan does not reflect the best interests of the fishermen themselves and that if it does do so, it is by happenstance. This, of course, was not the intent of the council; shrimpers find it difficult to attend regularly scheduled meetings even if they do find out about the meetings and their importance.

My impression of the public hearings, based on attendance at one such meeting and conversations with others who had attended many of the public hearings all along the Gulf Coast, is that the larger fleet owners were the ones who testified as to the needs of the shrimp industry. At the meeting I attended, fleet owners came to the podium with prepared statements to make their opinions known. A few captains also made some remarks, but they were less impressive than the owners because they lacked experience in public speaking (while one captain was speaking only a few of the members paid him any attention). Because shrimpers in different ports throughout Texas, and the rest of the Gulf, are not represented by any organizations that could furnish experienced spokesmen, their voice went largely unheard. This is not to imply that shrimpers do not possess expertise about the industry; rather, it is to suggest that the interests of boat owners and shrimpers are not necessarily the same. Regulations that might positively benefit the owners might not necessarily have the same effects on shrimpers working in the Gulf.

There remains, then, an unfortunate but significant information and communication gap between shrimpers and the regulatory body

[2] See Gulf of Mexico Fishery Management Council, *Draft Environmental Impact Statement and Fishery Management Plan for the Shrimp Fishery of the Gulf of Mexico, United States Waters.*

empowered to design laws that directly affect them. The owners have done an excellent job of making their opinions heard, but the shrimpers have remained an anonymous work force although they are the mainstay of the shrimping industry.

The composition of the Gulf of Mexico Fishery Management Council represents a final impediment to direct representation in the interests of shrimp fishermen. The council is composed of political appointees named by state governors, including executives of large fish companies, representatives of state park and fisheries commissions, and others with particular vested interests; a variety of scientific experts, including a sprinkling of social scientists, make up the subcommittees that prepare the various studies and carry out research that is required. Thus while a wide range of interests with extensive experience and expertise in the fishing industry is represented, shrimpers have no direct influence on the council.

The Growing Battle over Texas Shrimp Fisheries

In the last few years there has been a growing struggle over the uses of the shrimp fishery in Texas. While a complete discussion of the nature of this struggle is beyond the scope of this work, the role that the Gulf shrimp owners and shrimpers play will be given some attention.

Gulf shrimp trawler owners and bay shrimpers have never gotten along very well.[3] Although bay shrimpers are often former Gulf shrimpers, or part-time Gulf shrimpers, hostilities between the two groups have mounted in recent years. Basic to this conflict is the use of the shrimp fishery. Both sides have recognized that the resource is limited; as productivity per trawler has continued to decrease, Gulf fleet owners have sought to put the blame on the bay shrimpers.

Each side mounts its own arguments and defenses. In a nutshell, the Gulf owners believe that the bay shrimpers deplete the shrimp population by netting the crustaceans in the bays. They offer ample

[3] For example, in a letter to the editor of the *Brownsville Herald*, June 6, 1980, a longtime bay shrimper outlines what he sees as discrimination against bay shrimpers by Gulf shrimpers, the Texas Parks and Wildlife Department, and the state legislature.

scientific research in support of their assertions, plus the support of the Texas Parks and Wildlife Commission. The owners point out that it makes much more economic sense to wait to net the shrimp when they have gotten to the Gulf, by which time they are larger and bring a higher price. The Gulf owners, therefore, argue that to close or partially close the bays to commercial shrimping would be one way to increase their productivity. Then, they say, more shrimp could migrate out of the channels and passes to be netted by the big shrimp trawlers.

The bay shrimpers believe strongly that such arguments are nonsense, that the Gulf fleet owners simply want to put them out of business because the Gulf owners do not like and have never liked the competition. The bay shrimpers point out that natural predation is responsible for the greatest amount of decline in shrimp population from the bays to the Gulf; some biologists support this assertion. Bay shrimpers believe there are enough shrimp for everyone but that, since the number of Gulf trawlers continues to increase each year, each trawler is netting less. They ask why the bay shrimpers should suffer just because the Gulf shrimpers are, in their eyes, greedy to get all the shrimp and, because of their overcapitalized operations, require larger catches than do bay shrimpers to stay in business.

As some fleet owners have perceived their economic troubles to intensify, they have put increased efforts into lobbying the state legislature to limit commercial bay shrimping. Bay shrimpers are not well organized; in fact they seem to be even more independent than Gulf shrimpers and have had difficulty in forming organizations to represent their interests.[4]

There are extreme differences between the Texas bay shrimpers and the Mexican shrimp fishermen of South Sinola, but McGoodwin's description of the development of the Mexican Gulf fishery at the expense of the bay and estuarine fisheries warrants consideration.[5] In the Mexican case, the bay fishermen lost their means to earn an income when bay shrimping was severely limited by the needs of the govern-

---

[4] See chapter 4 in J. Anthony Paredes, James C. Sabella, and Marcus J. Hepburn, "Human Factors in the Economic Development of a Northwest Florida Gulf Coast Fishing Community."

[5] See James R. McGoodwin, "The Decline of Mexico's Pacific Inshore Fisheries," *Oceanus* 22 (1979): 52–59.

ment-supported Mexican Gulf shrimper. Because alternative employment opportunities were lacking, and because job skills and education
were minimal, Mexican bay shrimpers were reduced in the 1930s to a
subsistence living even though an abundant fishery was literally at
their doorstep.

Certainly, if commercial bay shrimping in Texas were curtailed,
these fishermen would, unlike the Mexicans, find alternative employment. But the effects of these changes on the fishermen and their families would be severe. Many of these men, and their fathers before
them, have been fishing the bays for fifty years or more. It is more than
historically noteworthy to consider that the very biological justifications that the Mexican government made some years ago to their bay
shrimpers are now being duplicated by the lobbyists for the Gulf
owners.

The majority of the Gulf shrimpers interviewed did not believe
that bay shrimpers should be excluded from fishery use, however.
Their opinions were quite biased; some were bay shrimpers themselves, while others had close family who worked as bay shrimpers.
Very often bay shrimping was viewed by those men as a viable employment option, especially since the price of a trawler had skyrocketed in
the last several years. To Gulf shrimpers, bay shrimping is a last path to
upward mobility. Gulf shrimpers view bay shrimpers as fellow fishermen with an equal right to net shrimp.

The Texas Parks and Wildlife Department has played an important
role in the growing struggle between Gulf fleet owners and bay shrimpers. Its researchers have gathered extensive biological data that support the Gulf trawler owners' position. The biological weight of the
evidence falls resoundingly on the side of the Gulf boat owners. The
conflict between the two groups has not taken place in a political void,
but within the context of Texas politics. As such, the Gulf interests
have been very successful in using the bureaucratic weight of the Parks
and Wildlife Department to their own ends.

Bay shrimpers are in a particularly negative position vis-á-vis the
Parks and Wildlife Department because on a daily basis it is this
agency that enforces existing statutes regarding use of the bay shrimp
fishery. It would be difficult for the bay shrimpers, even if they were
organized, to influence the same agency that routinely policed them.

Political clout is the name of the game; bay shrimpers will lack the important support of the department when the final legislative decisions are formulated.

From the perspective of the department, scientific research has dovetailed nicely with bureaucratic rationalism and political expediency. Parks and Wildlife is a politicized bureaucracy (its board of commissioners is appointed by the governor), and Gulf shrimping is by far the most important fishing industry and interest in the state. As a result, the bureaucratic decision has been reduced, somehow, to an all-or-nothing proposition; the human component has been neglected in favor of the economic and biological evidence, and issues other than agroeconomic ones have not been consistently raised. These neglected issues can be summarized by means of a few questions, which remain unsatisfactorily answered: (1) Are bay shrimpers a primary cause, or even an important cause, of the financial problems that Gulf owners now face? (2) What is the impact of bay shrimpers on the local economies of the communities in which they reside, and how would these communities be adversely affected by an elimination of bay shrimpers? (3) What kinds of compromises can be worked out between the two groups that would avoid a complete curtailment of bay shrimping? and (4) What kinds of alternative employment or training programs should be made available to the bay shrimpers to help in the transition if and when the bay fishery is closed?

As of this writing, legislative bills have placed a moratorium on new licensing of bay shrimp boats. Public hearings are being held along the Texas coast to discuss the moratorium and what, if any, new policies should be adopted regarding the bay fishery. The Texas legislature is expected to enact new legislation affecting bay shrimpers in its next regular session.

The possible displacement of bay shrimpers and the consequential psychological and socioeconomic impact on these Texas fishermen should not be ignored because they are relatively few in number; these men merit a high priority in future decision making. It would be a terrible waste of human lives to reduce Texas bay shrimpers, who have worked so long and hard for so many years, to the status of outlaw fishermen, to poachers.

Vietnamese Bay Shrimpers

Even less is known about a significant number of Texas bay shrimpers who are Vietnamese refugees. Beginning with the fall of Saigon in 1975, refugees were resettled by private and public placement agencies in several Texas coastal fishing communities.[6] Presumably the idea was to relocate Vietnamese in the traditional occupational areas of their homeland, with an approximate climate and proximity to the sea, although no real federal policy toward resettlement was ever to emerge. In practice, many of the First Wave and Second Wave, as they were to be called, were less likely to be peasant fishermen than urban middle-class and upper-middle-class educated men and women, who could not hope, at first, to find the same kinds of employment in the United States that they held in Vietnam.[7]

One particularly tragic case was the resettlement of Vietnamese in Port Isabel. While the employment arrangement seemed to satisfy a majority of the refugees—the women worked in a fishhouse and the men worked as Gulf shrimpers—their acceptance into the community was disastrous. The Vietnamese felt unwelcome, and the residents of the community felt invaded by a strange culture. The refugees found insurmountable difficulties in language acquisition and assimilation of community values, attitudes, and life-style. They were finally relocated after reconciliatory efforts by community and religious groups failed.

The problems that emerged in Port Isabel have unfortunately been duplicated in a number of other Texas coastal communities.[8] The Vietnamese have become quite adept at fishing the bays for crab, shrimp, and other commercial fish, but their acceptance into the com-

[6] See Gene Lyons, "The Newest Americans," *Texas Monthly*, June, 1976, pp. 96–101, 141–146.

[7] Darrel Montero, *Vietnamese Americans: Patterns of Resettlement and Socioeconomic Adaptation in the United States*, is still the best source for this subject.

[8] See John Bloom, "A Delicate Balance," *Texas Monthly*, October, 1979, pp. 124, 256–258; Louise Flippin, *The Indochinese Situation: America's Newest Wave of Immigrants*; Barry N. Stein, "Occupational Adjustment of Refugees: The Vietnamese in the United States," *International Migration Review* 13 (1979): 25–45; and Paul D. Starr, "Troubled Waters: Vietnamese Fisherfolk on America's Gulf Coast," *International Migration Review* 15 (1981): 226–238.

munity setting has been beset with problems. The killing of an Anglo shrimper in self-defense by two Vietnamese fishermen in Seadrift in 1978 brought the resettlement situation to state and national attention. Based on my interviews with Gulf shrimpers and other community members, including social workers, and with religious and political leaders in several coastal towns, hostility between Vietnamese fishermen and local fishermen and residents is intensifying as of this writing despite both local efforts and the governor's Texas Indo-Chinese Task Force, which was initiated to help solve some of the problems that have arisen.

In addition to the possibilities for conflict between Vietnamese and indigenous Texans because of cultural differences and problems in communication, there are real differences in the two groups' attitudes toward use of the fishery. Such differences are compounded by the fact that the fishery is increasingly viewed as a limited resource. Added to this are the Vietnamese penchant for hard work and a pooling of extended-family resources, which have enabled Vietnamese fishermen to purchase new bay fishing boats in a fairly short time. This has caused a certain amount of resentment among local fishermen. There seems to be a definite feeling on the part of some in the communities that real trouble will come if and when the Vietnamese can legally own and fish Gulf trawlers.

A large variety of negative characteristics is attributed to the Vietnamese bay shrimpers, similar to the labeling that occurred in Port Isabel.[9] These characteristics range from the barely believable to the fantastic, but they are all grounded in an unfamiliarity with Vietnamese culture and tradition as well as in what appears to be a need to believe the worst. Vietnamese refugee fishermen are beginning to serve as community scapegoats, blamed for whatever ills befall the residents and their towns.

Almost nothing is known of the reaction of the Vietnamese to their treatment in these communities. They are viewed by others as a homogeneous group, though they are composed by now of a variety of different socioeconomic classes that escaped in the Third, Fourth, and Fifth waves from Vietnam. There is among them an inter- and intra-generational conflict, which is reflected in different attitudes toward

[9] Bloom, "A Delicate Balance," p. 124.

use of the fishery. The younger fishermen have become more highly assimilated into some of the materialistic aspects of our culture, while the older adults, as have generations of American immigrants before them, have clung to their former cultural values and traditions.

To date there has been no adequate social-scientific assessment either of the real needs and problems of the bay shrimpers, of their lack of acceptance by many in the communities (although various armchair theories have been offered up by those unfamiliar with the situation), or of possible ways to dilute present and future hostilities. The governor's task force is, unfortunately, burdened with a tremendous challenge and has had little time to direct its efforts to the Texas coastal fishermen. The Texas Department of Human Resources has, in effect, been delegated the problem, but it remains understaffed, underfunded, and overworked.

10. Unions, Shrimpers, and the Shrimping Industry

"The Bible says you came into this world with no clothes and leave that way. But while you're here you have a brain and a heart and you don't want to get messed with."

Texas shrimpers have reacted to the economic pressures of their occupation and the inroads of corporations and government in a variety of ways. In the good times, when they felt they were getting a price for their shrimp that allowed them to live well relative to others in the community, they did not complain. But in the bad times, when they felt in common either that the owners were not treating them fairly or that the work was no longer providing them a decent income, they have not stood by quietly. Instead they have sought to protect their jobs and their incomes as best they can.[1]

One particular case in point is the strike by Port Brownsville shrimpers in 1973. While the strike and the subsequent attempts at formation of a shrimpers' union were largely unsuccessful, the events in which the shrimpers were involved from the Christmas holidays of 1973 to the spring of 1974 are illustrative both of the socioeconomic stresses with which shrimpers have contended over the last thirty-five years and of their relationships with owners and the communities in which they live. The strike and the events surrounding it also suggest how shrimpers may react in the coming years.

Attempts at unionization of shrimpers in Port Brownsville began in earnest in 1960, although undoubtedly there were less substantial

---

[1] Fishermen, like other American workers, historically have fought for higher wages and safety in the workplace and have challenged innovations that have threatened to alter their patterns of work. See, for example, Carl Gersuny and John J. Poggie, Jr., "Luddites and Fishermen: A Note on Response to Technological Change," *Maritime Studies in Management* 2 (1974): 38–47.

efforts at organization many years earlier. The Rio Grande Fishermen's Association had been organized by several fleet owners in 1948,
shortly after Gulf shrimping began in South Texas. The association
functioned as a company union, with the role of mollifying the fishermen and preempting any organization of real influence or power. In
late 1959 its then president resigned in disgust and began working with
other dissatisfied fishermen to form a real union.

In 1960 the fishermen went to the San Antonio local of the International Brotherhood of Teamsters, which filed a petition on their behalf to have an election called by the National Labor Relations Board
(NLRB). At a hearing before two NLRB examiners the two sides presented their cases. The attorney representing the owners at Port
Brownsville branded the former president of the Rio Grande Shrimp
Fishermen's Association a "turncoat" and stated that the existing association represented the fishermen's best interests.[2] In the owners'
opinion there was no real need for a union because of the existence of
the association. The leaders representing the shrimpers claimed they
had the signatures of 30 percent of the men in five of the largest
shrimping companies at the port. Briefs were filed by the attorneys for
both sides, but an election was never called by the NLRB.

There were several more unsuccessful and less organized attempts at forming a union in the next thirteen years. Grievances between shrimpers and owners increased despite the fact that the 1960s
were good years, in general, for both. The shrimpers complained of
unfair treatment by certain owners, of both a lack of job security and
being treated as "second-class citizens." Owners, on the other hand,
felt not only that they did pay their fishermen well, relative to the
average area income, but that formation of a union would totally ruin
the industry by driving them out of business. They were particularly
adamant about maintaining their right to pay shrimpers what they
wanted to pay and to hire and fire fishermen as they saw fit.

Most owners in Port Brownsville then paid their captains based on
a 60–40 wage-share split of the catch. Relative to other Texas ports,
shrimpers at Port Brownsville were getting more than other shrimp-

---

[2] For an extremely antiunion perspective, see the following issues of the *Brownsville Herald*: March 4, 8, 10, and 22, 1960.

ers; in Port Aransas, for example, most shrimpers were getting a 65–35 split at the time. At first glance it is surprising, then, that shrimpers in Port Brownsville struck the owners immediately after the Christmas season in 1973 because of the rumor that the owners were going to cut their wage agreement to 65–35. In the most orderly fashion to date, the shrimpers formed the Gulf Coast Trawler Captains' Association of Brownsville. They elected officers, collected dues from members, and set up picket lines at the gates to the port. A few weeks later they affiliated themselves with the National Maritime Union.

The major reason for the strike was, in fact, the shrimpers' concern over a reduction in the wage-share agreement. The owners, for their part, denied that they had any intention of a reduction; they said that they did not have an organized plan for such a reduction and had not even discussed it among themselves. According to one owner, every owner in port acted only on his own volition and put no pressure on other owners to act together. This same owner agreed with the shrimpers that a reduction to 35 percent was ridiculous. "If I was cut back to 35% I'd quit, too," he said.[3]

Why, then, did the shrimpers go on strike so readily when all they were reacting to was a rumor, the kind of talk that floats around many ports on a regular basis? The shrimpers struck because they were disgusted not only with what they saw as an eventual cutback in their wage-share percentage—a cutback, incidently, that the owners did invoke shortly after the strike was over—but also with the treatment they received from some of the owners.

In interviews with some of the shrimpers who participated in the strike, there was general agreement among them that they were as concerned about their status as employees as they were a possible pay cut. Many of them felt that they were professionals, that they worked hard and took risks only to return to the dock to be treated like children, or worse, by some of the owners. The fact that they felt the dockside price was rigged by the owners did not sit well with them either. They went on strike, then, as much out of years of frustration of being treated as "second-class citizens" as they did in reaction to the wage reduction.

[3] *Brownsville Herald*, December 31, 1973.

There were no outside agitators, no professional union organizers. The shrimpers went on strike because that was the only way they could show their dissatisfaction with the owners. They were flexing their muscles as organized fishermen, testing the owners to see how they would react. But they were also venting their emotions, demanding in effect that they be taken seriously as men and as fishermen. The rumor of the reduction in the wage was seen by many shrimpers as the last straw in the long, often tenuous working relationship with some of the owners.

Shrimpers with whom I talked did say that not all owners were indifferent to their needs; some companies had good reputations among shrimpers. But shrimpers who worked for the good companies felt that they had to show support for their fellow fishermen. Some shrimpers felt torn by the strike, their natural sympathies lying with the strikers but their loyalties with their owners, who had treated them fairly for many years.

There were many meetings and much planning, and a contract was drawn. The union claimed it had over two hundred captains signed up.[4] The picketing continued at the gates of the port. The owners took a wait-and-see attitude. Time was on their side: the Christmas season was a good time for the shrimpers to organize and strike, since all the boats were tied up at the dock for the holiday season, but it was also a good time for the owners to sit back and watch the strike, since they did not need to fish their boats until spring. The majority could afford to wait until then or even late summer if they were forced to by the strike. The owners accused some of the shrimpers of acts of sabotage. The union denied any knowledge or support of violence against owners or their property.

Many of the owners were surprised by the suddenness of the strike and the strikers' formation of a union. The owners claimed they themselves had no group strategy, but they reacted swiftly to the strikers. The owners repeatedly stated that they had not met, and would not meet, as a group, either to discuss the strike or to negotiate with the fishermen. There was, however, a cooperative, coordinated effort among them. Their strategy was to keep a low profile and let the

[4]Ibid., December 28, 1973.

media do their talking for them; the local media were strongly biased against the shrimpers, the strike, and the union.

The owners were successful in presenting their side of the strike to the community. They appeared as reasonable, responsible businessmen faced with unruly and ungrateful employees. One owner said, "I'm going to split the catches the way I want to. No association and no union is going to tell me what to do, that's between me and the captain."[5] Another responded, when asked what he would do if the strike continued, "If I can't work my boats the way I want to I'll leave. These boats have engines and rudders on them and I can move them. They're not nailed to the dock and they can damn sure go somewhere else."[6]

The strike continued through January and February, but the owners held on. They were not really losing much money, since the majority of the boats do little fishing in the winter months, and some of the men did continue to show up for work in spite of the strike. The owners continued to discredit the shrimpers in the local newspaper. In particular, they reiterated that they could not negotiate a contract with the union because each of the owners ran a separate business and there was no organization that represented them all. When a reporter asked about the possible role in the negotiations of the Brownsville–Port Isabel Shrimp Products Association (the local chapter of the Texas Shrimpers Association and an eventual supporter of the Tax Reform Act of 1976), one owner replied, "It's an association to work on industry problems. The owners are all different. They think differently. They won't get together to deal with the union."[7]

Through their new union, the shrimpers put all their efforts and energy into drawing up a general contract, an agreement that outlined the terms of their work relationship with the owners. The contract provided for a 60–40 wage-share split, guarantees against arbitrary firing of a captain ("all captains shall be entitled to one warning notice in writing for each offense before the captain may be discharged for any reason except dishonesty"), a guaranteed vacation, and collection of union dues from the paychecks for crew members.[8] In light of union

[5] Ibid., December 31, 1973.
[6] Ibid.
[7] Ibid.
[8] Ibid., December 28, 1973.

contracts in other parts of the country at the time, the demands were quite tame. The owners saw otherwise. One owner, when asked by the men who worked for him to sign a contract, said that the contract defined whom he could hire and whom he could fire. "If I decide to fire a man," he said, "I'm not going to sit around for 30 days while we argue it out."[9] The contract was amended to meet his objections, but the owner still refused to sign.

The shrimpers' enthusiasm began to wane when they could not get any of the owners at the port to sign the new contract. While they had the support of a majority of the crews, some of the men were hurting financially. Normally, in the winter months the shrimpers would be working or getting pay advances from the owners against their catches in the spring. The lack of extra income particularly affected those shrimpers who were not good money managers: part-time jobs were very hard to find, and, besides, shrimping was the only job many of the men knew.

These fishermen had no experience with the sustained efforts required by a prolonged strike. Their personal finances put increasing pressures on them. The needs of their wives and families could not be ignored. Some shrimpers who could tried to help those who needed food and their bills paid. The strike dragged into February. Some of the fishermen returned to the docks, although few boats went out, and more trawlers fished in March. By April the strike was over.

Seven Years Later

Many shrimpers who participated in the strike of 1973 still harbored resentment toward the owners when interviewed in 1980. At the same time, they felt that they had been naive in 1973—that the strike was doomed to failure from the start because of poor planning and because, according to one captain, "you just can't organize shrimpers." Most of the shrimpers who participated in the strike said that the problems that caused the strike in the first place had not disappeared but had instead worsened.

The shrimpers themselves blamed the rising costs of fuel. Several

[9] Ibid.

were quick to sympathize with the owners and their financial problems. Others were less sympathetic but resigned to their situation. Few shrimpers believed that another strike could be successful, although the majority believed that a union was the only answer to many of their problems. Many of the shrimpers mentioned the fishing unions on the East Coast and West Coast as examples of unions that had benefited fishermen.

One rigger, when asked why he went back to work in 1973, said, "I got to eat, I have to feed my family. Shrimping is the only thing I do good." This shrimper supported the strike, but when his money ran out he was among the first to go back to work. Another blamed the failure of the strike on Mexican illegal aliens. He said that although the owners did not actually recruit the Mexicans, many of the shrimpers believed that if they did not go back to work they would be replaced by these foreign workers. One shrimper told a story of how a boat manager and a former shrimper took a boat out for the owner during the strike but caught few fish and did considerable damage to the boat. The shrimper who told the story was disdainful of the strikebreaker, but he, too, felt that if he himself had not gone back to work when he did, the owner would have permanently replaced him, despite his years of experience in working for the company.

A majority of the shrimpers interviewed were very pessimistic about the future of the industry. Many believed that 1979, a bad year for many shrimpers, was the beginning of the end for shrimping as they knew it. Many foresaw in the next five years increasingly lower prices for shrimp and lower incomes for themselves. They spoke almost wistfully of the good years when they were paid well for their jobs. Not a few said that shrimping the old way was gone for good, that a man could no longer make a decent income from Gulf shrimping.

The strike, then, was an education of sorts to many of these fishermen. It was, for many, their first and last strike. They had joined willingly, each for his own reasons. For some it was a venting of many years of frustration with perceived discrimination, while for others it was strictly a dollars-and-cents proposition. Still others went along with it because there was no real fishing for the next several months anyway. For these men it was an adventure, a diversion. But, regardless of why they joined, the men did seem to feel that the strike had given them a sense of solidarity as shrimpers that they had not felt

before. They looked back on it and saw their mistakes in strategy, where they had gone wrong.

Shrimpers from Port Brownsville and Port Isabel formed a Crewmen's Association in 1980. The purpose of the organization is to lobby state and national politicians on issues that are important to the shrimpers. Although the organization is not a union—in many ways it emulates the Texas Shrimping Association and the owners' national organizations—its formation represents an increased political sophistication on the part of some of the shrimpers in these two ports. They realize that a union, for many reasons, is not feasible at the present time but that a lobby representing their vested interests is possible.

Representatives of the Crewmen's Association have gone to Austin and Washington, D.C., to speak up on fuel prices and other problems they are having. They sent a busload of shrimpers to Washington in the spring of 1980 to put pressure on the federal bureaucracy to help them through their hard times. They have met with state and national politicians and have been heard. Their sporadic monthly meetings have generated support and enthusiasm from many shrimpers, who, in the future, could serve as the basis for membership in a functioning union.

Why There Are No Unions

At a glance it would seem that Texas shrimpers would be among the first to organize a strong union movement. Strong unions stand to be a major defense against owners, certain economic trends, and government. This case study of one strike suggests several factors that have precluded the unionization of shrimpers in all of Texas. These factors include a regional business climate traditionally antagonistic to unions; the sociopolitical isolation of the communities in which most shrimpers reside; the fragile economic status of shrimpers, which works to fractionalize their group cohesiveness; and the real and perceived threat of a surplus labor force willing to function as strike breakers.

It is no secret that Texas and Texans in general do not get along with unions. There are a variety of historical and economic reasons why unions are to be found only in a few of Texas' largest metropolitan areas. Others have documented the efforts of the private sector to exclude unions from Texas and the South in general and the success of their efforts.[10]

To a great extent the general public has supported business's efforts to keep unions, any unions, from spreading. Certainly this was evident in the lack of support that was forthcoming from the communities during the shrimpers' strike in 1973. Of course, since the local paper was and is strongly antiunion, its role in shaping and manipulating opinion should not be discounted. The paper did an excellent job of presenting the owners' sides to all the issues in the strike and neglected any real coverage of the shrimpers themselves.

Yet even if the media had done a better job in reporting the strike, there is doubt that Brownsville, Port Isabel, and the other surrounding communities would have been wholeheartedly in favor of the strikers. To this extent the strikers' communities are very similar to all Texas shrimping towns, from Sabine Pass to Freeport, Port Lavaca, Aransas Pass, and south. These towns, like most similar-sized Texas communities, have traditionally seen little need for unions and less for strikes.

What community support the strikers did have came from friends and neighbors of the shrimpers themselves. One would expect that in Port Isabel, for instance, community political pressure might have been applied to the owners to end the strike by negotiating a contract. But shrimpers, as suggested, lack any real political power even though in numbers they represent a dominant political force. Thus, even though shrimpers and their families compose a sizable majority in towns such as Port Lavaca, Aransas Pass, Freeport, and Port O'Connor, they nevertheless exert a minimum of political influence compared to that of the owners. With a few exceptions, it is the owners who serve on the city councils, the chambers of commerce, and the bank boards.

These Texas coastal communities, moreover, are in the backwaters of major sociopolitical movements and trends. Their geographical isolation has been matched by their detachment from major political events. Almost all the shrimping communities are distant from large metropolitan centers from which an impetus to unionize might be expected. Consequently, shrimpers' strikes in these Texas communities

---

[10] Alfred J. Watkins, in "From a Colony for Northern Industry to a Battleground in an Economic War," *Texas Observer*, October 3, 1980, pp. 3–9, does an especially sound job in outlining the posture of Texas businessmen toward unions.

have been few and far between. That is not to say that shrimpers have been content with their work; it is instead a comment on the ultraconservative attitude of these communities in an antiunion state.[11]

The attitudes of many shrimpers themselves reflect the antiunion sentiment of the communities and region in which they reside. These shrimpers do not see unionization as a reasonable way to solve their problems. I remember, in particular, one shrimper who said that he was all for a union but that he would never go on strike. Striking, to him, was not an alternative; he viewed it as un-American.

The negative public image that many people have of shrimpers certainly was reinforced by the strike of 1973. This negative image, when juxtaposed against the backdrop painted by the owners and the media, worked to undermine the legitimacy of the strike and the strikers' demands. The shrimpers' negative status in their own communities, when combined with their public labels as deviants, certainly hurt what little public support they could muster.

That the strike lasted only three months before shrimpers said they were forced by their finances to return to work underscores once again the precarious economics upon which shrimpers must base their lives, their families, and their life-styles. Some shrimpers, mainly captains, have found ways in which to minimize their up-and-down monthly incomes, largely because on an annual basis they make a considerable amount of money. Riggers, and especially headers, are less likely to be as adept at managing their money, and they also have less money with which to buffer themselves and their families against the winter months. The dependency of shrimpers on their fluctuating catches and the prices they receive for their shrimp means, ultimately, that they are highly vulnerable during a strike. Thus, even in a good year, their ability to sustain a prolonged strike would be problematical.

Texas shrimpers are all too aware, as evidenced in the strike of 1973, that there are many men who would willingly serve as strikebreakers. These include those who unload the shrimp at the dock, those who help to sort and grade it in the fishhouses, those who truck it to market, and those who have desk jobs with the companies. These men in normal times either are unsuitable as fishermen, are too old, do

---

[11] The impetus for these comments comes out of a series of conversations with William Kuvlesky.

not want to fish, or lack experience. But when a strike comes, as in 1973, they are called or pressured into service on behalf of their companies.

The other, more significant reservoir of potential strikebreakers is composed of undocumented Mexican workers. Increasingly these men are taking jobs as headers and riggers and, more rarely, are serving as captains. Texas shrimpers recognize the fact that, in general, Mexican shrimpers are hard workers who are willing to work for less money and are far less demanding as employees. They are less likely to complain about safety conditions on the boat, including old and dangerous equipment. When injured, they will not bring suit because they want to keep their jobs. They represent a surplus of relatively passive workers who are available at any time.[12] These four factors, among others, have minimized the attempts and the successes of shrimpers at unionization.

In contrast to these important pressures against unionization stand the shrimpers' strong feelings of commonality among other fishermen, a commonality based on an intense shared work experience. As noted earlier, the demands, risks, and dangers of the work and the workplace create a strong sense of occupational identification.[13] Furthermore, many shrimpers not only work together but also live next door to each other in shrimpers' neighborhoods, especially in some of the smaller coastal towns. Their wives look out for each other when their husbands are gone. Their kids grow up together playing on the same school teams and heading shrimp together during summer vacations. Their family ties are strong, and their identification with shrimping as an occupation, a life's work and livelihood, is equally strong.

The Future of Unions

Unionization of Texas shrimpers is closely tied to future developments within the industry as a whole. Texas shrimpers are more likely,

[12] There is a growing literature on the effects of the undocumented worker on the U.S. economy. See, for example, Shelby D. Gerking and John H. Mutti, "Costs and Benefits of Illegal Immigration: Key Issues for Government Policy," *Social Science Quarterly* 61 (June, 1980): 71–85.

[13] See, for example, Arthur B. Shostak, *Blue Collar Stress*, for a discussion of the frequency and implications of stress in the workplace.

at this point, to leave their work as fishermen—in effect, to vote with their feet—than they are to form unions. Many shrimpers I interviewed told me about friends of theirs, former shrimpers, who had found or were finding alternative employment because of a basic dissatisfaction with the recent income reductions. Shrimpers are not leaving in droves, but some definitely are seeking other work. These men have found jobs in the booming Texas economy. Even if the jobs do not pay as well as shrimping, they are more satisfying.

For some shrimpers this has meant moving their families to the larger Texas metropolitan areas and job markets. This change from a rural, small-town setting to Houston, Dallas–Fort Worth, or other urban areas has undoubtedly been a considerable adjustment for these men. Some of these former shrimpers have found work in the growing offshore oil industry, where their experience as pilots and familiarity with work at sea have qualified them for jobs. They have found jobs as worms and roughnecks, maintenance men, deckhands, and cooks and in other semiskilled jobs that provide a regular work schedule with overtime. Others have gone into new kinds of work in the cities in fields in which they could use their mechanical abilities, knowledge of electronics, or welding experience. In general, the captains have been more successful in finding work in which they can approximate their incomes as shrimpers, but the riggers, and especially headers, less so. A few have come back to shrimping because they miss the life and the life-style; some are unwilling, for example, to put up with Houston traffic.

Many shrimpers, however, will stay with the industry regardless of what happens to it. These men are more likely to be older and less educated and to have fewer transferable job skills. As long as they can support their families, they will keep fishing. They are more willing to take continued pay cuts because their job options are fewer and/or they see themselves as being totally committed to shrimping. They feel that they are too old or unskilled to change jobs at this point in their lives. One shrimper said, "I don't like what's happening, but what else can I do?"

Shrimpers who leave seeking other work are being replaced by those with less experience, fewer skills and qualifications, and less commitment to shrimping as an occupation and a life-style. There are two major components in this replacement work force: Texans who are more marginal to the labor force than the shrimpers they are replacing and undocumented Mexican workers. The first group is comprised of Anglos, blacks, and Mexican-Americans who are sometimes vaulted into positions as riggers and captains without extensive fishing experience. This is particularly true in Aransas Pass and Freeport, ports that have seen a recent rapid increase in the numbers of trawlers and nearby labor-intensive industries.

The other growing labor force that now comprises a significant segment of all Texas shrimpers, as evidenced by the survey, is the undocumented Mexican worker. Usually in his twenties, hard working, he is willing to work as a header for several years, learn the skills, and then progress up the occupational ladder to the better-paying job of rigger. He is willing to make four, five, or six thousand dollars a year for up to five or six years, before his income jumps to that of a rigger.[14] He saves his money, he is ambitious, and he is patient.

The undocumented Mexican's presence in the labor force has been most visible in South Texas. He is likely to make his home in Matamoros or Brownsville, more rarely in Cuidad, Victoria, Tampico, or the smaller towns and villages of the state of Tamaulipas, Mexico. Gradually this kind of worker will migrate, with or without his family, to ports farther away from the border as more jobs in shrimping become available. Mexico has an enormous rate of unemployment, especially among its youth, and the pressures to migrate north will continue for the foreseeable future. It is now not rare to see such men in Aransas Pass, Freeport, and even Louisiana and Florida ports. They will follow the jobs, although they would prefer to remain as close to the border, their families, and their culture as possible.

The eventual effects of these two components of the replacement labor force are detrimental to future unionization. Both segments of this new labor force are much less likely to be dissatisfied with their incomes, working conditions, or treatment by the owners.

[14] See Ellwyn R. Stoddard, *Patterns of Poverty along the U.S.–Mexican Border*, for a complete discussion of why undocumented workers are willing to work for far less than their American counterparts.

Concluding Remarks

"It's an unpredicting [*sic*] life. . . ."

The men who fish for shrimp play a crucial role in the Texas shrimping industry. The overcapitalized trawlers; the huge dockside freezers, fuel depots, and repair shops; the owners, wholesalers, or brokers—none of these are as central to the industry as the men who actually harvest the shrimp. Perhaps the industry's best-kept secret is the capability of its work force.

Shrimpers themselves are the ones who take the personal risks at sea, spend large amounts of time away from their friends and family, and then return sometimes to find an ambivalent acceptance from their communities. Conceptions of deviance regarding shrimpers, and the labeling and stereotypes that perpetuate them, have arisen out of the interplay between the particular historical and social setting of each community and the subjectively perceived superficial characteristics of fishing as an occupation and life-style. Beliefs about shrimpers, sometimes held and reified by the fishermen themselves, are exacerbated by shrimpers' political powerlessness. At the center of this powerlessness is an occupation that, in addition to its harsh demands, creates a severe short-term financial insecurity for the fishermen and their families. Each season shrimpers know they will financially survive, but they rarely know whether they can meet today's bills.

Shrimpers return to the dock with boxes of shrimp it took them twenty days and nights or longer to catch. They watch as the shrimp are unloaded into the fishhouse, sorted, and graded. They get the poundage weight of each count, then wait around for their pay advances or checks. I have seen their exhausted faces turn from anger to frustration to resignation as they look at their paychecks. They talk about what they used to earn in better years.

In fact, shrimping for many men of limited education and job skills has been, since the late 1940s, a gateway to upward mobility. By hard work and a willingness to risk more than inconvenience, men with sixth-grade educations have earned up to forty thousand dollars or more a year. Some have bought expensive houses, furnished them, raised families, and sent their sons and daughters to college.

It has not been an easy life, but those shrimpers who stuck to it seem grateful, in a sense, that they have had the opportunity to make a decent living. A few have become millionaires for all their hard work, diversifying their investments and becoming leaders in their communities and powerful local political forces. Others have passed through the industry on their way to some better job or, in some cases, to something worse: alcoholism remains an occupational hazard.

I have talked, too, with owners who are feeling, or beginning to feel, the big squeeze on their own businesses. Those who follow current trends can see the writing on the wall; while they might not have been hurt in 1978, 1979, or even 1980, the probability of sustaining real losses in future years has become a reality. Others feel that they are still getting by, regarding the last few years as reflective of a temporary downturn in the industry. They are misleading themselves.

Few would disagree that the industry is going through hard times. The real question, however, is the extent to which these hard times are inextricably tied to financial practices within the industry itself and to trends outside the industry, to world economic forces. Fuel prices have gone up, as have operating costs. Imports, too, play an important role. Finally, inflation has certainly influenced the industry, not least in its effects on consumer demand for shrimp. All these variables would have far less influence on the shrimping industry, however, if the dockside price and the wholesale price were more elastic, more reflective of real-money costs to both the shrimper and the owner-wholesaler. Monopolistic practices in the shrimping industry retard elasticity of price at these two important levels; costs are disproportionately distributed. The shrimper to date has borne the burden through a reduction in percentage of wages. As the conditions grow worse, it is now the owner's turn.

The recent hard times have radically decreased the possibilities of rapid economic mobility for those willing to make the sacrifices that are required in this capitalistic system, and both owners and fishermen have become relatively fixed in their economic niches. What will the outcome of these developments be? Assuming present trends, the first possible outcome is a rearrangement of work relationships on shrimp boats within the next ten years. The income differential between captain, rigger, and header is considerable, but, because of the nature and demands of the work, differences in status traditionally have been far less rigid than one might expect. Many tasks are shared, and, depending on the preferences and personality of the captain, there is a definite camaraderie among a crew working together to net the shrimp. Such work arrangements could change, however. The captain could become much more of a foreman, a supervisor, the man in the middle between management, the owner, and labor, the crew. In this new role, the jobs of rigger and header would become less distinct. Riggers and headers would become general deckhands, paid a piece rate for their work, while the captain continued to earn a percentage of the catch.

There are several factors pressuring shrimping and shrimpers in this direction. There are an increasing number of boats captained by able and experienced Anglos and Mexican-Americans with Mexican riggers and headers. On these boats the role of captain is already much more like that of job foreman than like that of the traditional Texas shrimp captain. This is especially true on boats with Anglo captains and a Mexican crew that speaks little or no English. In this situation, language and cultural differences accentuate the distinctions in roles. Anglo and Mexican-American captains appear to become more authoritarian, in a sense, to fulfill both their own and their crews' role expectations: from the American captain's point of view, the Mexican shrimpers want and need more supervision; on the Mexican fishermen's side, stronger status differences in their work on shrimp boats seem to be welcome.

The second possible outcome is the elimination of headers. Several boats on which I interviewed were crewed only by a captain and a rigger. In each of these cases the captain and rigger had worked together for some time and felt that hiring a header was a luxury they could do without. These shrimpers said they could not only handle the work but also that, since they did not have a header on board, they made more money. They pointed out that it made sense to have a header if you were catching five or more boxes a night, as in the old days, but that since a normal night's work in recent years had been more in the range of two or three boxes, a header simply was not that necessary.

These fishermen explained that experienced headers were harder and harder to find and that when you did get a good one he often worked for only a few trips before changing boats. They thought that headers were troublesome and not worth the money they sometimes demanded, up to twenty dollars or more a box in 1980. In each of these headerless boats the captain and rigger seemed perfectly satisfied with their working arrangement.

Working without a header means that the captain and rigger must work that much better together. This in turn means that they must get along well with each other when at sea, for the stresses put on the two men are of far greater intensity than with three. (The captain, for example, has less time to spend in the warm pilothouse because he must spend more time on the rear deck helping the rigger work the nets and head shrimp.) The men who have developed this work relationship split the boat's share 50-50 instead of the traditional 55-45 or 60-40. They are more likely to be very experienced fishermen: in three out of four cases the rigger had worked for some years as a captain on his own boat.

This kind of headerless shrimping does not preclude unionization; in fact, it makes it a more likely outcome. First, men who worked on headerless boats would be more likely to support the values inherent in creating and sustaining a union for shrimpers. Second, a sense of professionalism, of skills learned and mastered over years of experience, would increase with headerless boats. Finally, the captain, because he is less foremanlike, is apt to perceive himself more as a shrimper than as a representative of the company who is looking out for their and his best interests. Headerless boats, however, do raise the question of how men will learn to become captains and riggers without the apprentice role of headers.

Shrimpers soon may be adversely affected by the impact of shrimp mariculture. Efforts to cultivate shrimp commercially appear to be making major advances. Although the future of domestic shrimp mariculture remains problematic (seasonality is a major impediment), the effect of foreign production could be disastrous: conceivably, it could force shrimpers out of their jobs. This is neither to prophesy doom for shrimpers nor to discourage the efforts of the scientists engaged in this current research; rather, it is to signal an alarm that developing technologies may make the shrimper obsolete. It is possible that both efforts could coexist, but it is unrealistic, if not naive, to believe that shrimpers would be able to keep their jobs when tasty large shrimp could be raised on "farms" much the same as those for commercial trout and catfish. Surely the elimination of shrimping as we know it is probable, given a critical appraisal of technological innovation and its effects on American labor. Thus, at the very least, it would seem appropriate, at the same time that research efforts are involved in the development of technologies which may eventually replace shrimpers, to make an effort to explore alternative job possibilities for shrimpers, programs to assist in job transition, and other ways in which shrimpers could be helped.

The federal government, as evidenced by its seeming lack of concern in negotiating with Mexico on behalf of U.S. fishermen, seems to set a low priority on the shrimping industry. Although in dollar value shrimping is the major U.S. fishery, the government seems minimally interested in its day-to-day problems or its future. Mexican oil is, as discussed earlier, certainly more important than the shrimping industry, but the government's lack of interest seems to extend not only to the shrimp fishery but to the American fishing industry as well.

Should shrimp boat owners receive fuel subsidies from the federal government, they will have a lot of explaining to do to shrimpers. As mentioned earlier, a majority of shrimpers explain their recent percentage reduction as a direct result of increased fuel prices, an argument reinforced by many owners. If federal fuel subsidies become a reality, then shrimpers, naturally enough, will expect to see the results in terms of higher paychecks. This is unlikely to happen, however, since increased fuel prices, as discussed, are but one reason for reduced percentage shares.

Should the price of oil become even tighter, it is quite possible that the federal government could drive the shrimping industry out of business, given present trends. Shrimp trawlers consume large amounts of fuel—in excess of ten thousand gallons or more for a two-week trip—but produce only three or four thousand pounds of shrimp. Some in the government will most likely argue that the industry cannot be justified in terms of its mass fuel consumption and minimal poundage of landings. What this kind of argument neglects, though, is both the dollar value of the production and the multiplier effect of the industry on local economics.

A tariff on imports would affect the industry in a number of ways. In addition to causing profound economic and social changes in Mexico, it would result in a greater number of illegals, some of whom would seek work as shrimpers. Unionization in such a case would be retarded.

Research into alternative fisheries has intensified in the last several years. Again, however, the needs of shrimpers have been relatively ignored. In one prominent example, some owners have, at considerable expense, outfitted their boats for long-lining. This involves installing a very large reellike contraption on the rear of the work deck. The line that is wrapped around this spool is fed out over the stern. Regularly spaced along the line are large baited hooks. A series of floats with attached poles, topped by bright flags, marks the line and keeps it in place.

Shrimpers with long-lining rigs fish predominantly for swordfish. Results have been mixed. Several owners with whom I talked who had invested in the required rigging said they had, in the first season, made a good profit on their investment. Several others claimed that they had lost a considerable amount of money in the deal. The consensus among owners seems to be that for those willing to make the investment, long-lining can be a viable but small fishery, an alternative when shrimping is bad. The owners say that they are still learning about the techniques and that the lack of consistent market channels is one of the major problems.

Shrimpers seem also to have mixed feelings about long-lining and its future. Of the men I interviewed, a few who had gone long-lining enjoyed the work and saw it as a nice change from the routine of shrimping. Others felt it was much more exhausting work than shrimping. Several captains were very conservative in their reactions toward long-lining, saying that they were shrimpers, not long-liners, and that they would stick to shrimping.

Besides an unwillingness to change from shrimping to something new, the major impediment to long-lining from the shrimper's view is that he can go out on two-week trip, come back after working hard, and actually lose money. This is because many owners are requiring that the fishermen themselves pay a majority of the costs for a trip, including fuel, ice, groceries, and gear. When the crew does run into good fishing, they can make more money than they do shrimping. But they also may lose up to five hundred dollars or more per man, say the shrimpers, for two weeks' work.

In some respects the shrimping industry is little different from other American industries in its often dubious economic arrangements, its worker-management disputes, and its attitudes toward issues like unionization or safety in the workplace. This is said not by way of apology but rather to emphasize that the shrimping industry is, in fact, a prototypical American industry, even though it would seem a distant cousin. We are all, as workers, increasingly finding ourselves on the rear deck of a shrimp trawler, adrift in the same economic waters, with no easy solutions in sight. Governmental and technological solutions are most often sought as short-term solutions, but what is good for the owners is not necessarily good for the crews; certainly that was the lesson learned by Texas shrimpers after the Tax Reform Act of 1976.

One must conclude that the shrimping industry should be scrutinized as closely as any other. The policies formulated by the industry's own public-relations experts, research institutes, and legislative lobbies must be carefully examined. The overriding consideration must be whether the impact of proposed aid indeed benefits the work force, the fishermen themselves. The data and issues that have been presented in these pages are intended to be a first step toward both an understanding of these men who fish for a tiny crustacean deep in the Gulf waters and an assessment of the socioeconomic and political variables that directly influence both their work and their daily lives.

Bibliography

Abrahams, Roger D. *Deep the Water, Shallow the Shore*. Austin: University of Texas Press, 1974.

Acheson, James M. "Anthropology of Fishing." *Annual Review of Anthropology* 10 (1981): 275–316.

Agee, James, and Walker Evans. *Let Us Now Praise Famous Men*. Boston: Houghton Mifflin Co., 1960.

Akers, Ronald L., et al. "Social Learning and Deviant Behavior." *American Sociological Review* 44 (1979): 635–655.

Alvarez, Humberto Romero. *Health without Boundaries*. Mexico City: United States–Mexico Border Public Health Association, 1975.

Alvarez, José; Chris O. Andrew; and Fred J. Prochaska. *Economic Structure of the Florida Shrimp Processing Industry*. State University System of Florida Sea Grant Program Report No. 9. Gainesville: Food and Resource Economics Department, Institute of Food and Agricultural Sciences, University of Florida, 1977.

Aransas Pass Chamber of Commerce. *Aransas Pass, Texas*. Aransas Pass: Biography Press, 1976.

Arbingast, Stanley A., ed. *Atlas of Texas*. Austin: Bureau of Business Research, University of Texas, 1976.

Ballard, Chet. "The Control of Small Community Growth/Nongrowth." Paper presented at the annual meeting of the Association for Humanist Sociology, Louisville, Ky., October 14, 1980.

Bernard, H. Russell, and Peter D. Killworth. "Scientists and Mariners at Sea." *Marine Technology Society Journal* 10 (April, 1976): 21–30.

Bloom, John. "A Delicate Balance." *Texas Monthly*, October, 1979, pp. 124, 256–258.

Blumberg, Leonard V.; Thomas F. Shipley, Jr.; and Stephen F. Barsky. *Liquor and Poverty*. New Brunswick, N.J.: Rutgers Center of Alcohol Studies, 1978.

Bok, Sissela. *Lying*. New York: Vintage Books, 1974.

Bottom, Jim. "Research Increases Profits for Shrimp Industry." *Sea Grant Today* 10 (November–December, 1980): 304.

Bryant, Clifton D., and Donald J. Shoemaker. "Briney Crime: An Overview of Marine and Maritime Law and Deviance." Paper presented at the annual meeting of the Southern Sociological Society, Washington, D.C., April 9, 1975.

Cahalan, Don; Ira H. Cisin; and Helen M. Crossley. *American Drinking Practices*. New Brunswick, N.J.: Rutgers Center of Alcohol Studies, 1969.

———, and Robin Room. *Problem Drinking among American Men*. New Brunswick, N.J.: Rutgers Center of Alcohol Studies, 1969.

Caillouet, Charles W., and Dennis B. Koi. "Trends in Ex-vessel Value and Size Composition of Annual Landings of Brown, Pink and White Shrimp from the Gulf and South Atlantic Coasts of the United States." *Marine Fisheries Review*, December, 1980, pp. 18–27.

———; ———; and William B. Jackson. "Relationship between Ex-vessel Value and Size Composition of Annual Landings of Shrimp from the Gulf and South Atlantic Coasts." *Marine Fisheries Review*, December, 1980, pp. 29–33.

Campbell, Angus; Philip E. Converse; and Willard L. Rodgers. *The Quality of American Life: Perceptions, Evaluations, and Satisfactions*. New York: Russell Sage Foundation, 1976.

Christensen, James B. "Motor Power and Woman Power: Technological and Economic Change among the Fanti Fishermen of Ghana." In *Those Who Live from the Sea*, ed. M. Estellie Smith, pp. 71–95. St. Paul: American Ethnological Society and West Publishing Co., 1977.

Cox, Bruce A. "The Economic Impact of Commercial Fisheries on Cameron County." Unpublished paper, 1977.

———. Statement before the U.S. International Trade Commission, Brownsville, January 27, 1976.

Crompton, John L.; Dennis D. Beardsley; and Robert B. Ditton. *Marinas on the Texas Gulf Coast*. College Station: Texas Agricultural Experiment Station, 1976.

Danowksi, Fran. *Fishermen's Wives: Coping with an Extraordinary Occupation*. University of Rhode Island Marine Bulletin No. 37. Narragansett: University of Rhode Island Marine Advisory Service, 1980.

Davidson, Chandler. "The Culture of Poverty, the Culture of Wealth, and the Culture of Shiftlessness: Notes on the Distribution of Laziness among Social Classes." Paper presented at the meeting of the Southwestern Social Science Association, Dallas, Tex., April 8, 1976.

Denzin, Norman K. "Notes on the Criminogenic Hypothesis: A Case Study of the American Liquor Industry." *American Sociological Review* 42 (1977): 905-920.

———. *The Research Act*. Chicago: Aldine Publishing Co., 1970.

Ditton, Robert B.; Richard M. Jarman; and Steve A. Woods. "An Analysis of the Charter Boat Fishing Industry on the Texas Gulf Coast." *Marine Fisheries Review*, August, 1978, pp. 1–7.

———; Thomas J. Mertens; and Martin P. Schwartz. "Characteristics, Participation, and Motivations of Texas Charter Boat Fishermen." *Marine Fisheries Review*, April, 1978, pp. 8–13.

"Economist Advises Fishermen about Alternative Fishing." *Texas Trawler* 7 (1980): 3.

Eisley, Loren. *The Excavation of a Life*. New York: Charles Scribner's Sons, 1975.

Fehrenbach, T. R. *Fire and Blood*. New York: Macmillan Publishing Co., 1973.

Ferguson, Henry N. *The Port of Brownsville*. Brownsville: Springman King Press, 1976.

Flippin, Louise. *The Indochinese Situation: America's Newest Wave of Immigrants*. Mimeographed. Austin: Center for Asian Studies, University of Texas at Austin, 1979.

Frost, Susan, ed. *Texas Coastal Legislation*. 5th ed. Austin: Texas Coastal and Marine Council, 1982.

Gerking, Shelby D., and John H. Mutti. "Costs and Benefits of Illegal Immigration: Key Issues for Government Policy." *Social Science Quarterly* 61 (June, 1980): 71–85.

Gersuny, Carl, and John J. Poggie, Jr. "A Fisherman's Co-operative: Open System Theory Applied." *Maritime Studies in Management* 1 (1974): 215–222.

———, and ———. "Luddites and Fishermen: A Note on Response to Technological Change." *Maritime Studies in Management* 2 (1974): 38–47.

———, and ———. "The Uncertain Future of Fishing Families." *Family Coordinator*, April, 1973, pp. 241–244.

Gillespie, William C.; James C. Hite; and John S. Lytle. *An Econometric Analysis of the U.S. Shrimp Industry*. Economics of Marine Resources No. 2. Clemson: Department of Agricultural Economics and Rural Sociology, South Carolina Agricultural Experiment Station, Clemson University, 1969.

Gladwin, Hugh. "Decision-Making in the Cape Coast Fishing and Marketing System." Ph.D. dissertation, Stanford University, 1970.

Gouldner, Alvin W. *The Dialectic of Ideology and Technology*. New York: Seabury Press, 1976.

Graham, Gary, and Jim Buckner. *Hangs and Bottom Obstructions of the Texas/Louisiana Gulf: Loran-C*. College Station: Marine Information Service, Sea Grant College Program, Texas A&M University, 1980.

Grebler, Leo; Joan W. Moore; and Ralph C. Guzman. *The Mexican-American People*. New York: Free Press, 1970.

Griffin, Wade L. "Economic and Financial Analysis of Increasing Costs in the Gulf Shrimp Fleet." *Fishery Bulletin* 74 (1976): 301–309.

———. "Economics of Production and Marketing in the Commercial Fish Industry." In *Sea Grant College Proposal 1979–81*, vol. 2, pp. 65–76. College Station: Sea Grant College Program, Texas A&M University, 1979.

———. *Effect of Extended Jurisdiction on Landings and Value of Landings for the Five Gulf States*. Department Information Report 77-1, SP-9. College Station: Texas Agricultural Experiment Station, 1977.

———. *Time Trends in the Harvesting Section of the Gulf of Mexico Shrimp*

Industry. Department Information Report No. 77-1, SP-2. College Station: Texas Agricultural Experiment Station, 1977.

———, and Bruce Beattie. "Economic Impact of Mexico's 200-Mile Offshore Fishing Zone on the United States Gulf of Mexico Shrimp Fishery." *Land Economics* 54 (February, 1978): 27–38.

———; Melvin L. Cross; and George W. Ryan. *Seasonal Movement Patterns in the Gulf of Mexico Shrimp Fishery*. Department Technical Report No. 74-4. College Station: Texas Agricultural Experiment Station, 1974.

———; Ronald D. Lacewell; and John P. Nichols. "Optimum Effort and Rent Distribution in the Gulf of Mexico Shrimp Fishery." *American Journal of Agricultural Economics* 58 (November, 1976): 644–652.

Gulf King Shrimp Co. v. Wirtz, 407 F.2d 508 (5th Cir. 1969).

Gulf of Mexico Fishery Management Council. *Draft Environmental Impact Statement and Fishery Management Plan for the Shrimp Fishery of the Gulf of Mexico, United States Waters*. Baton Rouge: Center for Wetland Resources, Louisiana State University, 1979.

Hart, Kathy. "Of Nets, Towlines, and Tickle Chains." *Coast Watch*, September, 1981, pp. 1–7.

Hills, Stuart L. *Demystifying Social Deviance*. New York: McGraw-Hill Book Co., 1980.

Hinds, Dan H. *Maritime Liens and the Law: Creation and Enforcement*. Sea Grant Publication No. SG-79-501. College Station: Sea Grant College Program, Texas A&M University, 1978.

Hoese, H. Dickson, and Richard H. Moore. *Fishes of the Gulf of Mexico: Texas, Louisiana, and Adjacent Waters*. College Station: Texas A&M University Press, 1977.

Hollin, Dewayne. "Fishing Vessel Safety Tips." Mimeographed. College Station: Sea Grant College Program, Texas A&M University, 1979.

———, and Malon Scogin, eds. *Directory of Texas Shipyards*. Sea Grant Publication No. SG-80-507. College Station: Sea Grant College Program, Texas A&M University, 1981.

Hudgins, Shirley, ed. *A Reporter's Directory to Sea Grant Marine Research*. University of Southern California Sea Grant Program AS1-81. Los Angeles: Sea Grant Program Institute for Marine and Coastal Studies, University of Southern California, 1981.

Jedlicka, Davor, and Muncho Kim. "Population Redistribution and Socioeconomic Development along the South Atlantic Coast." Paper presented at the annual meeting of the Southern Regional Demographic Group, Myrtle Beach, S.C., 1979.

———, and Ray-May Hsun. "Coastal Farming and Fishing." Paper presented at the Fifth World Congress for Rural Sociologists, Mexico City, August 7, 1980.

Jessor, R.; T. D. Graves; and S. L. Jessor. *Society, Personality, and Deviant Behavior: A Study of a Tri-ethnic Community*. New York: Holt, Rinehart, and Winston, 1968.

Johnson, L. V., and M. Maitre. "Anomie and Alcohol Use: Drinking Patterns in Mexican-American and Anglo Neighborhoods." *Journal of Studies on Alcohol* 39 (1978): 894–902.

Johnson, Ronald N., and Gary D. Libecap. "Regulatory Arrangements and Fishing Rights in the Texas Bay Shrimp Fishery." Unpublished paper.

Jones, Lamar B., and G. Randolph Rice. "Agricultural Labor in the Southwest: The Post Bracero Years." *Social Science Quarterly* 61 (June, 1980): 86–94.

Jones, Lonnie L., et al. *Impact of Commercial Shrimp Landings on the Economy of Texas and Coastal Regions.* Sea Grant Publication No. SG-74-204. College Station: Sea Grant College Program, Texas A&M University, 1978.

Jones, T. M.; J. W. Hubbard; and K. J. Roberts. "Productivity and Profitability of South Carolina Shrimp Vessels, 1971–75." *Marine Fisheries Review*, April, 1979; pp. 8–14.

King, Lauriston R. "The Coastal Upwelling Ecosystems Analysis Program as an Experience in International Cooperation." *Ocean Development and International Law Journal*, Nos. 3–4: 269–288.

Knowlton, Clark S. "Causes of Poverty in San Miguel County, New Mexico." Paper presented at the annual meeting of the Rural Sociological Society, San Francisco, Calif., 1978.

Laurent, Eugene A. "Description of Industry: Economics." In *The Shrimp Fishery of the Southeastern United States: A Management Planning Profile,* Technical Report No. 5, ed. D. R. Calder, pp. 70–85. Charleston: South Carolina Marine Resources Center, 1974.

Lawrence, Addison L.; George W. Chamberlain; and David L. Hutchins. *Shrimp Mariculture.* Sea Grant Publication No. SG-82-503. College Station: Sea Grant College Program, Texas A&M University, 1981.

Layne, Norman R., and George D. Lowe. "The Impact of Loss of Career Continuity on the Later Occupational Adjustment of Problem Drinkers." *Journal of Health and Social Behavior* 20 (1979): 187–193.

Leap, William L. "Maritime Subsistence in Anthropological Perspective: A Statement of Priorities." In *Those Who Live from the Sea,* ed. M. Estellie Smith, pp. 251–263. St. Paul: American Ethnological Society and West Publishing Co., 1977.

Lee, Alfred McClung. *Toward Humanist Sociology.* Englewood Cliffs, N. J.: Prentice-Hall, 1973.

Living Marine Resources, Inc. *Spring Market Report.* San Diego: Living Marine Resources, Inc., 1980.

"Loran-C Completes Transition January 1." *Texas Trawler* 7 (1980): 1.

Lyndon B. Johnson School of Public Affairs, University of Texas at Austin. *Texas Coastal Zone Issues.* Policy Research Project No. 39. Austin: Lyndon B. Johnson School of Public Affairs, University of Texas at Austin, 1980.

Lyons, Gene. "The Newest Americans." *Texas Monthly*, June, 1976, pp. 96–101, 141–146.

McGoodwin, James R. "The Decline of Mexico's Pacific Inshore Fisheries."
    Oceanus 22 (1979): 52–59.

———. "The Human Costs of Development." *Environment* 22 (1980):
    pp. 25–42.

Madsen, W. "The Alcoholic Agringado." *American Anthropologist* 66 (1964):
    355–361.

Maril, Robert Lee. "Continuity and Change in a Texas Fishing Community."
    Paper presented at the annual meeting of the American Anthropological
    Association, Washington, D.C., December 7, 1982.

———. "Shrimping in South Texas: Social and Economic Marginality Fishing
    for a Luxury Commodity." Paper presented at the annual meeting of the
    Association for Humanist Sociology, Johnstown, Pa., 1979.

———, and Anthony N. Zavaleta. "Drinking Patterns of Low-Income Mex-
    ican-American Women." *Journal of Studies on Alcohol* 40 (1979):
    480–484.

Miller, Marcos, and John Van Maenen. "Situational and Cultural Uncertainties
    Surrounding Government Regulation of a New England Community." Pa-
    per presented at the annual meeting of the Society for Applied Anthropol-
    ogy, Mérida, Yucatán, Mexico, 1978.

Miller, Michael V. *Economic Growth and Change along the U.S.–Mexico
    Border: The Case of Brownsville, Texas.* Austin: Bureau of Business Re-
    search, University of Texas at Austin, 1982.

———. "Industrial Development and an Expanding Labor Force in Browns-
    ville." *Texas Business Review* 55 (November–December, 1981): 258–261.

———. Personal correspondence, August 15, 1981.

———, and Robert Lee Maril. *Poverty in the Lower Rio Grande Valley of
    Texas: Historical and Contemporary Dimensions.* Technical Report No.
    78-2. College Station: Texas Agricultural Experiment Station, 1978.

———, and William P. Kuvlesky. "The Farm Labor Movement in South Texas:
    Historical Development, Current Status, and Implications for Change."
    Unpublished paper, 1975.

Montero, Darrel. *Vietnamese Americans: Patterns of Resettlement and Socio-
    economic Adaptation in the United States.* Boulder, Colo.: Westview
    Press, 1979.

Mullen, Patrick B. "The Function of Magic Folk Belief among Texas Coastal
    Fishermen." *Journal of American Folklore*, 1969, pp. 214–225.

———. *I Heard the Old Fishermen Say: Folklore of the Texas Gulf Coast.*
    Austin: University of Texas Press, 1978.

National Fisheries Institute. *Year-End Report.* Washington, D.C.: National
    Fisheries Institute, 1980.

Nichols, John P. Correspondence to Ed Wolfe, National Shrimp Congress,
    June 11, 1980.

———, et al. *Marketing Alternatives for Fishermen.* Sea Grant Publication
    No. SG-1-80-204. College Station: Sea Grant College Program, Texas
    A&M University, 1980.

————, and Larry Johnston. *The Influence of Alternative Pricing Methods on Ex-vessel Shrimp Prices.* Department Information Report 77-1, SP-7. College Station: Texas Agricultural Experiment Station, 1979.

————; Wade L. Griffin; and Vito Blomo. "Economic and Production Aspects of the Gulf of Mexico Shrimp Fishery." In *Drugs and Food from the Sea,* P. K. Kaul and C. J. Sindermann, pp. 83–101. Norman: University of Oklahoma Press, 1978.

Nix, Harold L., and Muncho Kim. *A Sociological Analysis of Georgia Commercial Shrimp Fishermen, 1976–77.* Athens, Ga.: Institute of Community and Area Development, 1982.

Orbach, Michael K. *Hunters, Seamen, and Entrepreneurs: The Tuna Seinermen of San Diego.* Berkeley: University of California Press, 1977.

————. "Making Extraordinary Decisions in Ordinary Ways: Decision-Making as a Natural Process." Unpublished paper, 1978.

Orth, Frank, et al. "Minority Participation in the Fisheries of the Gulf and South Atlantic." Report prepared for the Gulf and South Atlantic Fisheries Development Foundation, Tampa, Fla., 1981.

Paine, H. J. "Attitudes and Patterns of Alcohol Use among Mexican Americans: Implications for Service Delivery." *Journal of Studies on Alcohol* 38 (1977): 544–553.

Paredes, J. Anthony; James C. Sabella; and Marcus J. Hepburn. "Human Factors in the Economic Development of a Northwestern Florida Gulf Coast Fishing Community." Unpublished paper, 1977.

Penn, Erwin S. *Price Spreads of Fish Products among Producers and Distributors.* Marine Fisheries Review Paper 987. Washington, D.C.: Technical Information Division, Environmental Science Information Center, National Oceanic and Atmospheric Administration, 1976.

Perez, Lisandro. *Working Offshore.* Sea Grant Publication No. LSU-T-79-001. Baton Rouge: Center for Wetland Resources, Louisiana State University, 1979.

Pesson, L. L. *The Coastal Fishermen of Louisiana: Their Characteristics, Attitudes, Practices, and Responsiveness to Change.* Baton Rouge: Cooperative Extension Service, Center for Agricultural Sciences and Rural Development, Louisiana State University, 1974.

Peterson, Susan, and Leah Smith. *New England Fishing, Processing, and Distribution.* Woods Hole Oceanographic Institute Technical Report WH 01-79-52. Woods Hole, Mass.: Woods Hole Oceanographic Institute, 1979.

Poggie, John J., Jr. "Ritual Adaptation to Risk and Development in Ocean Fisheries: A New England Case." Paper presented at the annual meeting of the Society for Applied Anthropology, Mérida, Yucatán, Mexico, April 6, 1978.

————. "Small-scale Fishermen's Beliefs about Success and Development: A Puerto Rican Case." Paper presented at the annual meeting of the Society for Applied Anthropology, San Diego, Calif., April 7, 1977.

————, and Richard Pollnac, eds. *Small Fishing Ports in Southern New England*. Marine Bulletin No. 39. Narragansett: University of Rhode Island, 1981.

Pollnac, R. B. *Continuity and Change in Marine Fishing Communities*. Mimeographed. Kingston: International Center for Marine Resource Development, University of Rhode Island, 1976.

————. "Income Periodicity and Economic Gratification Orientation among Small-Scale Fishermen in the Gulf of Nicoya, Costa Rica." Unpublished paper, 1977.

————. "Sociocultural Aspects of Technological and Institutional Change among Small-Scale Fishermen." Paper presented at the International Symposium on Modernization in Fishing Industries and Communities, Greenville, N.C., April 28, 1978.

————. "Technological Change and Social Organization among Small-Scale Fishermen." Paper presented at the Seminar/Workshop in Investigation and Development of Marine Resources in the Eighth Region of Chile, Concepción, Chile, January, 1978.

————, and Roberto Ruiz-Stout. "Gratification Orientations among Small-Scale Fishermen in the Republic of Panama." Unpublished paper, 1976.

Prochaska, Fred J., and James C. Cato. *An Economic Profile of Florida Commercial Fishing Firms: Fishermen, Commercial Activities, and Financial Considerations*. State University System of Florida Sea Grant Program Report No. 19. Gainesville: Food and Resource Economics Department, Institute of Food and Agricultural Sciences, University of Florida, 1977.

Rawick, George P. *The American Slave*. Westport, Conn.: Greenwood Publishing Co., 1972.

Roberts, K. J., and M. E. Sass. *Commercial Fishing Industry Licenses in Louisiana in 1978*. Sea Grant Publication No. LSU-TL-79-002. Baton Rouge: Center for Wetland Resources, Louisiana State University, 1979.

————, and ————. *Financial Aspects of Louisiana Shrimp Vessels*. Sea Grant Publication No. LSU-TL-79-007. Baton Rouge: Center for Wetland Resources, Louisiana State University, 1979.

Rogg, Eleanor Meyer, and Rosemary Santana Cooney. *Adaptation and Adjustment of Cubans: West New York, New Jersey*. Bronx, N.Y.: Hispanic Research Center, Fordham University, 1980.

Rootes, Rebecca. "Who Has the Rights to the Redfish?" Unpublished paper, 1981.

Ross, Stanley R., ed. *Views Across the Border: The United States and Mexico*. Albuquerque: University of New Mexico Press, 1978.

Rubel, Arthur J. *Across the Tracks: Mexican Americans in a Texas City*. Austin: University of Texas Press, 1966.

Sass, M. E., and K. J. Roberts. *Characteristics of the Louisiana Shrimp Fleet, 1978*. Sea Grant Publication No. LSU-TL-79-006. Baton Rouge: Center for Wetland Resources, Louisiana State University, 1979.

Sea Grant Publications, 1969–75. Sea Grant Publication No. SG-76-604. College Station: Sea Grant College Program, Texas A&M University, 1976.

Shostak, Arthur B. *Blue Collar Stress.* Reading, Pa.: Addison-Wesley Publishing Co., 1980.

Skupien, Linda. "Fuel Studies to Aid Shrimpers." *Sea Grant Today* 12 (March–April, 1982): 16.

Smith, M. Estellie. "The 'Public Face' of the New England Regional Fishery Council: Year 1." Unpublished manuscript, 1978.

————. "Sociocultural Continuity: The Role of Tourism." Unpublished paper, 1980.

————, ed. *Those Who Live from the Sea.* St. Paul: American Ethnological Society and West Publishing Co., 1977.

Southern Exposure 10 (May–June, 1982).

Starr, Paul D. "Lebanese Fishermen and the Dilemma of Modernization." In *Those Who Live from the Sea,* ed. M. Estellie Smith, pp. 57–70. St. Paul: American Ethnological Society and West Publishing Co., 1977.

————. "Troubled Waters: Vietnamese Fisherfolk on America's Gulf Coast." *International Migration Review* 15 (1981): 226–238.

Stein, Barry N. "Occupational Adjustment of Refugees: The Vietnamese in the United States." *International Migration Review* 13 (1979): 25–45.

Stickney, Robert R., and James T. Davis, eds., *Aquaculture in Texas: A Status Report and Development Plan.* Sea Grant Publication No. SG-81-119. College Station: Sea Grant College Program, Texas A&M University, 1981.

Stoddard, Ellwyn R. *Patterns of Poverty along the U.S.–Mexico Border.* El Paso: Center for Inter-American Studies, University of Texas at El Paso, 1978.

Stuster, J. "Where 'Mabel' May Mean 'Sea Bass.'" *Natural History* 87 (November, 1979): 76–89.

Tarter, Ralph E., and Dorothea U. Schneider. "Models and Theories of Alcoholism." In *Alcoholism: Interdisciplinary Approaches to an Enduring Problem,* ed. Ralph E. Tarter and Arthur A. Sugerman, pp. 6–30. Reading, Pa.: Addison-Wesley Publishing Co., 1976.

Teller, C. H., et al., eds. *Cuantos Somos: A Demographic Study of the Mexican-American Population.* Austin: University of Texas Press, 1977.

Trotter, R. T., II, and J. A. Chavira. *El Uso de Alcohol: A Resource Book for Spanish-Speaking Communities.* Atlanta: Southern Area Alcohol Education and Training Program, Inc., 1977.

U.S. Bureau of the Census. *County and City Data Book, 1977.* Washington, D.C.: Government Printing Office, 1978.

————. *Statistical Abstracts of the United States, 1980.* Washington, D.C.: Government Printing Office, 1980.

U.S. Department of Commerce, Data Management and Statistics Division. *Fisheries of the United States, 1980.* Washington, D.C.: Government Printing Office, 1981.

————, National Oceanic and Atmospheric Administration, National Marine Fisheries Service. *United States Fisheries Systems and Social Science: A Bibliography of Work and Directory of Researchers*. Washington, D.C.: Government Printing Office, 1979.

U.S. Department of the Treasury, Internal Revenue Service. *Tax Guide for Commercial Fishermen*. Internal Revenue Service Publication No. 595. Washington D.C.: Government Printing Office, 1981.

Wadel, Cato. *Now Whose Fault Is That?* Toronto: University of Toronto Press, 1978.

Warren, John P., and Wade L. Griffin. *Costs and Returns Trends for Gulf of Mexico Shrimp Vessels*. Department Information Report 78-1, SP-4. College Station: Texas Agricultural Experiment Station, Texas A&M University, 1978.

Watkins, Alfred J. "From a Colony for Northern Industry to a Battleground in an Economic War." *Texas Observer*, October 3, 1980, pp. 3–9.

Weedman, Parmula K., comp. *Sea Grant Publications Index 1974. 2 vols*. National Sea Grant Depository Publication Nos. 1-74-002 and 1-74-003. Narragansett: National Sea Grant Depository, University of Rhode Island, 1975.

————, ed. *Sea Grant Publications Index 1975. 2 vols*. National Sea Grant Depository Publication Nos. 1-75-001 and 1-75-002. Narragansett: National Sea Grant Depository, University of Rhode Island, 1975.

————, ed. *Sea Grant Publications Index 1976. 2 vols*. National Sea Grant Depository Publication Nos. 1-76-001 and 1-76-002. Narragansett: National Sea Grant Depository, University of Rhode Island, 1977.

Weisbrod, Burton A., ed. *The Economics of Poverty*. Englewood Cliffs, N. J.: Prentice-Hall, 1965.

White, David R. M. "Environment, Technology, and Time-Use Patterns in the Gulf Coast Shrimp Fishery." In *Those Who Live from the Sea*, ed. M. Estellie Smith, pp. 195–214. St. Paul: American Ethnological Society and West Publishing Co., 1977.

Wolcott, Harry F. *The African Beer Gardens of Bulawayo*. New Brunswick, N.J.: Rutgers Center of Alcohol Studies. 1974.

Wright, Rita J., and Mildred C. Anderson. *Texas Fact Book 1980*. Austin: Bureau of Business Research, University of Texas at Austin, 1980.

Zarur, George. "Seafood Gatherers in Mullet Springs: Economic Rationality and the Social System." Ph.D. dissertation, University of Florida, 1975.

Zeitlin, Irving M. *Ideology and the Development of Sociological Theory*. Englewood Cliffs, N.J.: Prentice-Hall, 1965.

Zulaika, Joseba. *Terranova*. Philadelphia: Institute for the Study of Human Issues, 1981.

Newspapers

Brownsville Herald
Beaumont Enterprise
Corpus Christi Caller
Dallas Morning News
The Facts (Freeport, Texas)
Houston Chronicle
Houston Post
Port Isabel–South Padre Island Press

Index

age, 59, 60

alternative fisheries, 204

Anglo shrimpers: drinking patterns of, 108; and labor force, 53, 80, 198, 201

Aransas Pass, 116, 150, 163, 194, 198; social history of, 80, 84

attitudes: toward accidents, injuries, and safety, 69–71; toward future of shrimping, 64; toward government agencies, 172–75; toward work, 61–71; toward work and families, 67–69

bay shrimping: and coastal communities, 77; demographic characteristics of, 78; and Gulf shrimping, 179–82; history of, 77–78; and overcapitalization, 147–48; annual production of, 78; profile of, 78; with sailboats, 77; with skiffs, 77; and Vietnamese, 78, 183–85

Beattie, Bruce, 131

bidding, 155, 156, 158–59

black shrimpers: and bay fishery, 78; and boat's share, 30; and labor force, 54, 55, 80, 198

black spot, 48

boats: crew comfort of, 9, 11, 12; equipment of, 10, 11; layout of, 9–12; and safety, 9, 15

boat's share: and captain's income, 49; and operating costs, 134; and shrimper's income, 30

Bok, Sissela, 107

boots, 13

Breaux, John, 167, 169

Breaux and de la Garza bill, 165, 167–70, 172, 203, 204

brown shrimp: life cycle of, 3–4; migration patterns of, 43; profitability of, 23

Brownsville, 194, 198; drinking patterns in, 116–22

Brownsville Herald, 118 n, 123

Brownsville–Port Isabel Shrimp Products Association, 190

Cahalan, Don, 113 n.6

Cajun shrimpers: and boats, 79; history of, 79–81, 93; and labor force, 54; and owners, 160

"candy," 163–64

captain: age of, 59; attitudes of, toward work, 61–71; and boat's share, 49; and children, 60, 61; and condition of shrimp, 48; cooperation of, with other captains, 37; and crew efficiency, 150; and dragging, 36; economic strategy of, 141–42; education of, 59, 60; and fishing strategies, 42–47; and fatigue, 35; and fuel costs, 49; future of, 201–202; and harvesting of shrimp, 47–48; and hiring of crew, 38–40; income of, 12, 17, 49–52; income of, as captain-owners, 52; and job status, 58, 59; and luck, 51; major responsibilities of, 32; and maintenance of boat, 36, 37, 38, 49; marital status of, 60, 61; mechanical ability of, 36; preparations of, for fishing, 49; protective fishing strategies of, 44–47; and storms, 35; supplemental income of, 129–30; and technological aids, 32–34; and try net, 47, 49; and work with rigger, 41–42

captain-owner. *See* captain

Central American shrimpers: attitudes of, toward work, 63; and federal subsidies, 57; and labor force, 54, 55, 81

Chamber of Commerce, 123

children of shrimpers, 60, 91, 93, 196

coastal communities: and bay fisheries, 77–78; and bay shrimping, 77–78; and deviance, 116–24; history of, 75–83;